The Chinese
Defense Establishment

Also of Interest

China as a Maritime Power, David G. Muller

† *China Briefing, 1982,* edited by Richard Bush

China's Decision for Rapprochement with the United States, 1968–1971, John W. Garver

† *China: A Political History, 1917–1980,* fully revised and updated edition, Richard C. Thornton

† *China, the Soviet Union, and the West: Strategic and Political Dimensions for the 1980s,* edited by Douglas T. Stuart and William T. Tow

† *China in World Affairs: The Foreign Policy of the PRC Since 1970,* Golam W. Choudhury

China's Quest for Independence: Policy Evolution in the 1970s, edited by Thomas Fingar and the Stanford Journal of International Studies

† *The Chinese Military System: An Organizational Study of the Chinese People's Liberation Army,* second, revised edition, Harvey W. Nelsen

Military Power and Policy in Asian States: China, India, Japan, edited by Onkar Marwah and Jonathan D. Pollack

From Muskets to Missiles: Politics and Professionalism in the Chinese Army, 1945–1981, Harlan W. Jencks

Technology, Politics, and Society in China, Rudi Volti

† *China Among the Nations of the Pacific,* edited by Harrison Brown

† Available in hardcover and paperback.

The Chinese Defense Establishment: Continuity and Change in the 1980s

edited by Paul H.B. Godwin

Westview Press / Boulder, Colorado

Westview Special Studies on East Asia

Published in 1983 in the United States of America by
Westview Press, Inc.
5500 Central Avenue
Boulder, Colorado 80301
Frederick A. Praeger, President and Publisher

Library of Congress Cataloging in Publication Data
Main entry under title:
The Chinese defense establishment.
  (Westview special studies on East Asia)
  Includes index.
  1. China—Defenses. I. Godwin, Paul H.B. II. Series.
UA835.C449   1983   355'.033051   83-5834
ISBN 0-86531-568-X

Printed and bound in the United States of America

Contents

Part 1
National Security and Defense Policy

Part 2
The Industrial Base

Part 3
Leadership and Management

v

Part 4
The Militia

Tables and Figures

Preface

In late March 1980, the contributors to this volume organized a panel at the national meeting of the Association for Asian Studies that had as its central purpose a discussion of the modernization of China's defense establishment. It was evident at the time that such modernization was viewed by the Chinese as being part of a complex decision-making process that involved both their past experience in creating a modern military system and current issues of national security and economic development. As in the past, there were no easy choices. The process of determining the direction, pace, and cost of modernizing the defense establishment had generated considerable debate and disagreement since the early 1970s, and it was not until the end of the decade that reasonably precise predictions could be made about the choices that had been selected.

It was quite evident that even though the Chinese People's Liberation Army (PLA) had had considerable experience with modernization, both in terms of the utilization of external assistance between 1950 and 1960 and in terms of its own efforts after the split with the USSR, the decade of the 1980s had brought with it new problems. The effort of building a modern force structure and defense establishment out of the sprawling semiguerrilla army that had defeated the Nationalist forces in the civil war of 1946–1949 had resulted in a complex military system with a web of supporting defense industries. After 1960, however, with the exception of the nuclear weapons program, much of the defense establishment had stagnated. This stagnation was compounded by the involvement of the PLA in the politics of the Great Proletarian Cultural Revolution and by Lin Biao's aborted military coup in the fall of 1971. When the issue of defense modernization broke into open debate in the mid-1970s, it soon became evident that the entire military system was in need of extensive overhauling. In addition to the questions of weapon system and military equipment modernization, basic questions of national security strategy, military doctrine and strategy, professional military education, management of the military system, force structure, and relations of the military with society were all under review.

Changes in the relationship between the armed forces and the Party and government structures are also under way as the 1982 constitution continues the post-Mao policy of separating Party and state responsibilities. The constitutions of 1975 and 1978 had formalized the de facto authority of the Party over the armed forces by designating the chairman of the Chinese Communist Party Central Committee (CCP CC) as commander in chief of the PLA. Because the CCP CC chairman was also chairman of the Central Committee's Military Commission, real control of the armed forces was in the hands of the Party. The 1982 constitution created a Central Military Council, with a chairman elected by the National People's Congress, to head the armed forces. The chairman of the CCP CC is no longer designated commander in chief. Thus, under the new constitution, legal authority over the armed forces has been moved from the Party to the government. What this reorganization will mean in actual practice remains to be seen, but the changes that are under way are not without significance.

The decade of the 1980s, therefore, could well witness the second major transformation of the Chinese military establishment. A strategic alignment with the Western powers as part of the redefinition of China's national security strategy and a major overhaul of the PLA's military doctrine and strategy has led to a critical review of the Chinese military system. It is the purpose of this volume to analyze the changes being sought and to look at the problems and prospects of the Chinese defense establishment through this decade.

Paul H.B. Godwin

Part 1

National Security and Defense Policy

1
Rebuilding China's Great Wall: Chinese Security in the 1980s

Jonathan D. Pollack

Introduction

For China's leaders and external observers alike, the issue of national security is a pivotal and fascinating topic. China's vulnerability to external pressures or outright military attack has been a vital leadership concern since the earliest months of the People's Republic of China (PRC). At times of national crisis, these concerns have commanded the attention of Beijing's ranking decision makers. Security issues have frequently been the object of leadership debate and policy conflict in the PRC. Five key questions related to the acquisition and use of modern arms—what to acquire, how much, how quickly, by what means, and for what purposes—have recurrently been the source of disputes among political and military leaders. The form and extent of political alignments with external powers (both adversaries and allies) have also provoked controversy and division at the highest policymaking levels.

With the onset of the 1980s, leadership concern with the ends and means of military power shows few signs of abating. Although the central issues on China's national security agenda remain comparable to those of the past, the strategic, political, and economic contexts of such decisions have all changed dramatically. The framework of debate over defense and security affairs has been altered; the consequences for domestic, regional, and global politics have therefore been affected as well.

The views expressed in this essay are the author's own and should not be attributed to the Rand Corporation or any of its government sponsors.

Without question, the issues associated with national security are now more openly and candidly addressed than at any point in the past three decades. This phenomenon is not limited to an increased flow of discussion and debate in the Chinese press. External observers—including high officials of foreign governments—have gained access to Chinese officials and institutions that would have been unthinkable only a few years ago. The proliferation of literature on China's defense and security problems in the post-Mao era, amply indicated by the breadth and depth of research interests in this volume, has been extraordinary. Indeed, a field of Chinese security studies has begun to take shape. To make maximum use of the new research opportunities, the major analytical issues and research methods and materials require closer scrutiny.

The purpose of this chapter is to identify some of these central issues. Unlike military policy or national defense, the concept of security captures the full range of external imperatives impinging upon a state's decision-making process. As Arnold Wolfers noted in his classic essay, national security remains an "ambiguous symbol" laden with a range of objective and subjective connotations.[1] China's leadership is not alone in needing to ascertain the limits of a purely military conception to China's security, the complex interaction between the need to deter war as well as to defend against actual attack, and the values and interests to be secured, at what cost, and with what degree of risk.

Yet the historical continuities of the past three decades suggest a set of recurring concerns for Chinese decision makers. From the earliest months of the new regime, Chinese elites have had to respond to major military deployments directed against China by hostile, militarily superior external powers. On repeated occasions, China's armed forces have engaged in conflict, frequently beyond territory physically controlled by the PRC. China's leaders have sought to reduce their vulnerability to outside powers, but without mortgaging Chinese sovereignty or political control to any other state. In addition, China's security needs have been one among a number of competing budgetary and manpower priorities.

For all these reasons, the range of policy choice in China's national security strategy has always been somewhat circumscribed. Leadership sentiment has therefore tended to favor political, diplomatic, and psychological approaches to security planning rather than predominantly military ones. Decisions about and policies for security have also been crucial to the allocation of political power within China. Thus, a full understanding of the policy dynamics and choices in Chinese security must be attentive to both the human dimension of such decisions (the predominant focus of this volume) and the political and institutional consequences of elite-level decision making.

China's Security Environment

Three issues will dominate Chinese security planning during the 1980s. The first concerns the long-term Sino-Soviet political and military rivalry and the most appropriate means of deflecting Soviet pressure directed against the PRC. The Sino-Soviet conflict has followed a tortuous course since public evidence of political and ideological cleavages between Beijing and Moscow first surfaced late in the 1950s. If the conflict could once be assessed largely in historical, racial, or personal terms, such a framework no longer suffices. Nor does a predominant focus on ideological differences serve as an adequate basis for understanding the dynamics of this competition. The Sino-Soviet rivalry is now best understood within the context of the national security perceptions and policies of both elites.[2] On a public level, Chinese decision makers insist that the focus of Soviet expansion is not directed principally against the PRC. By this logic, means exist to ameliorate or limit the overall competition. Notwithstanding the self-serving view that China is the least likely target among the world's major powers for Soviet aggression, there is a core underlying logic that supports precisely this proposition.[3]

The increasing preoccupation in Chinese strategic assessment with the long-term trends in the growth and exercise of Soviet power bear comparison with U.S. conduct when the United States was the PRC's principal military adversary. Both the tenor of Chinese analysis and the corresponding tasks for the construction of an anti-Soviet security coalition are highly instructive.[4] There is an increasingly differentiated view of Soviet power and policy that delves far more deeply into the constraints and choices in Moscow's security planning.[5] Some Chinese analyses describe Soviet political-military behavior in ominous terms, deeming Moscow's conduct in various regions of instability the product of an underlying expansionist course intent upon global conquest. These views, however, are tempered in other interpretations that stress the constraints and limitations in the exercise of Soviet power. In this alternative view, the USSR is described as an increasingly beleaguered (if not enfeebled) military power faced with difficult choices in the allocation of its military forces and the application of its military power. These contrary judgments reflect disagreement within the Chinese leadership about the degree and nature of the threat of "Soviet hegemonism" to global security, the most appropriate means of deflecting such a threat, and the implications of such views for the security of China.

To what extent, for example, do international imperatives compel Beijing to pursue security arrangements with the industrialized nations of the West? Are the tasks implicit in the "international united front against hegemonism" divisible? Do these tasks presuppose active collaboration, coordination, and consultation with the West, or simply assertions of shared concerns? To what extent can Soviet preoccupations with more immediate security concerns (for example, Afghanistan and Poland) diminish the more direct Soviet threat to China? And is the Soviet threat most appropriately viewed as an immediate, frontal military challenge to the territorial integrity of China?

Despite the seemingly deterministic framework of Chinese strategic thought, these writings reveal considerable ambiguity, contradiction, and fluctuation. The task of strategic assessment concerns judgments about time, political consequence, and the virtual dialectic between short-run imperatives (the principal domain of the military planner) and long-run political, military, and economic trends. Such assessments thus reflect both China's long-standing tradition of strategic thought and the centrality of military power in both the Chinese revolution and the effort to protect Chinese security since 1949. Military leaders are central participants in this growing debate. The proliferation of Chinese research institutes on issues of global policy include the Beijing Institute for International Strategic Studies, nominally headed by Deputy Chief of Staff Wu Xiuquan and staffed principally by former active duty military personnel. Whether this institute offers a distinctively military viewpoint on issues of global and regional security remains to be seen. Undeniably, however, the emergence of such research organizations reflects the increasing awareness of a need for an intellectual and institutional framework for assessing vital security issues.

Judgments about global strategic trends possess immediate relevance to both the allocation of scarce resources within China and the distribution of internal political power. To the extent that a direct Soviet military threat to China is deemed less pressing than events in either Indochina or Afghanistan, the military component of a Chinese security strategy becomes less salient. The dominant political forces within China, beginning with Deng Xiaoping, are strongly committed to this view. The PRC's political leadership seeks to avoid the debilitating effects of a sustained military confrontation with the USSR—a confrontation that would be costly and draining in the context of China's broader developmental objectives. Nor can the

PRC hope to match the capabilities of Soviet armed forces deployed against China.

These considerations suggest the second key question on China's security agenda in the 1980s: the relationship between the international environment and the tasks associated with China's effort to progress toward the front ranks of the world's agricultural, industrial, military, and scientific powers by the year 2000. When compared with the experiences of other newly industrializing societies, the choices and constraints confronting the Chinese are far from unique. Yet differences are also apparent. No matter how underdeveloped China might seem, the magnitude of the PRC's military effort dwarfs that of all but a handful of the world's states. China, although still a largely agrarian, labor intensive economy, already possesses an indigenous defense industrial system larger than that of all but the superpowers. As David Shambaugh describes in great detail in Chapter 3 of this volume, the PRC currently produces large quantities of armaments across the entire range of defense needs. Although the sophistication of both the technological and the manpower bases is not at the world's most advanced levels, breakthroughs in the realm of defense design, innovation, manufacture, and quality control remain very much the preserve of the advanced industrial states. In view of China's profound economic and political dislocations of the past two decades, it is hardly surprising that China continues to lag behind.

If this gap is to be narrowed significantly in the coming decade, the technological and economic ties that China fosters with the outside world will be critical. The nature of the international situation affects defense modernization in three significant ways: (1) the relative priority accorded national defense in relation to other budgetary, manpower, and investment needs; (2) the opportunities (political as well as budgetary) for Chinese military commanders and defense industrial managers to gain access to advanced defense systems or defense-related technology from abroad; and (3) the terms and extent of such technology transfers and managerial assistance, especially the degree of indigenous control over these processes.

The relative priority accorded defense construction as opposed to economic construction has been a recurring political issue within China. China's economic rehabilitation and societal transformation were anticipated at the end of the 1940s, but the outbreak of the Korean War and the demands on China's available resources abruptly altered such expectations. Indeed, the tranquillity of global and regional politics has been a decisive factor in determining the direction and pace of China's overall modernization effort ever since. If armed conflict involving China was deemed likely or even imminent, then preparations against war had to assume singular importance. If war was judged unlikely, attention could turn to the long-term tasks of China's agricultural, industrial, and scientific development, with defense modernization ultimately a beneficiary of progress on other levels rather than an immediate claimant of scarce resources. Chinese leaders have grappled with these questions for much of the past three decades. There has been a virtual dialectic between the short-term imperatives of the military planner, who must unavoidably prepare for war, and the broader, evolutionary trends in the international strategic system that have frequently enabled China to enhance its security through nonmilitary means.

Since the death of Mao Zedong, rival positions have been articulated by proponents of both "development first" and "defense first." For a time, military commanders (having presumably played a vital role in the arrest of the Gang of Four and the simultaneous appointment of Hua Guofeng to the Party chairmanship) took advantage of the opportunity to address the long-neglected tasks of defense modernization. Their emphasis on the urgent need to prepare for war—and the extensive and highly publicized visits of Chinese military delegations abroad—led many observers to expect a vastly expanded Chinese defense effort, including significant purchases of defense technology.[6]

These expectations, however, were greatly overstated, both in terms of the opportunities for a "quick-fix" solution to China's military deficiencies and in terms of the prospects for rapidly unleashing China's economy from the shackles of the previous decade. The "leftist line in economic work," which was evident in 1977 and 1978 and to which military interests were closely linked, has since been discredited.[7] At the same time, the ominous talk of 1976 and 1977 about the race against time to prepare for an inevitable war has disappeared from the Chinese press. International conditions—in particular, the growing political accommodation between the PRC and the states of the West—would permit a more measured approach to defense modernization. As then-Minister of National Defense Xu Xiangqian argued in the fall of 1979:

> The modernization of national defense cannot be divorced from the modernization of agriculture, industry, science and technology and, in the final analysis, is based on the national economy. . . . Blindly pursuing large-scale and high speed development in building national defense will invariably and seriously hinder the development of the national economy and harm the base of the defense industry. Subsequently, "haste makes waste."[8]

Since "current international conditions" enabled China to conduct "economic, scientific, and technological exchanges with other countries," and since "we believe that it is possible to delay the outbreak of war," China "should build and develop the defense industry step by step."[9]

The effects of these decisions find ample support in the greatly diminished visibility of "purely military viewpoints," the lower priority accorded the defense sector in China's "four modernizations," and in the still-tentative framework of security collaboration between the PRC and the major Western powers. In its own way, each of those areas illustrates the continuing problems in maintaining a leadership consensus on an overall security strategy in the coming decade. Somewhat ironically, the building of security links to the outside world has reduced rather than heightened the leverage of military leaders in the Chinese political process. Unlike the various strategies and activities discernible in other areas of China's program of agricultural, industrial, and scientific development, those in the defense sector remain principally the subject of conjecture by outside analysts. There is no detailed available statement of precisely how the Chinese see enhanced military power contributing to the goal of a strong and secure China. Rather, as China has become increasingly linked to the international strategic system, the PRC's military leadership has had to forgo any immediate opportunities for widespread technological advancement. The PLA thus had to acquiesce to a continuation of the long-standing disparities between Chinese military capabilities and those of the PRC's potential adversaries. Leaders in the high command may also have felt that they have had to bear a disproportionate sacrifice in China's continuing economic retrenchment and reappraisal—even as the *political* leadership in China defined the international environment of the 1980s as one of increasing turbulence, turmoil, and danger.[10]

It is nevertheless difficult to document a specific grievance list offered by the Chinese high command. The technological, organizational, and budgetary imperatives that the PRC leadership began to articulate at the peak of their political prominence and visibility in early and mid-1977 are now regarded as deferrable.[11] Such a reduction in the PLA's voice in Chinese policy debate is also reflected in diminished political, institutional, and budgetary prerogatives. The March 1981 appointment of Vice-Premier Geng Biao as Xu Xiangqian's successor as minister of defense, purportedly in the face of severe resistance within the military ranks, amply testifies to this reduction in political power. For the first time in the history of the People's Republic, the ranking defense official is not a man whose principal post-1949 career was in the military ranks. Nor could the spectacle of some of Lin Biao's surviving, but dispirited, confederates standing trial for their alleged role in the attempted coup of September 1971 have been particularly edifying to veteran commanders. Finally, the severe downgrading of Hua Guofeng's political role and power constitutes a humiliation to Hua's political patrons within the armed forces.[12]

At the Twelfth Party Congress, however, Geng lost his membership in both the Central Committee and the Politburo, and in November 1982 he was replaced as defense minister by Zhang Aiping, a senior military commander long associated with China's strategic weapons effort and the development of more sophisticated defense technologies. Geng's demotion, Zhang's appointment, and the continued high levels of military representation in both leadership bodies reflected a reassertion of PLA prerogatives within the political process. Defining an appropriate security strategy, therefore, cannot be isolated from issues of political position and institutional influence. The PLA has been instructed to accept uncomplainingly its diminished role in Chinese domestic politics.[13] The diminished expectations from the early post-Mao modernization effort continue to find the PLA among the principal "losers," especially as blind expansion of capital construction and the prospect of rapid gains in industrial productivity have been supplanted by efforts to balance the various economic sectors and increase attention to "the entire social economy and the people's material and cultural levels."[14]

Even if military policymakers chafe under such restraints and limitations, an incremental approach to upgrading China's defense industrial capacities makes eminent sense. Voices within the high command no doubt argued that the severe curtailment in capital construction and the importation of technology and equipment threatens to put Chinese security at risk. However, the leadership sees defense expenditure as a principal area where China's budget deficits can be reduced. The defense industries have increasingly been ordered to turn their attention to producing goods for civilian use, reflecting a belief that threats to China are waning or are at least manageable.[15] Under such conditions, attention can focus on achieving proportionality and balance in the Chinese economy. As a *Red Flag* editorial observed in January 1981:

> Ours is a country with a population of nearly one billion, 800 million of whom are peasants. We have a poor foundation to start with, our economic development is uneven and the level of our labor productivity and per capita national income is very low. After ensuring the livelihood

needs of the nearly one billion people, few financial and material resources are left for accumulation. If we divorce ourselves from this basic fact and arbitrarily try to increase accumulation and go after excessively high speed, we are bound to . . . aggravate the economic unbalances left by history. . . . Although we may not be able to achieve quite so high a speed for the time being, in the long term point of view . . . we will have a solid foundation.[16]

Such trends have additional implications for Chinese security cooperation with the outside world, in particular with the United States. The dramatic forward movement in the security realm, as testified by a flurry of high-level exchanges and consultations over the course of 1980, reflected the increasing effort to institutionalize Sino-American relations across the entire spectrum of government departments and agencies. Even at the peak of expectations of a U.S.-Chinese security relationship, China's leaders never called for highly formalized security ties. Rather, they asserted an underlying parallelism of interest between Beijing and Washington on various issues of strategy and security. The renewed intrusion of the Taiwan issue has complicated such dealings, leading China to disavow substantial interest in the acquisition of U.S. weapons. Even prior to the deterioration of U.S.-Chinese strategic relations, China remained highly equivocal about its intentions in this area.[17] Inasmuch as the PRC did not wish to appear the supplicant, Chinese officials remained somewhat ambiguous about their intentions, even after U.S. policy changes permitted the sale of lethal weaponry on a case-by-case basis. But stronger Chinese opinions were rarely ever heard; any solicitation of access to such technology was frequently implied rather than explicit and demonstrative.

The gap between such speculation in the West and the reality of China's present and foreseeable budgetary, investment, and manpower capabilities remains profound. Where, when, and how would the funds for such weapons transfers materialize? How would China fully and effectively absorb and utilize a major infusion of sophisticated defense technology, especially in areas (such as electronics) where China's experience is very limited? Who is to produce such equipment, on what scale, and with what controls and stipulations with respect to end use? Chinese commentaries reflect a clarity of understanding on this issue, a clarity that is frequently lacking in the United States. As *People's Daily* observed at the time of Geng Biao's visit to the United States in May 1980:

The Chinese position [on sales of weaponry] is clear. . . . The consistent principle of Chinese socialist construction is to take self-reliance as the essential factor. It is essential to rely on our own resources, technology, and wisdom. . . . The Chinese people deeply understand that we cannot rely on "buying" to achieve the socialist "four modernizations," including modernization of national defense.[18]

Thus, although China will clearly benefit over the coming decade by assistance from the West, the utilization and enhancement of China's indigenous human, material, and institutional resources remain far more important. The current emphasis on buying time rather than racing against it seems an appropriate and sensible course. Under such conditions, Chinese officials can devote considerable thought to the third key dimension of the PRC's security strategy: the creation of a modernized force posture, defense doctrine, and institutional structure.

The tasks associated with "becoming modern" in the realm of national defense are sensitive, complicated, and potentially very contentious. Institutional modernization is best viewed as a process, not a terminal policy objective. The tasks are partly independent of the acquisition of more-advanced defense technology per se. The cultivation of skills and an institutional attitude appropriate to more-sophisticated techniques, equipment, and relationships are at least as important. These steps encompass the introduction of new ideas and leadership practices, the supplanting of overly rigid approaches to military thought and organization, and the recruiting or more rapid advancement of younger leaders into the decision-making process.

If a single factor is likely to impede this process, it is the continued influence of political leadership over professional military development. Although Chinese leaders profess an interest in emancipating the mind and in making practice the sole criterion of truth, political criteria and imperatives will continue to affect what military leaders view as their independent and legitimate professional concerns. The consequences of a full-scale commitment to military modernization would be far-reaching. Other institutional and societal needs compete heavily for leadership attention; political interventions will continue to serve as a brake on institutional change over the next decade.

Although the officer corps might resent such intrusions, many leaders in China retain strong suspicions about the potential consequences of military autonomy. There seems no other interpretation of Deng Xiaoping's continued leadership of the CCP Military Commission. Deng's leadership role and editorial exhortations for the army to follow official policy do not suggest great confidence on the part of the Party or state leadership in the managerial capacities and political loyalties of the high command.

Thus, political rather than institutional reasons explain the difficulty of fully assessing organizational reform and innovation within the Chinese armed forces. The understanding of the institutional structure of the national security establishment and both the formal and the informal ties of decision making also remains very sketchy.[19] The framework of debate has therefore focused largely upon disputes over resource allocation, allegorical discussions of military strategy, and other indirect indicators of pressures for new policies and practices.[20]

As several contributors to this volume suggest, however, evidence of division and tension within the military leadership has grown. William Heaton, for example, notes that Chinese military officers have openly acknowledged the PLA's acute need for a more modern institutional structure for training and educating soldiers who are more attuned to the potential needs of future warfare—what the Chinese term "the doctrine of people's war under modern conditions." Since such needs have been voiced by some of the most-senior and prestigious generals in the high command, discussion and debate on lower organizational levels are probably far more heated, if still virtually invisible to the external observer.[21]

Yet there is no prospect that the Chinese will rapidly dismantle their institutional doctrines and structure. Many past practices have served China extremely well; in the absence of available resources, other doctrines may have to suffice for the foreseeable future. Ingrained institutional habits (not to mention divergent organizational constituencies seeking to guard their political and economic prerogatives) further limit the scope and pace of change. For example, should one expect a ground force commander to acquiesce readily to significant reductions in personnel? Indeed, in view of the pivotal role such forces play along both the Sino-Soviet and Sino-Vietnamese borders, their relevance for China's security needs remains indisputable.

We should therefore resist the temptation to impose an "externally approved" model of a force structure and doctrine upon the PRC. In the future, as in the past, the Chinese themselves will seek to define strategies and practices attuned to China's opportunities, constraints, and abilities. This procedure will continue to serve a set of underlying goals or principles—principally the goals of deterrence, defense, assertion, and demonstration.[22] One can add to this list the military's still very extensive involvement in the areas of economic and social management as well as social control. Any major modifications in practices, doctrines, and programs must prove compatible with a prior organizational mandate—unless such long-standing norms themselves are subject to criticism or revision.

Our objective in this section, however, is not to describe a modernization agenda in any detail, but to indicate the political context of such decisions. All three dimensions in China's security effort will be affected by a range of political, economic, technological, and institutional constraints. Such constraints will serve as mediating factors preventing the singular pursuit of a particular option, strategy, or goal. Thus, evidence of strategic reorientation, enhanced attention to military needs in the resource allocation process, or significant institutional innovation may well prove discontinuous and intermittent: The range of factors at issue is simply too broad and diverse. And, in view of the decidedly long-term nature of many of these issues, it may well be years before incontrovertible evidence of new approaches or strategies is available. Such considerations are not trivial but central to an analysis of the dynamics of Chinese security in the 1980s. What does modernization look like, especially from afar? Can we deem China "strong and secure" only when (and if) the Chinese themselves make such an assertion?

In Search of an Analytical Framework

All the chapters in this volume share an underlying interest in the role of military power, both within Chinese society and as a pivotal institution in its own right. Yet the role of organized coercive power in a socialist society is a highly ambivalent issue in Marxist theory. The Chinese Communist Party has also sought to impose a subordinate role upon the PLA in the governance of China. In the original edition of Franz Schurmann's pioneering work, *Ideology and Organization in Communist China*,[23] for example, only the Party and state hierarchies were considered key institutions of state power.

How could an institution as pivotal to CCP history be neglected? The answer seems rooted less in one scholar's intellectual predilections and more in terms of the major limitations in evidence. The Chinese rarely depict the role of the various military institutions as organizations in their own right; to do so would violate the ethic of a Party-dominated political system that (with the exception of the Cultural Revolution era) has always governed China's political and institutional norms. Chinese leaders have also sought to avoid undue entrapment in the norms of an international strategic system. They have had to insulate China's national security elite, thereby limiting the opportunities for the development and expression of autonomous institutional attitudes, interests, and policies.

China's political leadership may be engaged in a losing battle. Even if such institutional independence is obscured or denied in public media, its existence is all too obvious. The centrality of military power in the victory of the Chinese revolution and in guaranteeing China's security since 1949 is not open to question. Equally important, as leaders in Beijing advocate an increasing technological and economic interdependence with the industrialized world, China's military leadership cannot possibly be insulated from such relationships.

The difficulty for external analysts is not so much to demonstrate the existence of distinctive organizational norms and policies, but to find a way to describe, document, and analyze these phenomena on a systematic, ongoing basis. Under present circumstances, the public expression of defense or national security policies seems likely to remain highly circumscribed. Scholarship on such a politically sensitive topic must still rely heavily on the Chinese media.

Attention to observable behavior, however, enables a significant broadening of insight. Although media attention on selected issues (notably shifts in defense doctrine) remains a key source of information, other sources of evidence have become far more accessible. China's interactions with external security elites, budgetary outlays and priorities, research and development objectives and activities, inquiries about and acquisitions of defense-related technology abroad, investment and manpower decisions, relationship of military activity to other levels of Chinese policymaking, and actual military behavior (for example, Chinese combat in Vietnam) all provide opportunities for significant research. China's search for a relevant security strategy for the 1980s cannot be wholly hidden from the external observer. These indications of organizational and political priorities within China provide a rich set of perspectives on the future of Chinese military power.

The Constraints on Policy Change

As China's leadership defines its security tasks for the decade of the 1980s, key changes will occur, but only slowly. The results of the PRC's defense modernization effort are not yet highly visible or pronounced. Many of the policy changes now under discussion will require sustained, long-term efforts. This need is especially important in the effective integration and utilization of more sophisticated technology in the weapons produced and deployed by the PRC. What factors will impede a rapid, far-reaching transformation of China's security policies and practices?

The first consideration concerns size. As noted earlier, the PRC's defense effort has hardly been negligible. In terms of the absolute size of the armed forces, the number of deployed weapon systems, and budgetary expenditure, China's military forces are already among the world's largest and most costly. In absolute terms, China maintains the largest complement of ground forces, the third largest navy and air force, a modest but growing array of strategic nuclear forces, an armed militia in excess of seven million, and an indigenous defense industrial system whose production capacities rank among the world's highest. No matter how one assesses the technological and organizational competence of these forces, they already reflect a very considerable institutional and budgetary effort. Sheer size does not preclude extensive change, but it tends to limit the scope and magnitude of a modernization effort.

The second consideration concerns the degree of autonomy in Chinese security planning. In a broad political sense, the PRC is independent of any other state's control. When the Chinese discuss security arrangements with other states, they speak almost exclusively about coalitions or united fronts; they do not speak about alliances. At the present time, the PRC maintains only one formal alliance commitment—the 1961 treaty with Pyongyang. As a result, Beijing does not have a large group of states from which China can expect outright assistance or formal security guarantees, nor are the Chinese for their part obligated to proffer assistance to others. At the same time, China's armed forces are almost wholly independent in terms of the sources of manufactured equipment for national defense. Even if this defense industrial system is increasingly outmoded by world standards, its existence constitutes a very significant accomplishment for a less-than-fully industrialized state. No Chinese decision maker seems prepared to mortgage this degree of autonomy unless the corresponding gains were all but certain.

A third set of constraints concerns the doctrines governing China's use of military power. The preponderance of Chinese defense policies have been devised in light of indigenous experiences; there is only scattered evidence of transplanted military doctrine. Many of these approaches have not only worked well in the past, but are still relevant in light of China's present or foreseeable security circumstances. For example, it is clear that the Chinese are prepared to live with far greater ambiguity and uncertainty in their security planning than many nations in the West would find acceptable. Visitors to China have recurrently been struck by the low level of Chinese military preparedness in the face of the USSR's mobilization of a far more impressive array of forces. Although the Sino-Soviet military confrontation is both very real and very costly to the PRC, no major outbreak of hostilities occurred during the 1970s. Yet the order of battle on the Sino-Soviet border is no more balanced today than it was a decade ago; if anything, the disparity in relative forces has grown. As in dealing with the U.S. threat to China in the 1950s and 1960s, however, China will seek to manage and ameliorate the present and future Soviet threat by predominantly political means. Although not excluding the military factor, the PRC cannot realistically expect to win, let alone control, a purely military competition with the USSR.

A fourth consideration concerns the leadership characteristics and attitudes at the highest levels of the military command structure. The preponderance of the PRC's key security planners are aged men. An effort is under way to bring younger leaders into positions of increasing responsibility, but the results of this effort remain limited. Thus, the predominant leaders represent "military generations" that are somewhat resistant to substantial policy change, given that such change will inevitably diminish their influence in the decision-making process. The question of who might be able to generate greater pressure for policy change may not be answered until the actuarial tables fully catch up with China's most-senior generals.

A fifth constraint concerns China's levels of scientific, technological, and economic achievement. In terms of the industrial, technological, and manpower base upon which any defense modernization effort must draw, China, in relative terms, remains a poor society. According to official data, China's 1981 per capita gross national product (GNP) amounted to $261, ranking China among the poorest third of the world's states.[24] Although there are inherent problems with such a measure (and U.S. estimates of Chinese GNP are considerably higher), this figure does not suggest an abundance of available resources for a heightened defense effort. China's prospects for military modernization will be greatly affected both by the degree and nature of external assistance and by the progress of China's overall economic development program. Even assuming major economic breakthroughs, substantial improvements in weapon systems will take even longer. As noted earlier, it is far from certain whether China's available manpower base would be capable of fully absorbing and utilizing a significant infusion of advanced military technology from abroad. Given the magnitude and complexity of China's defense needs over the next decade—priorities upon which Chinese military commanders and security planners are not yet fully agreed—the Chinese may have to further modulate the introduction of newer technologies.

A sixth and final consideration concerns the underlying assumptions of China's security strategy. As noted earlier, China's leaders rely on political or even psychological approaches to national security rather than depending heavily on the acquisition of modern military power. Not only do alternative resource needs seem more compelling to

China's development, many people question excessive reliance upon military power per se as an instrument of foreign and security policy. China's security needs do not seem driven by a technological imperative. Although some decision makers may argue for a more technologically based approach to security planning, China is (and will remain) a weaker, more vulnerable state in relation to its adversaries. Yet weakness can be turned to advantage, as China's growing political and diplomatic links to the West attest. A highly political approach also helps constrain overly assertive military voices within the decision process.

Despite the pressures for policy change in China, powerful historical legacies and the suspicions of other leaders in the Chinese power hierarchy constrain these developments. The issues addressed in this volume are not casual or ephemeral considerations for China's leaders. The objective of a strong and secure China remains a pivotal policy goal. The complicated and contradictory tasks of planning a security strategy for the 1980s and beyond will remain a fascinating issue, both for China and for the outside world.

Notes

1. Arnold Wolfers, "National Security as an Ambiguous Symbol," in Wolfers, *Discord and Collaboration* (Baltimore: Johns Hopkins Press, 1962), pp. 147–165.

2. For a fuller exploration of the shifting context of Sino-Soviet relations, see Jonathan D. Pollack, "Sino-Soviet Relations in Strategic Perspective," in Douglas Stuart and William Tow, eds., *China, The Soviet Union, and the West: Strategic and Political Dimensions in the 1980s* (Boulder, Colo.: Westview Press, 1982), pp. 275–292; Pollack, "China's Agonizing Reappraisal: Foreign and Security Policy in the 1970s," in Herbert Ellison, ed., *The Sino-Soviet Conflict: A Global Perspective* (Seattle: University of Washington Press, 1982), pp. 50–73; and Pollack, *The Sino-Soviet Rivalry and Chinese Security Debate* (Santa Monica, Calif.: Rand Corporation, R-2907-AF, October 1982).

3. For a more extended analysis of this topic and the evidence furnished in Chinese writings, see Jonathan D. Pollack, "Chinese Global Strategy and Soviet Power," *Problems of Communism* 30:1 (January–February 1981), pp. 54–69.

4. For an extended discussion of Chinese assessments of U.S. political-military strategy in Asia and its possible parallels with PRC views of Soviet conduct, see Jonathan D. Pollack, *Security, Strategy, and the Logic of Chinese Foreign Policy*, Research Papers and Policy Studies Monograph no. 5 (Berkeley: Institute of East Asian Studies, University of California, 1982).

5. See in particular, Special Commentator, "The Military Strategy of the Soviet Union for World Domination," *Renmin ribao* [People's daily], January 11, 1980, in Foreign Broadcast Information Service, *Daily Report—People's Republic of China* (henceforth FBIS-PRC), January 15, 1980, pp. C1–6.

6. These issues and developments are thoroughly discussed in Paul H.B. Godwin, "China's Defense Dilemma: The Modernization Crisis of 1976 and 1977," *Contemporary China* (Fall 1978), pp. 63–85.

7. Indeed, one recent commentary has argued that "in 1978 another 'Great Leap Forward' nearly took place" (Wang Jiye and Wu Kaitai, "Resolutely Implement the Strategic Policy of Readjustment," *Renmin ribao*, December 23, 1980, in FBIS-PRC, January 6, 1981, p. L19).

8. Xu Xiangqian, "Strive to Achieve Modernization in National Defense— In Celebration of the 30th Anniversary of the Founding of the People's Republic of China," *Hongqi* [Red flag] no. 10 (October 1979), in FBIS-PRC, October 18, 1979, p. L13.

9. Ibid., pp. L14, L18.

10. Commentator, "The 1980s—Full of Promise," *Renmin ribao*, February 5, 1980, in FBIS-PRC, February 6, 1980, especially p. L8.

11. Compare, for example, "A Great Call for Accelerating the Revolutionization and Modernization of our Army," *Jiefangjun bao* [Liberation Army daily], Editorial, June 5, 1977, in FBIS-PRC, June 6, 1977, especially pp. E7–9; Editorial Department, "Chairman Mao's Theory of the Differentiation of the Three Worlds is a Major Contribution to Marxism-Leninism," *Renmin ribao*, November 1, 1977, in *Peking Review* no. 45 (November 4, 1977), especially pp. 22–23, 33–35; and Xu Xiangqian, "Heighten Our Vigilance and Get Prepared to Fight a War," *Hongqi* no. 8 (August 1978), in *Peking Review* no. 32 (August 11, 1978), pp. 5–11.

12. For various Western accounts, see Michael Parks, "Policy Changes in China Stir Opposition in Military," *Los Angeles Times*, December 1, 1980; Fox Butterfield, "China's Army Grumbles Over Loss of Political Power," *New York Times*, December 16, 1980; Butterfield, "High Military Post in Peking Reported Taken Over by Deng," *New York Times*, January 4, 1981; and James P. Sterba, "China's Army Follows New Marching Orders, Not Happily," *New York Times*, March 1, 1981.

13. See, for example, Commentator, "Continue to Emancipate the Mind, Have a Correct Understanding of Present Policies," *Jiefangjun bao*, October 26, 1980, in FBIS-PRC, October 27, 1980, pp. L8–10, and the excerpts of the speeches of Hu Yaobang and Wei Guoqing to the All-Army Political Work Conference in FBIS-PRC, February 2, 1981, pp. L3–4, and February 4, 1981, pp. L4–8.

14. See the revealing article by economist Xue Baoding, "The Theory of Viewing the Modernization Program as a Whole," *Hongqi* no. 24 (December 1980), in FBIS-PRC, January 6, 1981, pp. L40–46.

15. See Vice-Premier Yao Yilin's report on the readjustment of the 1981 economic plan delivered to the seventeenth session of the Fifth National People's Congress, February 25, 1981, in FBIS-PRC, March 9, 1981, especially pp. L10–11.

16. "Strive to Accomplish the Task of Readjusting the National Economy," *Hongqi* no. 1 (January 1981), in FBIS-PRC, January 22, 1981, p. L9.

17. Shortly before leaving office, Defense Secretary Brown asserted that the PRC had at some unspecified point made a request to purchase U.S.

weaponry, but no other official sources confirmed this claim (Richard Halloran, "Defense Secretary Sharply Critical of Allies and Dissenting Officers," *New York Times,* December 7, 1980). Indeed, another Defense Department official, in commenting on possible Chinese interest in purchasing U.S. aircraft, insisted that "the effort is . . . strongly aimed at self-sufficiency. China does not want to buy aviation hardware; it wants licensing and coproduction arrangements." (Clarence A. Robinson, Jr., "China's Technology Impresses Visitors," *Aviation Week and Space Technology,* October 6, 1980, p. 26).

18. Wang Fei and Zhou Zexin, "A Successful Visit," *Renmin ribao,* June 8, 1980, in FBIS-PRC, June 18, 1980, p. B4.

19. See Harvey W. Nelsen, *The Chinese Military System* (Boulder, Colo.: Westview Press, 1977), and Harlan Jencks, *From Muskets to Missiles: Politics and Professionalism in the Chinese Army, 1945–1981* (Boulder, Colo.: Westview Press, 1982).

20. On a number of these issues, see Harry Harding, "The Domestic Politics of China's Global Posture, 1973–78," in Thomas Fingar, ed., *China's Quest for Independence: Policy Evolution in the 1970s* (Boulder, Colo.: Westview Press, 1980), pp. 93–146.

21. For three revealing assessments from several of China's most senior military leaders, see Su Yu, "Great Victory for Chairman Mao's Guideline on War," *Renmin ribao,* August 6, 1977, in *Peking Review* no. 34 (August 19, 1977), pp. 6–15; Ye Jianying, "Developing Advanced Military Science of Chinese Proletariat," *Peking Review* no. 12 (March 24, 1978), pp. 6–9; and Xu Xiangqian, "Strive to Achieve Modernization in National Defense."

22. I have discussed these goals more extensively in Jonathan D. Pollack, "The Evolution of Chinese Strategic Thought," in R. J. O'Neill and D. M. Horner, eds., *New Directions in Strategic Thinking* (London: George Allen and Unwin, 1981), pp. 137–152.

23. Berkeley and Los Angeles, University of California Press, 1966.

24. *China Business Review* 9:4 (July–August 1982), p. 55.

2
Mao Zedong Revised: Deterrence and Defense in the 1980s

Paul H.B. Godwin

Introduction

Since the Chinese communist armed forces were founded in 1927, the basic military dilemma facing them has been that of developing strategies for defeating adversaries that have superior weapons and equipment. That this dilemma should continue into the 1980s is no doubt frustrating to members of the current military hierarchy, many of whom have served continuously since 1927, but it in no way changes the centrality of the dilemma. In some ways, this predicament has become more difficult to resolve, for whereas in the 1930s and 1940s the communists could afford to surrender their base areas in order to maintain fluid battle fronts, the Chinese leadership concluded in the late 1970s that the defense of cities had to become an important aspect of China's defense strategy. Thus, in the 1930s, Mao could accept the destruction of China's "pots and pans" in order to maintain the fluid fronts and mobility essential to his concept of strategic defense, but by the 1970s, these pots and pans had become centers of industrial development critical to a China seeking to achieve a new stage of industrial development under the leadership of Deng Xiaoping and his cadre of political and economic pragmatists.

If the military dilemma remains the same, does the solution also remain the same? Has the current iteration of the PLA's historical

The opinions expressed in this chapter are those of the author and are not to be construed as representing the views of the U.S. Air Force, the Air University, or the Department of Defense.

problem led to solutions that differ in any major way from the concepts of "people's war" presented by Mao in the Kangda lectures he delivered between 1936 and 1938? Those classic statements of military strategy ("Problems of Strategy in China's Revolutionary War," "Problems of Strategy in Guerrilla War Against Japan," "On Protracted War," and "Problems of War and Strategy") remain the reference points for the concept of "people's war under modern conditions" that emerged during the military modernization debate of the 1970s and became the current statement and definition of China's new strategy. Out of the debate have come two widely held beliefs: first, that contemporary warfare is quite different from any war fought by the PLA in the past and, second, that the basic concepts of military strategy utilized in the past must be extensively modified before they can be applied to contemporary warfare. These two beliefs raise the question of whether or not people's war under modern conditions is war as it was fought in the early days of the Chinese communist armed forces.

In a very real sense, the espousal of people's war under modern conditions represents not only a reluctance to depart from Mao's concepts of strategic defense, but also a recognition that some of the underlying principles of people's war do remain applicable to the military threat currently posed by the USSR. The Chinese recognize that these concepts have to be modified, but modification has to take place within the limitations established by the weapons and equipment deployed by the PLA. The interaction between military technology and military strategy cannot be overlooked or treated lightly. It would be an error of major proportions for the Chinese military hierarchy to develop strategies that were beyond the capabilities of the nation's military resources. Since the Chinese leadership has decided to modernize the PLA's weapons and equipment slowly, whatever changes are made in the underlying strategy and battlefield tactics of the PLA will have to be made within the constraints estabished by weapon platforms, weapon systems, and military equipment that, with few exceptions, are of Korean War vintage.

The Soviet Military Threat

An equally important factor that has to weigh heavily as the Chinese reconsider their military strategy is the realization that the imbalance between China's capabilities and those of the USSR was far greater in 1982 than it was a decade earlier. Even though the Chinese have increased the total number of ground forces they have deployed against the USSR from forty to sixty-nine main force divisions—nine armored and sixty infantry divisions—supported by forty-one regional force divisions[1] and those of the USSR still number approximately forty-five, static comparisons are misleading. By 1973, the USSR was constructing roads, railroad spurs, barracks, and family housing and undertaking other construction activities, and all this work indicated that the forces in the Far East were viewed as a permanent garrison rather than as temporary relocations to face a local, short-term threat. Furthermore, there is no evidence that these forces were transferred from Europe or the western USSR. The deployment facing China is composed of newly formed units and units transferred from Central Asia and southern Russia.[2] The network of supply depots, logistic support facilities, command and control centers, and barracks capable of housing fully mobilized units leaves the impression that these Soviet forces are, as Edward Luttwak so aptly described them, like "coil springs fully compressed."[3]

The Soviet ground forces are complemented by equally improved capabilities in strategic weapons and air and naval forces. In the late 1970s, the USSR began to deploy MIRVed (multiple independently targeted reentry vehicles) SS-20 mobile intermediate-range ballistic missiles (IRBMs), into its force structure facing the PRC. With an estimated range of 2,700 nautical miles, these missiles are capable of blanketing China,[4] which means that the Soviet intercontinental ballistic missiles (ICBMs) can be reserved to counter the United States' strategic capabilities. The USSR has therefore created what could well be a nuclear capability dedicated to Chinese targets. This improvement in the USSR's nuclear forces has been accompanied by increased capabilities in its air force. The USSR now deploys approximately 2,060 aircraft in the Far East, including some 1,450 fighters, 450 bombers, and 160 patrol aircraft.[5] Although China is capable of utilizing about 50 percent of its more than 5,000 combat aircraft to face the Soviet deployments, the Chinese air force suffers because of the age of its aircraft. The obsolete equipment flown by the PLA air force and deployed by China's ground-based air defense systems would be woefully inadequate against a sustained Soviet attack. Chinese naval forces suffer from the same problem. Although large in size, the PLA navy would be inadequate to challenge Soviet naval units. Chinese antisubmarine warfare (ASW) capabilities are crude at best and could be easily defeated, and the navy's surface combatants lack the necessary weapons to successfully engage the Soviet navy in anything but a limited coastal defense action. In any sustained combat, it may be assumed that the USSR could quickly gain both air and naval superiority.

Under such ominous conditions, any strategies developed by the Chinese are of interest because the imbalance between the two force structures makes the task faced by China's military leaders extremely difficult. There is, however, another facet of their task that needs to be taken into account. The decision of the political leadership to place the modernization of the armed forces among China's lowest priorities indicates that as ominous as the Soviet military capabilities may be to the external observer, they are not viewed with any immediate alarm by the dominant faction within China's Politburo. This view contradicts the impression left by a number of senior Chinese military officials during the modernization debate of 1975–1978. During the public phase of that debate, military officials and representatives of the military-industrial complex clearly expressed concern about Soviet capabilities. Thus, it is at least plausible that many senior officers of the PLA have a somewhat different view of the Soviet military threat than that implied by the decisions of the dominant faction within the Chinese political elite.

That such a difference could exist is quite understandable because the people who are responsible for establishing specific military policy in support of China's overall national security objectives are also responsible for the deployment of the military forces in support of those objectives. These military leaders are required to prepare for war with the Soviet Union and are therefore responsible for developing military strategies and battlefield tactics to be used in engaging the Soviet forces. Such responsibilities tend to make them hypersensitive to Soviet military capabilities and lead them to prepare worst-possible-case scenarios. The fact that military preparations are only one part of a far wider political strategy to assure Chinese security does not relieve the military hierarchy of having to plan for war, but the most immediate effect of the larger political strategy has been military budgets that are far smaller than the military establishment would prefer.

The military modernization debate demonstrated the concern of at least a major segment of the Chinese military hierarchy about the demands of contemporary warfare, both conventional and nuclear, and the implications of such warfare for a force structure armed almost entirely with weapons and equipment dating back to the Korean War. It is also likely that the 1979 incursion into Vietnam demonstrated the impact of both equipment deficiencies and a lack of training in combined arms operations on the battlefield performance of the PLA. By the summer of 1979, the PLA high command had settled into a pattern in which training was to substitute for extensive reequipment of the conventional forces. During the two years following the PLA's military operations in Vietnam, reports from China emphasized the importance of improving the battlefield effectiveness of the PLA through intensive training in combined arms operations, battlefield command and control, and battlefield tactics. In the fall of 1979, the minister of national defense was especially critical of the PLA's inability to fight a "modern war" and to effectively conduct combined arms operations on the battlefield.[6] Throughout 1980, these same concerns were expressed, and it was not until the fall of 1981 that any real confidence in the PLA's capabilities was expressed in the public media. For two years and more, the PLA reported that it was attempting to improve its potential battlefield performance by training its officers to meet the demands of modern combined arms warfare.

In November 1980, an all-army conference was called to discuss ways to improve the PLA's training. Particularly noteworthy was that conference's decision that the training of officers (cadres) was to be the focus of a revised program.[7] Perhaps reflecting this decision, the approximately 1,000 commanders attending advanced courses at the PLA military academies in 1981 were pointedly described as studying "modern military science" and improving their "command skills and capabilities."[8] The curriculum was reported to have included not only the history of the PLA, but also the study of foreign armed forces. Contemporary warfare was analyzed through the study of "nuclear weapons, guided missiles, electronic confrontation [warfare?],"[9] and other aspects of the modern battlefield. Demonstrating the PLA's concern about armored operations, Zhang Zhen, a deputy chief of staff, reported that the 1981 training program shifted the PLA's focus from infantry to tank warfare. This shift was declared to be one of the three major changes in the PLA's training, the other two being the focus on combined arms warfare and the special emphasis on the training of officers.[10]

The culmination of the 1981 training year was a massive combined arms exercise, the largest ever reported, conducted in North China during the early fall. The importance of these maneuvers is indicated by the wide coverage they received in the press and the large number of senior officials who observed the exercise and attended the post-maneuver review. Deng Xiaoping, in uniform as chairman of the Military Commission, was accompanied by a group of China's most-senior Party and government officials led by Hu Yaobang, the Party chairman. Reports of the postmaneuver review introduced a new dimension into descriptions of the PLA, for not only did they carefully distinguish among the three service arms of the armed forces, but they also carefully identified specific branches, such as the artillery, paratroops, engineering corps, motorized infantry, and armored forces. The entire pattern of the commentaries describing the exercise and the review stressed that the PLA had now mastered combined arms warfare.[11]

Accepting the maxim that "you fight as you train," improvements in the capability of China's armed forces to conduct combined arms warfare do not overcome the limitations imposed by their weapons and equipment. The past two years of training exercises may well have improved the capabilities of the various service arms and branches of the PLA on the battlefield, but they have not transformed the PLA into a modern army. The addition of the Sagger AT-3'(assuming that it is in series production)[12] will increase the ground forces' antiarmor capability, for example, but this antitank weapon is only one item in an entire range of battlefield equipment that the PLA "needs" to face the USSR on equal terms. The decision not to invest scarce resources in the rapid modernization of the PLA means that for the foreseeable future, the imbalance between Soviet and Chinese military capabilities will be a permanent condition. For Chinese defense planners, this imbalance means that the forces they deploy against the USSR will have to be utilized according to a set of military strategies that must take into account the superior capabilities of the Soviet forces across the entire range of nuclear and conventional weapon systems. This is not a new dilemma for Chinese defense planners; it is just the most recent manifestation of their traditional predicament.

The Defense of China:
Mao's Concepts and the "New" Strategy

The extent to which Mao's concepts of war and strategy influence current strategic analyses presented by China's military leadership is certain to cause considerable debate among those people who seek to determine what is new in those analyses and what is not. Furthermore, it is evident that within China, there is still debate about the relevance of Mao's strategic concepts to the problems faced by the PLA today. There is, however, a dominant view that Mao's basic tenets remain valid, even though they can only be used as a guide and cannot be applied in a mechanical and dogmatic manner. Many people argue that it was Mao's own view that his concepts of military strategy would have to be revised, or even rejected, as the actual conditions of war changed.

What is certain is that the language used by the senior members of the military hierarchy in those strategic analyses is taken directly from Mao's essays, which are published collectively as the *Selected Military Writings of Mao Tse-tung*.[13] There are two obvious and complementary explanations for this usage. First, until very recently, only Mao's concepts of war and strategy were politically acceptable. Second, and equally important, the basic military problem, if not its solution, faced by China's defense planners is remarkably similar to the problem faced by the Red Army as it contemplated war with Japan. Song Shilun, the commandant of the PLA's Academy of Military Science, presented an analysis of China's current defense strategies in a 1981 article in which he discussed the possibility of a large-scale war with the USSR and noted that "we still have to deal with a superiorly equipped enemy with our inferior equipment."[14] But, in reviewing the applicability of Mao's principles to the current situation, Song was quick to make the point that some conditions are different now so Mao's concepts must be supplemented and revised. Before reviewing the changes Song believes to be necessary, and which give a clear indication of China's current military strategy, it is necessary to review the basic strategic thought that Song draws upon for his own analysis— Mao's "On Protracted War."[15]

In the late spring of 1938, Mao saw the advantages held by the Japanese forces as a result of their superior military equipment and training, which made each enemy unit much more lethal and gave them much greater mobility than the units the Red Army could put into the field. Japan's primary disadvantage was that the number of combat units it could deploy was far smaller than those potentially available to the communist forces.[16] In addition to size, Mao believed that the Red Army had the additional advantage of extensive maneuvering space. The strategic and tactical problem to be resolved, therefore, was how to take advantage of the only two advantages accruing to the communist forces. Mao argued that operations against the Japanese should take the form of "quick-decision offensive warfare on exterior lines"[17] and that the military dilemma to be resolved was how to determine the appropriate tactics and strategy for such operations.

It must be recalled that Mao was not thinking primarily in terms of guerrilla warfare when he delivered the lectures that were to become the essay "On Protracted War." In late 1938, he was arguing that the militarily decisive actions would be taken by the main force units of the Red Army. Guerrilla warfare would play a secondary, but important, role in support of the main forces. The basic military strategy Mao formulated was one of a protracted, defensive war. The problem was how to develop supporting strategies and tactics to prevent a defensive strategy from turning into a stalemate in which neither side could achieve a military victory. Mao's solution was based on the concepts of "active," or "positive," defense and on dividing military operations into those conducted on "exterior lines" and those conducted on "interior lines."

The concept of an active defense (*jiji fangyu*) consists of taking tactically offensive action within a basically defensive strategy. The defending forces undertake offensive operations in order to wear down the adversary while he is strategically on the offensive and attacking. It is the opposite of passive defense (*xiaoji fangyu*), which means the defending forces simply resist without attempting to weaken the adversary as he prepares to attack or is actually on the offensive.

The concept of interior lines (*nei xian*) and exterior lines (*wai xian*) is as important to protracted defensive warfare as the concept of active defense. Military forces on exterior lines control considerable space and the communication lines within that space. When operating on exterior lines, military units are usually dispersed and on the offensive. Forces on interior lines are usually on the defensive, control less space, and are quite concentrated. The concentration of forces that characterizes operations on interior lines permits units to be shifted from one defensive point to another quicker than the attacking forces can redeploy their units. The defense of the Pusan perimeter during the Korean War is an example of defensive operations on interior lines, and the amphibious assault of Inchon, which outflanked the Korean People's Army, is an example of operations on exterior lines. The Chinese attacks on the two wings of the UN forces as they advanced up the east and west flanks of North Korea in 1950 are examples of "quick-decision offensive warfare on exterior lines." The UN forces were on the offensive and on the move; the Chinese forces made a surprise attack with overwhelming numbers, and both wings were forced to retreat.

Although Mao clearly favored mobile warfare on exterior lines, there are clearly recognizable advantages to fighting on interior lines. Communications and supply functions are easier, defensive forces can be redeployed in response to changing tactical situations more quickly than the attacking forces can be shifted, and the defender can choose what to defend and prepare his positions. The limitation of a defensive strategy is that it cannot assure military victory; victory requires offensive actions. Mao postulated that offensive mobile warfare on exterior lines was needed to complement the defensive strategy on interior lines. The enemy (in this case the Japanese), on the offensive and using exterior lines, would be relatively dispersed and, while approaching, on the move. Given the military inequalities between the opposing forces, the communists needed to create tactical situations in which they would be able to combine an overwhelming advantage in numbers with surprise in order to defeat the Japaneses forces. This immediate, or local, advantage would permit Mao's commanders to fight short battles of annihilation—"quick-decision battles on exterior lines." Because Mao's army was unable to fight extensive and protracted engagements due to limited logistic support, and because it needed Japanese supplies and weapons to restock its own forces, short battles were essential.

The communist forces' limited weapons and equipment meant that only surprise attacks, made possible by the flexibility provided by mobile warfare, would permit them to defeat the Japanese units. The necessary flexibility would not have been possible if the underlying strategy of a defensive, protracted war on interior lines had dominated the tactics of the war with Japan. The main force units were to utilize the essence of mobile warfare—outflanking, encircling, and attacking the enemy while he is on the move—in order to turn defensive warfare into a war-winning strategy. Mao was seeking to utilize both the advantages of a defensive strategy based upon interior lines and the advantages accruing to mobile warfare on exterior lines. This policy would make the best possible use of the two advantages held by the Red Army: size and space.[18]

In Mao's concept of strategy and tactics, positional warfare played only a minimal role. Such warfare had its place in defending key points within a strategic area, in wearing down an attacker and eroding his capability to continue an assault, and in instances in which an enemy force was encircled and cut off from assistance. Positional warfare, however, could not become a major component of the Red Army's strategy for two reasons. First, the army had neither the weapons nor the logistic base to fight sustained positional warfare. Second, Japanese forces could also use China's space to bypass any fortified positions the communists chose to establish.[19] Positional warfare therefore played a supplemental role.

The ultimate objective of Mao's strategy and tactics was to protract the war until the Red Army was equal or superior in weapons and equipment to the Japanese forces. When this condition had been reached, the Red Army would enter the final stage of the war and defeat the Japanese in a series of strategic offensives. In fact, the communists never achieved that stage, and at no time were field armies used against the Japanese forces in the manner prescribed in "On Protracted War."

The transition from guerrilla to regular warfare envisioned by Mao never occurred, and by the end of 1941, the Japanese had terminated offensive operations and were following their own defensive strategy. Because the Japanese held most of the major cities, the only way the communist forces could return some fluidity to the war would have been to attack those cities. But the Chinese forces did not have the equipment or the logistic support to do so. Rather, the communists set about their primary political task, which was to expand the territory and population under the control of the Chinese Communist Party. Nonetheless, even though the level of warfare discussed by Mao in "On Protracted War" was not used against the Japanese, it was employed against Chiang Kai-shek's forces in the last two years of the civil war. Furthermore, "On Protracted War" has remained, along with Mao's other major essays, the core of the strategic thought used by the Chinese military hierarchy. As I shall show, Mao's concepts are still used as the basis for analyzing contemporary strategic problems. What has changed, however, is that today, questions are raised as to how to modify and supplement Mao's concepts of war and strategy in light of modern battlefield technology. Indeed, it is probably not overstating the case to say that Mao's concepts are used in China's military academies much as Karl von Clausewitz's concepts are used in Western war colleges.

Revising Mao's Strategic Concepts

It is evident that revisions of Mao's concepts of war and strategy have already been quite extensive. The development of China's nuclear arsenal, the creation of an air force and a navy, and the overall modernization of the Chinese armed forces since 1950 have raised questions that are simply not answered by the strategic concepts developed by Mao in the 1930s and 1940s. Since Mao's death in 1976, there has been extensive public discussion of the strategic options available to the Chinese as they face the USSR. This section will focus on an essay by Song Shilun because it incorporates much of the public discussion that has occurred since 1975.

Song is in many ways typical of most of China's senior officers. He is an experienced ground force commander, having served in the Eighth Route Army, the New Fourth Army, and as commander of the eastern front during the Korean War. As a combat commander, he has had only limited experience in combined arms warfare, but it is important that in Korea, he had direct experience with such warfare as it was fought by the forces of the United States. When ranks were introduced to the PLA in 1955, Song was made a Colonel General. He began his association with the Academy of Military Science in 1958 as deputy head of the school and became its commandant in 1973.[20] With a background in both combat command and China's professional military education system, Song's interpretations of the modifications that must be made in Mao's strategic thought will reflect both his past experiences and the debates about military modernization.

The basic problem is, as Song defines it, that the PLA would not be currently capable of fighting quick-decision warfare on exterior lines against invading forces from the USSR.[21] Because such operations are a critical dimension of Mao's strategy of protracted war, this situation places a severe restriction on any strategy the PLA may choose to implement. Song's solution is that during the first stage of a war, the PLA will have to fight "positional defensive warfare, with powerful support and coordination of mobile warfare and guerrilla warfare in order to gradually consume and annihilate the enemy's strength."[22] The major difference between Song's and Mao's strategies is Song's emphasis on positional warfare, which Mao placed in a secondary role.

The emphasis Song places on positional warfare is derived from two critical problems. The PLA's inferior mobility and lack of weapons needed to fight on a modern battlefield would not permit it to conduct extensive mobile warfare against Soviet forces. In addition, even at the level of modernization now achieved by the Chinese armed forces, a continuous supply of fuel, ammunition, and spare parts would be essential if the Chinese were to conduct a protracted defensive war against the USSR. These two problems of technology and logistics mean that the PLA must defend China's industrial bases.

City defense is not a new element in the revision of Mao's strategic concepts. In 1978, Nie Rongzhen, one of China's senior soldiers and a member of the Politburo, stated in a particularly realistic analysis of a future war with the USSR that "the defense of cities is of great significance to stabilizing the war situation, preserving our war potential and supporting a protracted war."[23] Less than one year later, Deputy Chief of Staff Wu Xiuquan, in a discussion of China's plans to fight a war with the USSR, observed that the PLA would not attempt to defend the entire border but had selected some "key points" along the border and inside China that would be defended.[24] Song's essay expands on these positions, pointing out that although the Red Army's bases were important in the past, none were essential for the kind of war then being fought against the Japanese. In a "people's war under modern conditions," however, the PLA would be dependent on China's cities as industrial bases supplying a continuing flow of parts, ammunition, fuel, replacement weapons, and equipment.[25]

The shift in basic strategic principles involved in the decision to defend the cities creates an image of a people's war that is distinctly different from that provided in Mao's essays and by his conduct of the war against Japan. For Mao, mobile warfare was the heart of a protracted war, but Song places more emphasis on defensive strategies and interior lines. The problem Song raises is that future wars will require strong logistic support for the main force units, for without such logistic support, the PLA would be unable to conduct sustained operations in the intensive type of warfare created by modern weapons and military equipment. The PLA is clearly not as dependent as the Soviet forces are on logistics, but even the PLA would require extensive support for its tanks, armored personnel carriers, artillery, and aircraft. Song notes that this kind of warfare is different from past wars, when it was possible to apply "the principle that 'our army's sources of manpower and material are mainly at the front.' "[26] The PLA's ability to sustain combat on supplies scavenged from the battlefield is obviously limited. Contemporary conventional warfare utilizing offensive operations on exterior lines requires the mobility and lethality of tanks, mechanized infantry, self-propelled artillery, close air support, battlefield interdiction, air defense systems, and command, control, and communications systems capable of maintaining coordinated actions in multifront battle areas. The Soviet forces are designed and equipped to fight in this manner; the Chinese forces have only a limited capability to conduct such warfare. But even the PLA's limited capability makes China's forces more dependent upon their logistic tail than they were half a century ago.

Song's analysis places the PLA in much the same logistics crunch China's military hierarchy believes to be a major weakness of the Soviet forces. Nie Rongzhen describes a future Soviet assault on China as a sudden attack involving large numbers of technologically advanced conventional and nuclear weapons. Nie predicts that the USSR will "attack and penetrate deeply," using large numbers of tanks and mechanized forces in conjunction with air attacks, airborne assaults, and naval units. He believes the primary objective of the Soviet assault would be China's cities—"our political, economic, and cultural centers and pivots of communication."[27] The major weakness of this Soviet strategy, and here Nie is clearly drawing on the 1945 Soviet campaign in Manchuria, is defined as its dependence on mechanized and armored units. Nie defines these units as the USSR's "tortoise shells" and states that without them, the Soviet forces are too weak to be effective. "Our enemies feel reassured by their modernization and mechanization. In fact, as men must eat, machines must 'eat' too."[28] It is the Soviets' heavy dependence on their logistic support system that Nie argues would be exploited by China's guerrilla forces through continual disruption of Soviet supply lines, thereby rendering Soviet armored and mechanized units impotent. In Song's analysis, China's forces have the same dependence, though to a lesser degree.

This importance of China's industrial bases has led to a major revision of the PLA's military strategy and, it seems, to a careful review of possible Soviet strategies in an assault on China's northern and northeastern provinces—essentially those incorporated into the Beijing and Shenyang Military Regions. The most obvious place for the Chinese to search for Soviet strategic concepts is in the analyses the USSR's military establishment made of the Soviet Union's 1945 campaign against the Japanese Kwantung Army in Manchuria. The Russian military hierarchy believes that this campaign was a model of surprise attack using combined arms operations and has published extensive analytic reviews detailing the operations and the concepts behind them.[29]

If China's defense planners have carefully analyzed the Soviet army's Manchurian campaign they will have noted that surprise, numerical superiority, advanced weapons, and air superiority were the keys to the Soviet success. They will also have noted that the lack of prepared, in-depth defenses was critical in the failure of the Japanese to defeat the Soviet forces when they were stalled deep in Manchuria because of a shortage of fuel.[30] This assessment may well mean that the Chinese will conclude that a defense of northern and northeastern China is feasible. But an extremely important factor in the early successes of the Manchurian campaign was the ability of the Soviet air force to bombard fixed fortifications, supply depots, railroads, and command and control centers.[31] If China's main force units are as dependent upon their logistic base as Nie Rongzhen and Song Shilun indicate they are, then they are just as susceptible as the Japanese Kwantung Army was to the effects of Soviet aerial bombardment. The Chinese advantage, to the extent they have one, will depend more on the size of their forces and their strategic position, which permits them to fight a defensive war on interior lines while the Soviet forces are dependent upon ever-lengthening supply links to maintain mobile warfare on exterior lines.

It is this advantage that leads Song to outline a strategy of protracted defense even though, as he describes the problem, such a strategy will be difficult to implement "because of the development in weapons and technical equipment."[32] Positional defense supported by mobile and guerrilla warfare is the only option open to the Chinese if they wish to defend their cities. The limitations of the PLA's weapons and equipment do not permit a more desirable strategy, which would place primary emphasis on the main force units' fighting a mobile war on exterior lines in order to destroy the Soviet forces before they can threaten China's cities. Rather, mobile and guerrilla warfare will play supplemental roles. There is the distinct possibility that to some extent,

China's cities are the "bait" to draw the Soviet forces into known approaches. Xu Xiangqian, the minister of national defense in 1978, stated that luring the enemy deep "does not mean letting enemy troops go anywhere they like but we will force them to move as we want them to; at key places we will put up a strong defense, prevent them from penetrating inland unchecked and systematically lead them to battlefields of our own choice so as to wipe them out piecemeal."[33] Because Chinese forces do not have the mobility required to maneuver the Soviets onto battlefields the PLA would prefer, they will rely on the size of their forces to cover all primary avenues into northern and northeastern China, including the approach to Beijing.

There appears to be an assumption underlying the Chinese analyses that because they believe the Soviet forces will head for the cities, the PLA can use its forces both to harass the approaches with mobile and guerrilla warfare and to prepare in-depth defenses to slow down and weaken the attacking forces. By the time the Soviet forces are converging on China's cities, they will have extended their supply lines and, to that extent, will have been "lured deep." At that point in the campaign, both guerrilla and main force units will have separated the Soviet armored and mechanized units from their logistic support. Weakened by Chinese harassment and separated from their rear services, the Soviet forces will then be susceptible to destruction by Chinese counteroffensives. This part of the strategy, of course, assumes that the PLA will be able to sustain the counteroffensives in the face of Soviet air power.

Much of the Chinese strategy depends on China's capability to prepare and sustain in-depth defenses along the most likely avenues of attack. It may also be that the strategy depends on the conflict's remaining at the subnuclear level. Nuclear war raises a very real dilemma for Chinese defense planners, and a 1980 article in the *Liberation Army Daily* approaches this issue quite directly.[34] The question raised is what would the PLA be able to do if the aggressor chose to use low-yield nuclear weapons to breach China's defenses? Would China be willing to resort to strategic weapons? The author implies that to respond with strategic nuclear weapons raises the level of warfare unnecessarily and that it would be far better if the PLA had the capability to respond with battlefield nuclear weapons. If the response could be kept on the tactical level, "the enemy would then hesitate to resort to strategic weapons."[35] Although no doubt written in part to provide a case for the introduction of tactical nuclear weaponry into the PLA's order of battle, the article raises the whole problem of China's strategy of nuclear deterrence.

Deterrence: Conventional and Nuclear Forces

Chinese analyses over the past four years depict a PLA preparing to fight a conventional war in defense of China's northern and northeastern provinces. The basic doctrine is drawn from Mao's principles, but the strategy to be employed has little to do with the strategy of protracted war developed by Mao Zedong. In terms of deterrence, this revised strategy is designed to influence any potential Soviet decision by denying Soviet forces any realistic chance of gaining the quick military victory they would seek and are designed to achieve. Nuclear warfare presents a more difficult problem. First, even with the deployment of full-range ICBMs in eastern China,[36] the Chinese nuclear arsenal does not give Beijing the capability to launch a preemptive first strike against the USSR or to threaten to devastate the Soviet Union with a MAD (mutually assured destruction) strategy. The deterrent value of the arsenal is based solely on a punitive second-strike capability.

The essence of deterrence is to reduce the adversary's incentive to attack. China's conventional forces contribute to deterrence by threatening to subject the USSR to a costly conventional campaign should it contemplate an attack that goes much beyond China's border. The nuclear forces contribute to this deterrence by threatening a high cost should the USSR contemplate a nuclear assault. The dilemma faced by the Chinese is that no matter how "defensive" they may state their nuclear posture to be, they cannot continue to deploy nuclear weapons without increasing their threat to the USSR. The result is a mutually hostile interaction, with forces on both sides reacting to each other. Thus, it is almost certain that the USSR's deployment of the SS-20 east of the Urals reflects an increasing concern about China's growing nuclear capability. Deterrence for one adversary is almost always perceived as a threat by the other, especially when the adversary is faced with multiple threats. The USSR has to adopt a strategy that is capable of responding to nuclear threats from the United States, the United Kingdom, and France as well as China. Beijing simply aggravates this situation by basing its contemporary national security strategy on an alignment with the Western powers and creating what the USSR sees as a pseudoalliance with the United States. A critical problem faced by Chinese defense planners in analyzing China's strategic relationship with the USSR is to determine what level or threshold they can achieve without creating an incentive for the USSR to seriously consider a preemptive attack on the conventional and/or nuclear level. The Chinese deployment of the CSS-4 and the massive maneuvers conducted during the fall of 1981 in northern China may indicate that they believe they have yet to reach this threshold.

China's public statements that constantly reiterate no "first use" pledges and official pronouncements that Beijing's missile forces are designed only to break the "superpower monopoly" of such weapons do not reassure the USSR. Chinese deployment practices are clearly designed to enhance the survivability of the nuclear force, indicating that the ability to survive a Soviet nuclear salvo and launch a punitive strike is at the base of China's current strategy. Nonetheless, this strategy may well change as China's nuclear forces become more numerous, survivable, and accurate over the years. Indeed, one can question the veracity of Chinese statements to the contrary.

It is certainly true, as Deputy Chief of Staff Wu Xiuquan has observed, that China has neither the capability nor the funds to compete with the United States and the USSR in the development of nuclear weaponry.[37] Even without competing, however, China continues to take steps that are designed to improve the range, accuracy, and survivability of its nuclear forces. Range has been improved by the deployment of the CSS-4 ICBM. Accuracy is assumed to be improving, and the launch in the fall of 1981 of three earth satellites from a single rocket booster[38] shows definite progress in the development of multiple reentry vehicles (MRVs) for the warheads. Testing and evaluation of solid rocket fuels continues, and when this testing is combined with the experience gained in the deployment of two nuclear-powered submarines,[39] a submarine-launched ballistic missile (SLBM) seems to be in the offing. SLBMs deployed in nuclear-powered submarines would add significantly to the survivability of Beijing's strategic forces. Current Chinese programs, therefore, although not competing with the USSR, are clearly designed to improve the competence of the nuclear forces in both war and deterrence.

Although the present nuclear force structure cannot do much more than launch a retaliatory strike against the USSR, the future force structure raises much more complex issues. Currently, China appears to have the ability to target every major urban-industrial complex in the USSR east of the Urals, with an additional but limited ability to strike at targets in European Russia with the few multiple stage IRBMs and ICBMs that are now deployed. This capability, combined with China's evident willingness to fight a conventional war in defense of its northern and northeastern provinces, provides the deterrent value of the current military posture adopted by Beijing. The direction now being taken by China's nuclear weapons and space programs raises the question of future Chinese attitudes to the role of nuclear weapons in China's strategic relationship with the USSR.

It is doubtful that future deployments will be seen by the USSR as anything but menacing, if for no other reason than in their analyses of Soviet military strategy and their assessments of East-West relations, the Chinese pay very close attention to the nuclear balance. In 1981, for example, one analysis noted that the USSR "has accelerated the development of multiple warheads and sophisticated SS-38 [*sic*] missiles and has manufactured 'Typhoon' grade submarines armed with guided missiles."[40] The analysis concludes that "the strategic situation with Moscow on the offensive and Washington on the defensive will not change overnight so long as the balance of military strength remains advantageous to the Soviet Union."[41] Beijing's public analyses of the global and regional military balance demonstrate a sensitivity to military capabilities that tends to undermine any self-serving statements that describe the Chinese nuclear weapons program as developing only a small number of weapons to break the superpower monopoly of nuclear weaponry.[42] It is far more probable that in the long run, China views its strategic weapons program as the core of an independent defense capability that will permit Beijing to deter any adversary without being forced to rely upon a strategic relationship with any other nation in order to assure its military security. In one sense, this strategy breaks the superpower monopoly, but it breaks it by making China an independent nuclear power.

If China is now in the transitional stage between having the capability of a minor nuclear power with weapons that are primarily useful only in regional exchanges, and the capability of a major power, with a full complement of survivable missiles of both regional and intercontinental range, then the issue for China is no longer to determine how stable is its relationship with the Soviet Union. The issue may now be to determine what nuclear force structure is necessary to create an independent deterrent capability. If so, then it is unlikely that short of a preemptive strike, the USSR can take any action that would limit future Chinese deployments. What is at stake in future deployments is not China's ability to deter the USSR, but Beijing's desire to create an independent defense capability. It is possible that the decision was made to weather a period of instability with the USSR in order to achieve the more important goal of military independence.

Conclusions

Since its founding in 1927, the PLA has had to wrestle with the problem of defeating a technologically superior adversary. The current iteration of this problem is that even though the conventonal forces of the PLA are modernized, with few exceptions only in terms of 1950s technology, they are now dependent on China's cities if they are to fight a protracted war. In addition, the industrialization of China over the past thirty years has led to the decision that these cities should be defended. Cities are no longer the "pots and pans" that could be surrendered in the 1930s in order to maintain the fluid fronts that made Mao Zedong's strategy of protracted war so viable. Both the demands of modern warfare and a conscious decision to preserve the industrial core of China against Soviet invasion have led to a major revision of Mao's original strategic concepts. Deterrence on the conventional level is now to be based on the ability to deny the USSR any chance of a quick military victory, such as it achieved in Manchuria in 1945.

Initially, the capability to deter the USSR on the nuclear level was based upon the same logic. Not having the capability to launch a disarming first strike, and being unable to threaten the USSR with wholesale destruction, China's nuclear deterrence takes the form of an ability to conduct a retaliatory and punitive second strike. Together the conventional and strategic forces could not necessarily defeat the USSR, but they could make any Soviet attempt to detach a major portion of northern and northeastern China from Beijing's control very costly. It is just possible that there has been a conscious attempt to balance the development of the conventional and the nuclear forces in order to achieve what China hopes will be a nonthreatening deterrent capability—nonthreatening in the sense that the joint force structures do not give Beijing an offensive capability against the USSR.

China's deployment of the CSS-4, when combined with programs that are intimately related to the development of more-advanced, accurate, and survivable nuclear weapons, appears to take China beyond simple deterrence of the Soviet threat. If this is the case, then it would be incorrect to interpret future missile developments in terms of the Soviet threat. It would appear that in the 1980s, China will be changing from a minor nuclear power concentrating on deterring a specific threat to a major nuclear power seeking more general deterrence. The dilemma for the people shaping China's defense policies is no longer, if it ever was, how to manage an unstable strategic nuclear relationship with the USSR, but to determine what China's nuclear force structure must be in order to create a credible, independent general deterrent.

Notes

1. *The Military Balance, 1981–1982* (London: International Institute for Strategic Studies, 1981), p. 74.

2. *Strategic Survey 1973* (London: International Institute for Strategic Studies, 1974), p. 65.

3. Edward N. Luttwak, "The PRC in Soviet Grand Strategy," in Douglas T. Stuart and William T. Tow, eds., *China, the Soviet Union, and the West* (Boulder, Colo.: Westview Press, 1982), p. 269.

4. *The Military Balance, 1981–1982*, p. 105.

5. Japanese Defense Agency, *The Defense of Japan 1980* (Tokyo: Japan Times, 1980), p. 51.

6. Xu Xiangqian, "Strive to Achieve Modernization in National Defense," *Hongqi*, no. 10 (October 2, 1979), pp. 28–33, in Foreign Broadcast Information Service, China (henceforth FBIS-CHI), no. 203, October 18, 1979, p. L15.

7. Beijing Domestic Service, November 21, 1980, in FBIS-CHI-80-229, November 25, 1980, pp. L24–25.

8. Beijing, Xinhua Domestic Service, January 15, 1982, in FBIS-CHI-82-012, January 19, 1982, p. K5.

9. Ibid.

10. Ibid., January 17, 1982, in FBIS-CHI-82-012, January 19, 1982, p. K11.

11. See, for example, ibid., September 26, 1981, in FBIS-CHI-81-187, September 28, 1981, pp. K1–4.

12. Jonathan Pollack, "The Men but Not the Guns," *Far Eastern Economic Review* 114:52 (December 18, 1981), p. 29.

13. Mao Zedong, *The Selected Military Writings of Mao Tse-tung* (Beijing: Foreign Languages Press, 1972).

14. Song Shilun, "Mao's Military Thinking Is the Guide to Our Army's Victories," *Hongqi*, no. 16 (August 16, 1981), pp. 5–15. Originally published in *Junshi xueshe* [Military science] no. 7 (1981), in FBIS-CHI-81-180, September 17, 1981, p. K20.

15. Mao Zedong, "On Protracted War," *Selected Military Writings*, pp. 187–267.

16. Ibid., p. 232.

17. Ibid., pp. 233–234, 241.

18. Ibid., p. 244.

19. Ibid., p. 248.

20. Wolfgang Bartke, *Who's Who in the People's Republic of China* (Armonk, N.Y.: M. E. Sharpe, 1981), p. 327.

21. Song Shilun, "Mao's Military Thinking," p. K21.

22. Ibid.

23. "Nieh Jung-chen's [Nie Rongzhen] 4 August Speech at the National Militia Conference," Beijing, NCNA Domestic Service, August 7, 1978, in FBIS-CHI-78-154, August 9, 1978, p. E7.

24. As reported by General André Marty, leader of a French military delegation to China, in an interview with Georges Bianic, Agence France Presse (AFP), Beijing, May 3, 1979, in FBIS-CHI-79-088, May 4, 1979, p. G1.

25. Song Shilun, "Mao's Military Thinking," p. K22.

26. Ibid., p. K23.

27. "Nieh Jung-chen's 4 August Speech," p. E7.

28. Ibid.

29. John Despres, Lilita Dzirkals, and Barton Whaley, *Timely Lessons of Manchuria: The Manchurian Model for Soviet Strategy*, R-1825-NA (Santa Monica, Calif.: Rand Corporation, July 1976), pp. 38–39.

30. Ibid., p. 39.

31. Ibid., p. 62.

32. Song Shilun, "Mao's Military Thinking," p. K21.

33. Xu Xiangqian, "Heighten Our Vigilance and Get Prepared to Fight a War," *Peking Review* no. 32 (August 11, 1978), p. 10.

34. This article is discussed in Cheah Cheng Hye, "Bridging the Strategic Gap," *Far Eastern Economic Review* 118:18 (April 25, 1980), pp. 30–31.

35. Ibid., p. 30.

36. Joint Chiefs of Staff, *United States Military Posture for FY 1983* (Washington, D.C.: U.S. Government Printing Office, 1982), Map II-2, p. 42.

37. *Mainichi shimbun* (Tokyo), July 15, 1979, p. 2.

38. Beijing, Xinhua, September 20, 1981, in FBIS-CHI-81-182, September 20, 1981, p. K1.

39. *The Military Balance, 1981–1982*, pp. 72–74.

40. Guo Ping, "A Review of the World Situation in 1981," Beijing, Xinhua, December 21, 1981, in FBIS-CHI-81-245, December 22, 1981, p. A4.

41. Ibid.

42. See, for example, Hua Guofeng's Tokyo speech following the first long-range tests of the CSS-4, Beijing, Xinhua, May 29, 1980, in FBIS-CHI-80-105, May 29, 1980, p. D6.

Part 2

The Industrial Base

3

China's Defense Industries: Indigenous and Foreign Procurement

David L. Shambaugh

Introduction

China's military industrial base supports a comprehensive and integrated program producing items from radios to thermonuclear weapons. The cornerstone of China's defense industrial establishment is the machine building industries. Today, there are a total of eight ministries of machine building, of which the second through the eighth produce for the military. The present production responsibilities can be found in Section 2 of this chapter.

Since the original establishment of two machine building industries in 1952, numerous structural and functional reorganizations have taken place.[1] Administrative control over machine building has varied over time, with an intricate mixture of responsibilities among ministries, central and local planning bodies, and industrial enterprises. Budgetary allocation and central policy have oscillated in response to perceptions of external threat and domestic political swings. Productive output has changed too, paralleling fluctuations in the economy as a whole. Significant geographical shifts have also taken place. Foreign assistance to the machine building industries has come and gone and returned again.

The first section of this chapter surveys the changes in the defense industries from 1949 to 1980. The second section examines the current status of the defense industries. The third section focuses on the

I wish to thank the following individuals who provided constructive criticisms of previous drafts: Robert Dernberger, Angus Fraser, Paul H.B. Godwin, Harlan Jencks, James Lilley, Harvey Nelsen, Michel Oksenberg, Jonathan Pollack, George E. Shambaugh, Jr., Allen S. Whiting, and William Zimmerman IV.

Chinese strategy and efforts to procure defense technologies and weapons systems from abroad, as well as Western options pertaining thereto. The final section raises questions about the defense industries in the decade to come. In conclusion, I found that despite impressive quantitative advances in defense production during the last thirty years, the qualitative gaps between indigenous output and the international state of the art will remain wide for the remainder of this century.

1. HISTORICAL OVERVIEW OF DEFENSE INDUSTRY POLICIES

During the first two years of communist control (1949–1951), the new regime concentrated primarily on restoring the war-damaged Manchurian industrial base. Limited ammunition, small arms, and artillery production were revived in these plants and others in the traditional industrial centers of Shandong, Shanghai, Beijing, and Tianjin. At this time, no administrative distinction was made between civilian and defense production. In 1952, however, two ministries of machine building (m.m.b.'s) were created. One specialized in civilian production, the other in military items.

The core of China's machine building industry was formed through the massive material and technical assistance provided by the Soviet Union during the 1950s. During the First Five Year Plan (1953–1957), nearly 100 of the 166 major Soviet-assisted industrial projects were undertaken in the field of machine building.[2] In addition to a broad range of civilian equipment, the Soviets supplied facilities for aircraft, naval vessels, electronic equipment, and land armaments and the know-how for nuclear weapons production. Many of these production facilities were constructed in China's interior as part of an effort to reduce vulnerability to (U.S.) attack and bridge traditional coastal-inland gaps in the industrial base.[3] Machine building plants were established in Taiyuan, Xian, Loyang, Lanzhou, Chengdu, Chongqing, Kunming, and Wuhan. This major effort to modify excessive reliance on Manchuria and the coastal provinces was hampered by China's poor transport network, which caused bottlenecks in delivery of raw materials and finished products. Structurally, the defense industries were configured in the Soviet organizational mode. They practiced vertical integration, whereby each plant was composed of as many departments as the whole manufacturing process required. The two ministries in charge of the machine building industry were also comprehensive in nature. As the organizational structure expanded, its efficiency declined.[4]

Defense production dropped also because of Mao's resolution of a heated leadership debate over external threat and defense needs. In his April 1956 speech, "Ten Great Relationships," Mao declared a reduction of defense expenditures so as to accelerate overall economic development, particularly heavy industry, which in turn would serve the needs of defense. In other words, military modernization would proceed but would not be allowed to inflict short-term disruptions on the overall economy. By taking this stand, Mao stood with a coalition of civilians—including Zhou Enlai, Liu Shaoqi, Li Xiannian, Chen Yun, and Deng Xiaoping—against those in the military establishment—Su Yu, Liu Bocheng, Ye Jianying, and Peng Dehuai—who favored significant expansion of defense production.

Additional erosion took place during the Great Leap Forward (1958–1960) when the construction of small plants and "backyard furnaces" diverted scarce raw materials from the heavy industrial sector. Decentralized planning and control of the small, locally controlled plants resulted in haphazard location and poor construction, poor quality control, and exaggerated output claims.[5] The Great Leap put much greater emphasis on the development of mining and steelmaking equipment. The agricultural crisis that followed forced China to shift machine building priorities once again to emphasize agricultural machinery, chemical fertilizer production equipment, and petroleum industry machinery.[6] This shift is evident in the machine building industry's growth among the branches of modern industry (28.7 percent), surpassed only by nonferrous metals (29.9 percent). Between 1957 and 1967, however, the machine building industry's rate of growth slipped to third behind the chemical fertilizer and petroleum industries.[7] Indicative of the increased attention paid to agricultural machinery was the establishment in the mid-1960s of an Eighth Ministry of Machine Building. The tenure of this ministry was brief, although it is not known exactly when it became defunct.

The failure of the Great Leap was compounded by the Soviet withdrawal of personnel, plans, and assistance in 1960. The aeronautic and nuclear programs were especially hard hit. The machine building industry retrenched with the rest of the economy from 1961 to 1963. Equipment stood idle, and capital formation was poor. Considerable evidence exists to indicate that the transfer of weaponry, especially nuclear assistance, was a central locus of friction and a cause of the Sino-Soviet split.[8] The fundamental change in economic development strategy in 1960–1962 meant rejection of the Soviet emphasis on heavy industry, especially to serve military needs. The new order of economic priorities, as formulated primarily by Chen Yun, relegated defense production along with heavy industry to a subordinate place behind agriculture and light industry. All sectors were meant to progress gradually and in a balanced fashion, unlike the "greater, faster, better" policies of the Great Leap Forward.

During these years (1960–1964), the machine building industries were reorganized and expanded. Their number increased from two to eight. Machinery for civilian use came from the First and Eighth Ministries, charging the Second through the Seventh Ministries with the following defense production functions.

Ministry	*Production Function*
2nd m.m.b.	Atomic energy and nuclear services
3rd m.m.b.	Munitions and assorted light armaments
4th m.m.b.	Electronics, radio, and telecommunication equipment
5th m.m.b.	Heavy weapons and artillery
6th m.m.b.	Naval equipment and shipbuilding
7th m.m.b.	Aircraft and missiles

To coordinate these six production lines, the National Defense Industries Office (NDIO) was established about 1960. Apart from its central coordinating role, the NDIO oversees local production facilities through its regional and provincial offices. Bureaucratically, the NDIO is responsible to the Military Commission (MC). Because of its very nature, details of NDIO functioning are obscure.[9]

Complementary to the NDIO is the National Defense Science and Technology Commission (NDSTC), which is the top military research and development (R&D) organization. Established in 1958, the NDSTC was originally responsible for overseeing nuclear weapons and delivery systems development. Through a series of reorganizations, its responsibilities were expanded to include oversight and coordination of all military R&D projects, allocation of funds, and personnel training. The NDSTC's primary responsibility is to direct the design, building, and testing of prototype military hardware. The NDSTC runs at least twenty research institutes and apparently some experimental factories within the machine building industry.[10] In addition to those run by the NDSTC, the service arms, General Staff Department, and General Logistics Department (formerly General Rear Services Department) operate their own research institutes. Certainly, civilian science and technological R&D must also be recognized for important contributions to research in the military field. These civilian institutes are located within the Chinese Academy of Sciences (CAS). Like the NDIO, the NDSTC is bureaucratically subordinate to the MC. Marshal Nie

Rongzhen, director of the NDSTC from 1958 to 1968, represented the personnel link between the two bodies as he served on both. Nie also sat on the Politburo and the MC, symbolizing the ties between Party and army in China's first-generation leadership. Nie was dismissed from all his posts during the Cultural Revolution, but he was restored to the Politburo and MC in 1977.

Peng Dehuai's purge following the 1959 Lushan Plenum and Lin Biao's subsequent ascension to the defense ministership was a turning point for the military's orientation, and concomitantly for defense production. Defense production and R&D were by no means halted, but the aforementioned reordering of economic priorities following the Soviet withdrawal caused their growth and output rates to decline. The PLA became increasingly involved in domestic political functions, to the detriment of professionalism and modernization. Lin intensified political training in the armed forces, rejuvenated Party branches throughout the military hierarchy, and reinforced the political authority of the political commissars attached to the General Political Department (GPD). As a result, Mao came to rely increasingly on the PLA as a power base and an organizational model to emulate, epitomized by the "Learn from the PLA" campaign of 1964. Thereafter, any proposal that the PLA withdraw from its domestic role so as to improve its military preparedness risked Mao's opposition. PLA Chief of Staff Lo Ruiqing made just such a proposal in 1965 and was consequently purged.[11] What did all of this emphasis mean for the defense industries?

Just as arms production had stabilized again in the mid-1960s, the political turmoil of the Cultural Revolution (1966–1969) upset the entire economy. The seizure of railroads and communications lines by Red Guards disrupted the flow of raw materials and parts to the machine building industries. Overall production dropped sharply, although some components of the defense industries (notably nuclear weapons production) were better insulated from the disorders by official decree and protection by Zhou Enlai. Military research was also hit hard as bureaucrats and scientists were purged. Overall, however, the curtailment in military production during the Cultural Revolution was not so severe or lengthy as during the Great Leap Forward.[12] By the second half of 1968, another period of growth in the defense industries had begun. The border clashes with the Soviets along the Ussuri River in 1969 added further impetus to this trend.[13] Defense production rose rapidly in the next two years, reaching an all-time peak in 1971–more than double the output of 1967.[14]

As might be expected, this trend was not to last. In mid-1971, a major policy debate between civilian and military planners surfaced in the press. The controversy went by the rubric of the "electronics versus steel" debate. At issue was not civil versus military production (guns versus butter), but rather, a more refined argument as to budgetary allocation within the defense industries; an important corollary being the relationship between defense production and overall heavy industrial production—which was to be the "leading factor." Within the military establishment, it appears that the ground forces and the Fifth and Sixth Ministries of Machine Building argued for large-scale investment in the "steel" (i.e., heavy) industries. On the other hand, the high-technology-oriented sectors (Second, Third, Fourth, and Seventh Ministries of Machine Building) conceivably lobbied for the rapid development of "electronics" technology.

The debate politically polarized national security planners on the elite level. Assessment of external threat was an integral part of the debate. Defense Minister Lin Biao, Chief of Staff Huang Yongsheng, Party ideologue Chen Boda, and other "radicals" took the electronics side of the debate,[15] arguing that the United States remained China's major adversary, hence the need for a strong air force and a nuclear deterrent. The steel faction was a coalition of party bureaucrats (headed by Zhou Enlai) and civilian economic planners. They identified the Soviet Union as the main enemy and advocated the strengthening of a conventional deterrent, i.e., bridging the chasm between "people's war" and a nuclear deterrent. This group was more closely in line with Mao's strategic outlook, and consequently, steel was favored over electronics.

In retrospect, this debate was a watershed for Lin Biao. In foreign policy, it included heated debate over China's opening to the United States and rejected the "dual adversary" stance taken by Lin.[16] In domestic politics, it signaled the beginning of a reassertion of Party primacy over the military.[17] In economics, the priority given to defense production was broadened in favor of an expanded overall industrial base. In ideology, the "expert" gained renewed respect vis-à-vis the "red."

During the night of September 13, 1971, a plane carrying Lin Biao and others, supposedly fleeing from an abortive coup d'etat attempt, crashed in the Mongolian desert. All aboard were reportedly found dead by Soviet soldiers.[18] Discussions of the intricacies of Lin's demise go beyond the scope of this study but suffice it to say that with Lin and his cohorts (including the ensuant purges within the PLA, especially the air force) went some of the opposition to army professionalism and conventional weaponry modernization.

Although Lin was gone, his political counterparts—the nefarious Gang of Four—were not. Inspired not only by their ideological views but also by the fear that a professionally inclined army would be less amenable to their influence than a highly politicized one,[19] the "radicals" attacked the campaign (begun after Lin's downfall) to promote professional values in the PLA and sought once again to upgrade political activities in the armed forces. The Gang of Four's Zhang Chunqiao took over the directorship of the GPD, which among other functions publishes the *Liberation Army Daily* (*Jiefangjun bao*). The "radicals" turned to a favorite medium—allegorical press articles—to criticize the growing trend toward a professional army, military modernization, and indeed the modernization program on the whole as put forth by Zhou and Deng. Indicative of the attacks were a series of articles by Liang Xiao, a pseudonym for a writing group of Qinghua and Beijing Universities that served as a spokesman for the "radicals."[20] In such articles as "On Salt and Iron" and "The Yang Wu Movement," the author(s) argued on behalf of "people's war" and building up the militia. The articles also attacked the importation of military and economic goods and technology on a large scale on the basis that such thinking was part and parcel of the "comprador" philosophy—an attitude that instead of augmenting China's security did just the opposite.

The exact effect of the arguments are difficult to document, but it appears that the "radicals" lost the debate on importation of foreign technology and equipment, as it became an integral part of the Fourth Five Year Plan (1971–1975). The plan also increased investment in basic industries such as mining, petroleum, chemicals, and electric power,[21] and it again reordered economic priorities. Defense production output figures were 25 percent lower than the peak 1970–1971 period. The aircraft industry bore the brunt of the cutback, but other sectors also suffered. Although the decision to curtail defense production was obviously linked to political and other economic allocation choices, it may also reflect decisions not to produce follow-on systems, which could only incrementally improve already obsolete Soviet designs. In economic lexicon, the Chinese began to encounter rapidly diminishing returns from large R&D outlays. The alternative, of course, was the Herculean task of incorporating foreign technologies into the existing (Soviet-based) serial-producing infrastructure.

Despite the enormous problems of absorption, a policy of acquiring technology from the West was activated in 1972. Foreign assistance became an integral part of Premier Zhou's plan for comprehensive economic modernization by the turn of the century. Negotiations for the transfer of a wide variety of technologies, goods and services, and whole turn-key plants from Western nations began in 1972–1973, and contract signing began in earnest in 1974–1975.

The critical question for policymakers was whether to favor the defense industries in such purchases (as they had during the 1950s) or to disperse imports so as to broaden the overall industrial base. To be sure, there is much overlap between civil and military industrial production. Initial purchases indicated the selection of a somewhat middle position. Right from the start, the Chinese made it clear that they were interested in minimizing dependency on foreign suppliers, which could only be done by acquiring the *means* of production, via prototype reproduction rights, and/or obtaining production rights under license. Indicative of this strategy was the 1975 purchase of fifty Rolls-Royce Spey turbofan jet engines with license to manufacture these engines at a plant near Xian. The Spey is a very durable engine with a low flight-to-maintenance ratio (600–1,000 hours of flight time before overhaul) and is suitable for fixture on small airframes (e.g., interceptors). Airframe production has always been a chronic problem for China's aerospace industry, but the Spey will reportedly be fitted on a modified version of the Soviet MiG-23 interceptor. Once this is done, China will have advanced its jet propulsion technology forward by ten years.[22] A more detailed review of China's procurement strategy, inquiries, and purchases from abroad is presented in Section 3 of this chapter.

Having been politically "rehabilitated" in 1973, Deng Xiaoping set as a central task the preparation of the PLA for combat under "modern conditions." Deng is generally held responsible for the drafting of Central Directive (*zhong-fa*) Number 18 of 1975, which included as a central element the bridging of the chasm in conventional weaponry between the AK-47 assault rifle and nuclear weapons. Deng's plan, and Deng, were shelved simultaneously in the spring of 1976 after Zhou's death. With the purge of the Gang of Four following Mao's death and Deng's subsequent second rehabilitation, calls for military modernization and PLA professionalism rose to a level unseen in China since the mid-1950s. Although the desire exists, as we shall see later, the allocations necessary to realize this goal do not.

Although there appeared to be a broad consensus among policymakers on the *need* to modernize the military, there has been much debate as to the *pace* and *modality* of this quest. Again, the central question has been whether the defense industries should lead industrial development or vice versa. This and other questions were debated openly in the press and at conferences in 1977 and 1978.[23] The debate was resolved in favor of those who argued that the modernization of defense is linked to the development of the overall economy, particularly the industrial base and science and technology (S&T) levels. This is an important distinction with direct impact on budgetary allocations. Chinese industry will not be "militarized" like its Soviet counterpart. Instead, the machine building industries have begun to diversify production by increasing sideline output of many light industrial products.[24]

These decisions were reflected in a definitive statement concerning military modernization by then-Defense Minister Xu Xiangqian in *Hongqi* [Red Flag], the party's theoretical journal, on October 1, 1979.[25] The entire article is worthwhile reading, but I quote selected salient sentences:

> The modernization of national defense cannot be divorced from the modernization of agriculture, industry, science and technology and, in the final analysis, is based on the national economy. . . . Blindly pursuing large-scale and high-speed development in building national defense will invariably and seriously hinder the development of the national economy and will harm the base of the defense industry. Subsequently, "haste makes waste." . . . We must lay stress on the development of conventional weapons while continuously developing some nuclear weapons and other sophisticated weapons. . . . Atomic energy, aeronautics, electronics, lasers, infrared rays and other techniques are extensively applied militarily, causing tremendous changes in weaponry. . . . We must actively design and manufacture new-type weapons and . . . selectively import advanced technologies which we urgently need.

In order to implement this strategy, wholesale personnel changes took place. The ministers of all defense industries were replaced during 1978. The Fifth National People's Congress (NPC) appointed Liu Wei, Lu Dong, Zhang Zhen, Chai Sufan, and Zheng Tianxiang to direct, respectively, the Second, Third, Fifth, Sixth, and Seventh Ministries of Machine Building. The minister of the Fourth Ministry, Wang Zheng, died in August 1979 and was replaced by Qian Min. With the exception of Liu Wei, these appointments clearly represent ongoing attempts to reinstitute civilian control over the military in general and the defense industries in particular.

This overview of Chinese defense industry policies during the past thirty years is really a prologue for a more detailed examination of the Chinese military-industrial complex as it enters the 1980s. In many ways, the decisions and choices made since 1978 are a continuation of policy choices made in 1956 and again in 1961. But perhaps today, given the gap between China's weapons and military prowess as compared with those of its potential adversaries, the issues have become more critical and the choices more narrow.

2. THE DEFENSE INDUSTRIES IN 1980

Budget

The major issues are those of budgetary allocation by the state to the defense industries on the whole and competing priorities within the various sectors. The regime has clearly decided to hold defense spending at a level that allows for the most essential aspects of deterrence while attempting to divert underutilized resources from military to civilian industrial production. This position was reflected in Hua Guofeng's address to the Fifth National People's Congress on February 26, 1978: "The national defense industries should turn their production to good account. . . . Serious efforts should be made to implement the policy of integrating military with non-military enter-prises and peacetime production with preparedness against war." This statement is in line with the conclusion that a strong defense requires a modern industrial base.

The process of estimating defense budgets always allows for a considerable margin of error, especially for "closed" command econ-omies, because of what one factors in or out.[26] The official Chinese defense expenditure figure, revealed for the first time as part of the 1979 national budget, was 20,320 million yuan (U.S. $12.9 billion), or 18 percent of planned state expenditure. This figure was cut to U.S. $9.92 billion for fiscal 1980–81 and U.S. $9.88 billion for fiscal 1981–82, and then rose incrementally to U.S. $10.5 billion for fiscal 1982–83. These figures differ markedly from Western estimates, which place the figure roughly at 10 percent of GNP, or approximately U.S. $40 billion,[27] the third highest figure globally. How this figure is earmarked for the various sectors of the defense industries is not exactly known.

However, the Central Intelligence Agency (CIA), in its publication *Chinese Defense Spending 1965–79*, divides defense expenditures into three categories: investment, operating, and RDT&E (research, de-velopment, testing, and evaluation). This report is worth reading in its entirety, but for our purposes, the following quotation summarizes its findings on sectoral investment.

> Investment expenditures reflect the flow of new or replacement equip-ment and facilities to the forces; operating expenditures are the costs associated with their day-to-day functioning; and RDT&E expenditures support activities concerned with future force modernization. About fifty percent of the estimated spending over the 1965–79 period went for investment in equipment (roughly forty percent) and facilities (roughly

ten percent). Operating costs absorbed about thirty-five percent of the total RDT&E (an average of about fifteen percent). Defense consists of both the procurement of weapons and equipment and the construction of military facilities. About eighty percent of investment spending has been for weapons procurement, with about one-half of this allocated for aircraft, missiles, and ships. . . . We estimate that operating expenditures between 1965 and 1979 grew at an average annual rate of slightly less than five percent. Operating expenditures include personnel costs and the cost of operation and maintenance (O&M) of equipment and military facilities. Within this category, O&M costs have grown somewhat faster than personnel-related costs—primarily reflecting a slow increase in weapons inventory. The Chinese have limited their RDT&E efforts to a few major products. They have generally included one or two models in each type of weapon system. The systems being developed show a substantial technological improvement over those currently being produced, but they still represent weapons technologies of the early 1960s. . . .

Another way of analyzing our estimated cost data is by use . . . into six functional components. Five are related to different types of combat forces: ground, naval, air defense, air attack, and ballistic missile. The sixth functional component includes activities—such as command, support and RDT&E—that provide common services to all the others. . . . Spending for the ground forces has gradually increased since 1965 and has averaged over twenty percent of total defense spending. Estimated spending for China's naval programs more than doubled between 1965 and 1972, primarily reflecting growth in the procurement of ships and boats. Since that time, the level of spending has been relatively constant, as a recent slowdown in the construction of submarines and small combatants has been offset by increased production of frigates and destroyers. Naval expenditures accounted for roughly twenty percent of military spending during the 1965–79 period. . . . Spending for air defense forces increased rapidly between 1965 and 1971, decreased sharply in 1972, and then increased gradually through 1978. Air defense expenditures represent nearly twenty percent of China's total defense spending for the 1965–79 period. The spending pattern for China's air attack forces reflects the uneven nature of Chinese aircraft production. Expenditures rose steeply during 1965–71 and began to decline in 1972. The trend continued slightly downward through 1974 and then followed a fluctuating pattern through 1979. Somewhat less than five percent of cumulative defense spending for 1965–79 has gone to these forces. The investment and operating costs for China's ballistic missile force have amounted to less than five percent of cumulative defense spending since 1965. We do not include in this figure the considerable expenditures associated with ballistic missile RDT&E, which accounts for about two-thirds of our total estimate for Chinese RDT&E. About thirty percent of Beijing's total defense expenditure was accounted for by the remaining activities, which include RDT&E and command and support components.

Command and support components include a variety of general rear-service functions such as logistics, security, intelligence, medical services, and administration. We estimate that military spending in China is taking a much smaller share of China's gross national product during 1979–80 than it did in 1965–71. GNP is now sixty percent above the 1971 level and industrial production is one hundred percent higher, but military spending is only now reaching the 1971 level.[28]

I quote this report at such length because it is the only sectoral breakdown of Chinese defense expenditure that I am aware of. Further, given the CIA's obvious advantages in estimating such things, one can be reasonably assured of the report's accuracy. What the report does not do, however, is to give a sectoral inventory of weapons in the Chinese arsenal—past or present. This breakdown is what follows in the ensuing ministry-by-ministry survey of the Chinese defense industries.

Organization

As the 1980s began, there existed a total of eight ministries of machine building, of which the second through the eighth produced for the military. Between 1981 and 1982, all were renamed, and the Eighth Ministry merged with the Seventh Ministry of Machine Building. Their present production responsibilities are as follows, and the defense-related industries fit into the broader planning structure as shown in Figure 3.1.

Ministry	*Responsibility*
Ministry of Machine-Building Industry (1st m.m.b.)	Civilian production
Ministry of Nuclear Industry (2nd m.m.b.)	Nuclear weapons
Ministry of Aviation Industry (3rd m.m.b.)	Aircraft
Ministry of Electronics Industry (4th m.m.b.)	Electronic systems
Ministry of Ordnance Industry (5th m.m.b.)	Munitions and armaments
China State Shipbuilding Corporation (6th m.m.b.)	Naval construction
Ministry of Space Industry (7th m.m.b.)	Ballistic missiles
Eighth Ministry of Machine Building (merged with 7th m.m.b. in 1981)	Space systems

FIGURE 3.1 China's Military-Industrial Complex

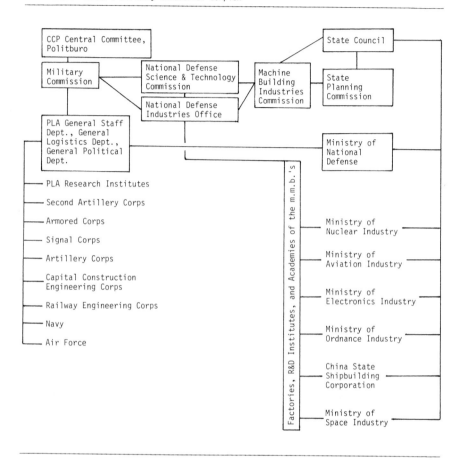

Ministry of Machine-Building Industry

The Ministry of Machine-Building Industry produces industrial equipment ostensibly for civilian use. It includes seventeen research institutes and seven industrial control bureaus.[29] It produces machine tools, power machinery and equipment, transportation equipment, metallurgical equipment, construction and mining equipment, petroleum drilling equipment, agricultural machinery, and a wide variety of general industrial equipment—such as pumps, compressors, bearings, motors, and welding equipment. Although this ministry does not produce military equipment per se, many of its products and design technologies "trickle down" to the military.

Second Ministry of Machine Building

The Second Ministry of Machine Building (renamed the Ministry of Nuclear Industry in 1982) is responsible for all nuclear research and weapons production. This ministry has probably received the most consistent support from the central government since its inception in 1959. The Soviet Union provided technical assistance in the late 1950s,[30] and the Chinese exploded their first nuclear device on October 16, 1964. There have been twenty-six tests since—the majority aboveground, much to the consternation of other countries. China's stockpile of thermonuclear weapons, both fission and fusion, probably amounts to several hundred and continues to grow. China has exploded nuclear devices ranging from twenty kilotons to four megatons. A gaseous diffusion plant at Lanzhou has been producing weapons-grade U-235 since 1963, and a reactor complex at Yumen has produced plutonium since 1967.[31] Most testing takes place at the Lop Nor site in Xinjiang Province. (Delivery systems are discussed later in this chapter.)

Third Ministry of Machine Building

The Third Ministry of Machine Building (renamed the Ministry of Aviation Industry in 1982) is responsible for aeronautic systems, except ballistic missiles. It does, however, produce tactical (e.g., anti-air, anti-tank) missiles. The Third Ministry supervises a significant industry that produces, maintains, and replaces over 5,000 military aircraft and at least 500 aircraft belonging to the civilian fleet.[32] China's largest aircraft production facilities are located in Shenyang, Liaoning Province. Other large aircraft manufacturing centers are in Xian, Beijing, Harbin, Nanchang, Chengdu, and Chongqing.

These facilities have produced virtually all of China's inventory of fighter-interceptor aircraft. The Chinese have made improvements on succeeding generations of the Soviet MiG-17, -19, and -21. Currently, the most advanced fighter in full production is the A-5 (also known as F-6bis and the F-9), which is based on the Soviet MiG-19 design. The F-8, which reportedly is a much-modified version of the Soviet MiG-21, is due to come on production stream in the early 1980s. Both planes are capable of Mach-2 speeds, but are hampered by propulsion problems and lack of all-weather capability (particularly navigation and weapons-aiming subsystems). The F-7 is an improved version of the MiG-21PF and has been in service since the 1960s. The Chinese have sold or given this plane to Bangladesh, Pakistan, Egypt, and Tanzania. The backbones of the Chinese fighter fleet, however, are the F-4 and F-6, which are based on the MiG-17 and -19, respectively. These planes compose nearly two-thirds of China's total interceptor inventory. Although it is not known to have gone into production, the Chinese are reportedly developing a modified version of the Soviet MiG-23 (to be dubbed the F-12), which they received copies of from Egypt in exchange for overhauling engines for Egypt's MiG-21s. Although it is at best in the prototype stage, it is this plane that the Chinese hope to fit with the aforementioned Spey engine. China also maintains about 500 antiquated MiG-15s.

Also antiquated is the bomber force of 300 IL-28s and 90 TU-16s, which also date back to Soviet designs of the 1950s. The TU-16/Badger, though antiquated, has the range to reach targets in the USSR as far as the Urals, as well as other states on China's periphery. The IL-28/Beagle's radius of action is so small as to limit its capability to nearby regional targets. Both aircraft can deliver nuclear weapons. The IL-28 is manufactured in Shenyang, and the TU-16 is produced near Xian, Shanxi Province. There is little chance that a new bomber with a strategic capability will be developed during the next ten years. However, the Chinese are capable of designing and producing a four-engine, long-range bomber, which would provide improved payload and range capabilities compared with the Badger.

All indications are that the aircraft industry has once again been designated as a "key-point" (*zhong dian*) and will receive a large portion of defense investment funds in the 1980s. The interceptor force is expected to reap most benefits, and substantial overall qualitative improvements are expected within the next decade. Further, the aircraft industry may be the recipient of foreign purchases. Indicative of this fact has been the purchase in the last few years of thirteen Super Frelon helicopters from France, four Messerschmitt helicopters from West Germany, the Spey engine factory from Great Britain, and Boeing jets from the United States. In addition, negotiations have taken place for the purchase of 70 Harrier (VSTOL) jets, with licensed production rights for 200 to 300 more, from Great Britain. During their European shopping trips of 1977–1979, the Chinese looked earnestly at French Mirage 2000 fighters, Italian Augusta helicopters, U.S. Lockheed C-130 and C-141 transport planes, and the P-3C Orion anti-submarine patrol plane. Optical guidance equipment and a variety of tactical missiles (air-to-air, air-to-surface, etc.) have also been of keen interest to the Chinese. These shopping excursions, purchases, and China's strategy for acquiring weapons and defense technologies will be discussed in greater detail in the next section of this chapter.

The Defense Intelligence Agency currently estimates that although the tactical air force has grown by nearly 70 percent since 1969, a much slower growth rate is expected during the 1980s. Current estimates project an overall increase of about 15 percent by 1989. During this time, older aircraft will be phased out of the inventory, and a new generation aircraft will begin to appear.[33] By its own admission, the Chinese air force currently lags twenty years behind state-of-the-art designs. Specifically, its problems lie in the highly sophisticated technologies associated with jet engine design and the production of special alloys for airframe construction.[34] China has sufficient competence to produce small quantities of superalloys, stainless steels, and electrical steels, but the key weakness in alloys needed for aircraft production are nonferrous metals: aluminum, magnesium, titanium, cobalt, and nickel.[35] China is receiving much assistance from abroad in mining and processing these metals plus copper, tungsten, and zinc. The Japanese and Europeans are also providing casting technology needed for jet engine housings, aircraft wings, brakes, bearings, and turbine blades. The enormous difficulties of incorporating new Western designs, technologies, and manufacturing facilities into the preexisting Soviet-based industrial infrastructure will perhaps be most acute in the aeronautics industries.

The aviation industry also produces tactical precision-guided missiles (PGMs): air-to-air, surface-to-air (SAM), etc. Production responsibility for some of these was taken over by the Eighth Ministry, but evidently air-to-air missiles remain with the Third Ministry.

Fourth Ministry of Machine Building

The Fourth Ministry of Machine Building (renamed the Ministry of Electronics Industry in 1982) is responsible for electronics, telecommunications, and navigational equipment. Electronics has truly been a growth industry in China, although again lagging in qualitative terms considerably behind advanced countries. Total value of output is estimated to be about U.S. $3 billion annually, with about one-half to two-thirds destined for military use.[36] To be sure, electronics is just such an industry where civilian and military development overlap and substantially complement each other. For the purposes of this book, I will focus on components used in military end products.

The most profound development in the field as far as the military is concerned has been the evolution from tubes to transistors to integrated circuits (ICs) during the 1970s. Transistors, diodes, and ICs of Chinese manufacture are being used in missile guidance and tracking systems, radars, sonar, avionics, nuclear equipment, and computers.

Foreign assistance, particularly Japanese, has been vital to the development of the electronics industry. In many cases, technology transfer has been the catalytic element enabling the Chinese to move from the laboratory stage to commercial output. Such was the case, for example, with ICs as in the late 1960s, the Chinese procured necessary material for the fabrication of ICs and other electronic devices from Japan. Japanese assistance has also been of critical help to the development and testing of large-scale integrated circuits (LSIs).

The development of LSI production capacity is critical to a wide variety of military systems, particularly sophisticated tracking and guidance systems. Some reports from knowledgeable foreign visitors confirm that China is fast approaching the world's highest performance levels in the development of high-capacity LSI circuits.[37] This ability, however, does not in itself mean the capability to mass produce the final chips in economic quantities. The process of mass production entails very sophisticated semiconductor materials technologies and precision testing equipment, most of which is under strict export controls by COCOM. (COCOM is the Coordinating Committee of the Consultative Group for the control of exports of strategic materials to communist countries. COCOM is composed of NATO members— minus Iceland—and Japan.)

The workings of COCOM and the subject of sensitive technology transfer will be dealt with at length in the next section of this chapter. Suffice it to say here that COCOM considers LSI a "critical technology" and has consciously attempted to minimize or restrict such exports altogether. This effort is particularly true of the U.S. government, as exemplified by two color television manufacturing plant deals—one by RCA and the other by Hitachi of Japan. Both sales were eventually made (in 1978 and 1977, respectively), but not before the U.S. Commerce and Defense Departments repeatedly sent designers back to the drawing boards so as to increase the gap between the LSI technology embodied in the television sets and the current state of the art—a gap of about ten years. Obtaining the export license was a very cumbersome, frustrating, and expensive endeavor for RCA.[38] This example is not only an illuminating case study in U.S. bureaucratic politics, but also an example par excellence of a dual-use technology, i.e., one that is ostensibly for civilian use but has direct military application. In the cases of LSI and infrared seismic scanning equipment, no real "reverse engineering" is necessary to convert them to military use, as is the case with computers. Infrared scanning equipment is used to search for mineral deposits, but it also has immediate utility in anti-submarine warfare (ASW) reconnaissance.

If IC production technology lags seven to ten years behind its counterpart in the West,[39] then the computer industry lags more than a generation. However, the improvement of IC production, especially

LSI circuits, will directly benefit the computer industry. The production capacity of the Chinese computer industry is hampered by archaic manufacturing techniques, such as manual soldering and by one-at-a-time, or batch, assembly rather than serial production. Memory storage capacity still relies primarily on magnetic drums and tapes. The principal forms of input continue to be keyboard and papertape readers.[40] The printout of most standard computers currently in production ranges from 100,000 to 500,000 operations per second. The DJS-11, DJS-260, and DJS-184 models all perform one million operations per second.[41] The 013 model can do two million, and a planned DJS-185 model will be capable of three million.[42] China's most powerful computer, the HDS-9, came on stream in 1978 and can perform five million operations per second.[43] Despite these advances, the Chinese computer industry has a long way to go to reach world standards.

To be sure, Chinese computer development has been severely hampered by strict COCOM controls on both hardware and software. The prototype purchases that have gone through have resulted in severe absorption problems because of China's poor design-engineering base. Attempts at reverse engineering have largely failed. The major effect of Western technology so far has been as a source of information and a starting point for R&D within the domestic computer industry. Insofar as military application of Chinese computers is concerned, they are used extensively in aircraft and missile guidance, tracking systems, and for radar and sonar. Digital computers are used for fire control and target analysis. Export controls in this area are loosening up. A British firm has reportedly sealed a deal for U.S. $94.8 million to equip the F-6 and F-7 with new navigation equipment.[44]

In addition to semiconductors and computers, the Fourth Ministry is responsible for all telecommunications production. For military usage, the Fourth Ministry produces a spectrum of equipment ranging from walkie-talkies to satellites, but it should be noted that virtually all civilian communications equipment has some military utility. The PLA regularly uses all forms of the extensive domestic communications network: microwave radio relay, multiplex wireless, telephone and telegraph, radio and television, telex, satellite relay, etc. During the 1970s, the Chinese were able to develop long-range, secure voice communication systems.

Nowhere in China's electronics industry has the impact of foreign technology and equipment been reflected more dramatically than in the telecommunications and detection/location fields. Defense has directly benefited. The Chinese have bought coding-decoding and electronic-intercept equipment, sonar and optical tracking equipment, navigation systems, and airborne and ground radar. The long-range surveillance radar system procured from Thomson-CSF of France has been deployed along the Soviet border.

The most notable assistance has come in the field of satellites. For example, the United States agreed during ex-Defense Secretary Brown's January 1980 visit to provide a LANDSAT-D ground station and a separate communications satellite. The ground station employs advanced computers and taping equipment, which could be used militarily, but the resolution of the imagery provided is not sharp enough for military use.[45] This sale surely supplements China's already existent reconnaissance satellite program. There has also been discussion of late of increased intelligence sharing from satellite detection with the United States and Western Europe (primarily information related to Soviet and Vietnamese troop deployments).

Finally, a few words about the location and organization of the electronics industry is in order. In sheer size, the Chinese themselves claim that the electronics industry "now has more than three thousand plants and units with more than ninety thousand scientific and technical personnel and more than one million workers and staff members."[46] The major plants are located in Shanghai, Wuhan, Beijing, Nanjing, and Tianjin. The ministry controls a large but unknown number of research institutes, many in conjunction with the Chinese Academy of Sciences (CAS).

Fifth Ministry of Machine Building

The Fifth Ministry of Machine Building (renamed the Ministry of Ordnance Industry in 1982) is responsible for producing all munitions and conventional military hardware. Production includes substantial quantities of infantry weapons, tanks, armored personnel carriers, ammunition, mortars, rocket launchers, anti-aircraft guns, and some tactical missiles.[47]

The AK-47 remains the PLA's standard assault rifle and is considered one of the finest infantry weapons in the world. Indigenous versions of pistols, recoilless rifles, light and heavy machine guns, and other semiautomatic and automatic weapons are also produced. Artillery weapons number about 16,000 of all types and use ammunition ranging in caliber from 14.5 mm to 160 mm. The PLA uses 20,000 mortars, rocket launchers, and anti-aircraft guns.[48] The RPG/7 is apparently the best launcher. Mortars use 82-mm, 120-mm, and 160-mm caliber shells. Anti-aircraft guns utilize 14.5-mm, 37-mm, 57-mm, 85-mm, and 100-mm caliber ammunition. Anti-tank weaponry uses 57-mm, 76-mm, 85-mm, and 100-mm ammunition. General-purpose field artillery use these caliber shells plus 107-mm, 122-mm, 130-mm, 140-

mm, and 152-mm howitzer cartridges. All are based on Soviet designs, although this situation is changing—particularly in anti-tank and anti-air weaponry.

The Chinese believe that the most likely form of Soviet attack will come as an armored blitzkrieg (with air support) through Xinjiang and/or Manchuria. To this end, the Chinese have paid closest attention to scouting anti-tank (AT) anti-air (AA) precision-guided missiles (PGMs) in Europe as a possible "quick-fix" means of augmenting immediate defense needs. In Great Britain, the Chinese have looked closely at the Rapier AA and the Swingfire AT missiles. Their main interest, however, has been in the French Crotale AA and the HOT and Milan AT PGMs (coproduced with West Germany). The Crotale, which can be mounted on trucks or patrol boats, is designed to bring down low-flying supersonic aircraft. The Milan is a PGM weighing twenty-four pounds with a range of just over 2,000 yards. The heavier HOT missile has twice the range and can be fired from a helicopter or tank. The Western press has carried conflicting reports about Chinese purchase of the Crotale, HOT, and Milan, but it appears at the time of this writing that no contracts have yet been signed.[49]

Indigenous anti-tank technology has been bolstered by the development of a grenade capable of piercing a steel plate 150 mm thick. On September 4, 1979, *Renmin ribao* [People's daily] reported that this compact, light, gun-fired, anti-tank grenade had been developed by Tang Zhaoning, a deputy chief of an ordinance section of a Lanzhou PLA unit. Tang got the idea at a "meeting on anti-tank technology innovation" in 1974; after five years and over 700 tests, the grenade has gone into production.

The PLA possesses about 11,000 battle tanks of heavy, medium, light, and amphibious variety.[50] Considerable numbers of the Soviet T-34, the supreme battle tank of World War II, are still deployed, but not produced. The T-34 chassis has been refitted with twin 37-mm AA guns and is sometimes referred to as the T-34AA. This model remains in production. The T-59 medium tank, which is a copy of the Soviet T-54, has been the main battle tank (MBT) since 1963. A T-62 light tank (25 tons, 85-mm gun) has been in service for many years and is deployed primarily south of the Yangtze River. This tank is particularly effective in rough terrain, as in southern China, and was used during the January 1979 incursion into Vietnam. The Fifth Ministry also produces a T-62 medium tank, which carries a 115-mm gun. This tank is modeled on its Soviet counterpart. The Chinese received samples of it from Egypt after that country's 1973 political rupture with the Soviets. The Chinese also produce T-60 and T-63 light, amphibious, reconnaissance vehicles, which superficially resemble tanks. They are both based on the Soviet PT-76 (76-mm gun). The Chinese modified that model by mating the PT-76 hull with an 85-mm gun turret similar to the one on the T-62 light tank (however the armor is welded, not cast). They also modified the amphibious propulsion system. The result is the T-60. Later, the water propulsion system was changed back to the PT-76 original version; this is the T-63.

Armored personnel carriers (APCs) number about 3,500, are indigenously designed, and are similar to the U.S. M-113.[51] The main APC is the M-1967 amphibious vehicle. China also produces STR-60 and T-56 open-top APCs, based on the Soviet BTR-60P and BTR-152, respectively.[52] APCs should be in for upgrading in the wake of the Vietnam incursion. Troop mobility was clearly hampered by inadequate battlefield transport support systems, both in number and quality.

Production facilities of the Fifth Ministry are spread throughout the country, as described in Section 1.

Sixth Ministry of Machine Building

The Sixth Ministry of Machine Building (abrogated in 1982 and replaced by the China State Shipbuilding Corporation) is responsible for shipbuilding and naval construction. The Chinese navy is basically a coastal defense force with little blue-water capability. It consists largely of patrol craft, frigates, light destroyers, hydrofoils, and submarines. The amphibious assault force has been steadily improved to the point where the Chinese navy now "has a sufficient number of conventional amphibious vessels to lift a force of over 30,000 men and equipment in a regional (less than thirty hours transit) amphibious assault."[53]

China's fourteen destroyers are primarily of the Luda class, are also armed with Styx surface-to-surface missiles (SSMs), and are composed as follows: three Jianghu class, five Jiangnan class, two Jiangdong class, and four ex-Soviet Riga class. The newer of these destroyers and frigates have a range of 2,500 to 4,000 nautical miles.[54]

The Hainan-class patrol boat is China's best. Also assisting in coastal defense are Osa- and Hola-class missile boats; Huangpu- and Shanghai-class gunboats—the latter having been produced in four versions and sold abroad. China also produces the Huchuan diesel hydrofoil and T-43 ocean minesweeper.[55]

China's submarine force consists of ninety-one diesel-powered Romeo, Whiskey, and Ming class subs. These vessels are equipped with six or eight 535-mm torpedo tubes, have a maximum cruising range of 7,000 nautical miles (or roughly forty days at sea), and travel at nineteen knots on the surface or fifteen knots submerged.[56] The Chinese also have one Golf-class ballistic missile submarine fitted with submarine-launched ballistic missile (SLBM) tubes—but no known missiles to deploy—and one Han-class nuclear sub.

It seems logical that naval construction will increase alongside the booming merchant fleet for escort purposes and protection of China's offshore oil. Competing needs in other service sectors will undoubtedly be a constraining factor, as will be problems of inputs from heavy industries. Specifically, problems of producing quality steels have been an inhibiting factor.[57] About a quarter of China's shipbuilding yards (including naval yards) are in the Shanghai region. Other centers are Guangzhou, Luda (Dairen), Guangzhi, and Huludao.

Seventh Ministry of Machine Building

The Seventh Ministry of Machine Building (renamed the Ministry of Space Industry in 1982) is responsible for ballistic missile production and satellite launching. It appears that satellite construction is the task of the Fourth and/or Eighth Ministries. Indeed, in the field of nuclear warhead production, there is much overlap with the Second Ministry. Further, the Second Artillery Corps (the PLA's equivalent of the Soviet Strategic Rocket Forces) appears to command the operation of strategic missiles.[58] The Second Artillery is responsible directly to the PLA chief of staff (currently Yang Dezhi) in the formal organizational structure, but the actual chain of command and control of its units and weapons is not clear.

All present missiles are liquid fueled (although solid propellants are being developed), use inertial guidance systems, and carry relatively large-yield nuclear warheads. The inherent slow reaction times and relatively poor accuracies of the following missile systems make them unsuitable for "counterforce" operations; however, they are effective for striking "countervalue" targets, i.e., cities instead of silos.[59]

China's medium-range ballistic missile (MRBM)—the CSS-1—has been operational since 1966, but it may be phased out and replaced by the intermediate-range ballistic missile (IRBM)—the CSS-2. The MRBM is based on the Soviet SS-2, carries a twenty-kiloton warhead, is deployed in soft sites or caves, and has a range of 600 to 700 nautical miles. The IRBM is also single staged and liquid fueled, carries a two- or three-megaton warhead, is deployed in caves or steel/concrete silos, and has a range of 1,500 to 2,500 nautical miles. The Chinese are working on a second-generation, solid-fueled, multistage IRBM. Development of an intercontinental ballistic missile (ICBM) has been completed, albeit slowly, and it is deployed in two forms. The CSS-3, a multistage rocket with a range of 3,000 to 5,000 nautical miles, was first flight tested in 1976. A full-range ICBM (the CSS-X-4) has been under development for years and is now operational. This missile, previously used as a launcher for satellites, was finally successfully full-range tested in May 1980. Launched in Xinjiang, the missile impacted over 8,000 kilometers away near the Solomon Islands in the South Pacific. This missile, similar to the U.S. Titan, can carry a multimegaton multiple warhead. When this missile is deployed, probably in hardened silos, it will considerably enhance China's nuclear deterrent vis-à-vis the Soviet Union. It should also be noted that this missile gives China, for the first time, the capability to strike the continental United States.

The Chinese also manufacture an air-to-air missile (the CAA-1), which is a version of the Soviet K-13A AA-2 Atoll. Also under manufacture is a surface-to-air missile (SAM), the CSA-1. However, as mentioned previously, the Chinese recognize the inadequacies of these missiles and have looked to foreign sources to fill their needs.

Lastly, the Chinese have been working for some time on the development of a submarine-launched ballistic missile (SLBM) for use in their Golf-class submarine. This SLBM, which is roughly comparable to the early U.S. solid-propellant Polaris, was successfully tested in November 1982. Once the SLBM is deployed, China will be able to complete the triad of strategic forces: submarines, bombers, and ICBMs. Although the Soviet Union assisted the Chinese in getting their program off the ground, much credit must be given to Chinese scientists for developing the nuclear and ballistic missile programs to their current levels.

Currently, the Chinese are estimated to possess forty to fifty of the CSS-1, fifty to seventy of the CSS-2, two limited-range CSS-3s, and an unknown number of the CSS-X-4.[60] China's major missile-testing facilities are located at Shuang Chengzi in northern Gansu Province and in the Wuzhai area in Shanxi Province. The Seventh Ministry was plagued by factional strife after Mao's death,[61] but judging by (the lack of) press reports since 1979, it now appears to have settled down.

Eighth Ministry of Machine Building

The Eighth Ministry (merged with the 7th m.m.b. in 1981) was created at the eleventh session of the Standing Committee of the Fifth National People's Congress in September 1979. The Eighth Ministry's mandate was not entirely clear. The communiqué stated only that it was "established to meet the needs of defense industry production."[62] It was believed, however, to be responsible for China's new space program[63] and its cruise missile development program[64] and probably took over some responsibility for satellite production and launching.

China has launched eight satellites since 1971 and has mastered the remote-control technology necessary for deceleration, reentry, and landing. This ability also shows that China can produce a heat-resistant alloy capable of withstanding the high temperatures of reentry. The mastery of retrieval technology is the prerequisite for launching manned spacecraft. China has begun to train astronauts and to do simulated biological experimentation.

Oversight

Responsibility for coordination of these production lines and allocation of funds continues to rest with the National Defense Industries Office (NDIO). The scope of the NDIO has been previously discussed, and as best one can tell, it remains essentially the same, although with the increased emphasis on coordination of industrial planning, the NDIO's role may be enhanced. Such is also the case with the aforementioned NDSTC.[65] Both of these bodies remain bureaucratically responsible to the Military Commission. Leading individuals in these bodies remain obscure. It was disclosed during Defense Secretary Brown's January 1980 visit that Zhang Aiping served concurrently as chairman of the NDSTC and PLA deputy chief of staff (in November 1982 Zhang replaced Geng Biao as defense minister). Qian Xuesen served as vice-chairman of the NDSTC; he is a noted scientist, professor, and author (*Theory of Engineering Control* and *Engineering Cybernetics*). The NDIO is now headed by Hong Xuezhi, former director of the General Rear Services Department (GRSD) and concurrently director of the General Logistics Department (formerly the GRSD).

What *is* new is the establishment of the Machine Building Industries Commission (MBIC) under the State Council. The MBIC was inaugurated at the thirteenth plenary session of the Fifth National People's Congress on February 12, 1980. In some ways, the MBIC appears to be the civilian counterpart to the NDIO and will concentrate primarily on coordinating the First Ministry's production, although its bailiwick appears to extend over defense production as well. In establishing the MBIC, Vice-Premier Bo Yibo generally outlined its tasks as follows:

> The main tasks of the Commission are to better implement the policy of readjustment, restructuring, consolidation and improvement, as well as relevant economic and technical policies in the machine building industry; to make unified planning and reasonable adjustment in accordance with the principle of combining specialization and coordination; to encourage the army and the people . . . to share the work and

cooperate with each other; to do a good job in turning out standardized, serial, and general-purpose products; vigorously improve the quality of machinery.[66]

The bureaucratic importance of the MBIC is underscored by its location alongside the State Planning Commission and just under the State Council.

Recent Trends

For the defense industries, the six-year period of economic readjustment (1979–1985), as formulated primarily by Chen Yun, means relative inattention. A key policy change of the readjustment period is to give priority to light industry over heavy industry. To this end, the defense industries are turning out light industrial products. Does this inhibit defense production? Logic says yes, the Chinese say no.

> National defense industries are completely able to guarantee fulfillment of military production while simultaneously carrying out production of light industrial products. . . . Of course, in promoting the production of the people's necessities, the military industry will encounter problems in raw materials, finance, production, and demand for products. These kinds of problems are to be solved by the efforts of the national defense industries.[67]

Premier Zhao Ziyang candidly assessed the fate of the machine building industries during the readjustment period in an authoritative article in *Hongqi* on January 1, 1980: "The machine building and metallurgical trades are among the first to bear the brunt. They are confronted with the problem of changing over to other products and undergoing reorganization to meet market needs."[68]

This trend of integrating defense and civilian production is evident in the nuclear field as well. At the first congress of the Chinese Nuclear Society in February 1980, then Vice-Premiers Fang I and Wang Zhen pointed out: "Atomic energy cannot be divided into two sectors, one for military use and the other for civilian use. It is hoped that scientists, while continuing military research to strengthen the national defense capability, will integrate military and civilian aspects."[69] The sideline production of civilian items has begun to show positive fiscal results in some machine building industries. For example, enterprises under the Third Ministry declared:

In 1979 it produced products for civilian use worth about 200 million yuan. The output value of products for civilian use in a number of its factories has accounted for about one-half of their total output value. . . . The Third Ministry of Machine Building has decided to set up networks or stations for exhibiting or marketing products for civilian use in such cities as Guangzhou, Hangzhou, Shanghai, Beijing, Nanjing, Xian, Wuhan, Fuzhou, and Guiyang. These networks and stations will promote sales for the production units, sell their products on a commission basis or become their sole agents.[70]

State Planning Commission Chairman Yao Yilin announced in his 1980 National People's Congress speech that "in 1979, the output of goods for civilian use accounted for twenty percent of the total output value of the defense industry."[71] Examples of such civilian products are "small-scale sports rifles, film projectors, ultrasonic diagnostic instruments, activated carbon and catalysts."[72] Although the Chinese maintain that "integrating military with non-military production is a long-term policy, not an expedient measure in any sense,"[73] that may also be a way of telling the defense industries that it will be well into the Sixth Five Year Plan before domestic investment or foreign procurement will be substantially increased. This seemed to be the message of a 1979 work conference of "the office in charge of the national defense industries" (presumably the NDIO):

> It is impractical to desire everything new or Western or to rely on the state for large sums of investments and foreign exchange whenever the word "modernization" is mentioned. Such mentality of "wait, depend on, and want" will only tie our hands and affect the expeditious development of the national defense industry.[74]

Thus, the first discernible trend in the defense industries is the stress on integration with the civilian economy and diversification of products.

The second noticeable trend is the increased glorification of people working in the defense industries. This trend is evident in numerous press articles, and the "army-people unity," "support the army," and "emulate Lei Feng" compaigns.[75] State leaders Fang I, Wang Zhen, and Geng Biao also honored "more than four hundred scientists, professors, chief engineers, and scientific and technical personnel who have made outstanding achievements in the most advanced branches of science for national defense" at a 1980 New Year's tea party.[76] The song-and-dance ensemble under the Political Department of the NDSTC entertained! At another meeting, Vice-Premiers Yu Qiuli, Wang Zhen, Geng Biao, Gu Mu, and Bo Yibo awarded medals to thirty-eight representatives of defense industry units "producing fine-quality war-industrial products."[77] Lastly, financial stipends and personnel promotions have been instituted. Indicative of the latter was a series of faculty promotions at the National Defense Science and Technology University in Changsha, Hunan Province.[78]

The third, and most important, recent trend is that the Chinese have made it explicitly clear to the military that they rank last among the "four modernizations" and will receive little, if any, increase in budget during the 1980s. After declines for fiscal years 1979-1982, as previously mentioned, there was a slight increase in the 1982-83 budget. Given the relatively low budgetary allocation to indigenous defense production and general PLA dissatisfaction over the reform policies (including the sweeping demobilization of veteran officers), one wonders if China's leaders may not attempt to placate the PLA with selected purchases of foreign weapons systems to meet pressing defense needs. It is this question to which we turn in the following section.

3. FOREIGN PROCUREMENT

Foreign assistance to China's defense industries has been a contentious issue for more than a century since the "self-strengthening movement" of the 1860s. Stimulated by the military training and techniques exhibited during the Westerners' cooperation against the Taiping, the anti-Taiping generals, Zeng Guofan and Li Hongzhang, launched the Tongzhi Restoration which sought to consolidate Qing power by introducing Western technology among other tactics. The movement was ideologically justified as "using the barbarian's superior techniques to control the barbarians."[79] From 1861 to 1872, the policy of building "shipyards and arsenals" as the catalytic element for industrial development was actively pursued, but from 1872 to 1894, the emphasis shifted from the weapons industry to a wider field of manufacture. As we saw in Section 1, this dichotomous argument has persisted to this very day. At the heart of the argument lie the notions of the militarization of industry and the army as a modernizing force in "authoritarian, transitional societies."[80] Chinese policymakers since Li Hongzhang have had to face this fundamental choice, not only in internal industrialization strategies, but also in foreign procurement.

We know that technology transfer from abroad plays a critical role in China's current quest for modernization by the year 2000, and we have noted the Chinese decision not to allow defense needs to dominate or "lead" industrial development, as well as the designation of military modernization as last among the four modernizations. What then *is* the role of foreign assistance in military modernization?

In brief, the Chinese seek to procure design technologies and, if possible, the means of production of defense equipment. By so doing, the Chinese hope to minimize the risk of dependence on and vulnerability to fluctuations in suppliers' policies and production capacities. In seeking to manufacture completed weaponry and components on their own soil, the Chinese utilize two basic strategies of acquisition: (1) prototype copying, which in some cases involves reverse engineering, and (2) importation of whole plants. To date, the Chinese record on prototype reproduction and reverse-engineering, "dual-use" technologies has not been good. Lack of specialized materials and a poor S&T infrastructure have been the main problems. Hence, the Chinese increasingly seek production rights under license—as was the case, for example, with the Spey engine and (if the deal is ever closed) will be the case with the Harrier VSTOL as well.

Does this foreign procurement strategy preclude a simultaneous quick-fix policy for China's military? Some observers believe so;[81] others do not. Those who do believe in the quick fix believe that since it will take at last ten years for imported production assistance to fully come on stream, the Chinese will probably meet their immediate defense needs with selected purchases of complete weapons systems from abroad. This possibility is particularly apt in the aforementioned areas of combat aircraft, anti-tank, and anti-air PGMs. Evidence of a quick-fix procurement strategy is currently scant, but if foreign exchange is accumulated in the next few years (and it has been rapid from 1980 to 1982), one might expect increased purchases. Such spot purchases would be a method of placating the defense sector in times of low budget allocation and political restiveness.

The Chinese have raised much speculation in the West about such purchases by their numerous window-shopping excursions.[82] Table 3.1 shows most, but not all, of the weapons systems the Chinese have examined, expressed interest in, or actually purchased. The table has been compiled from a variety of press reports, journals, books, and private discussions. Although the table is undoubtedly not comprehensive, it does point out China's primary areas of interest and, by inference, sheds some light on deficiencies in China's own defense production. Table 3.2 breaks down the inquiries/purchases into categories. It shows a predominance of interest in aeronautical items and items for tactical defense: ASW, AA, AT, and reconnaissance systems.

This is indeed an impressive shopping list, but so far few contracts have been signed. Given the strategy for military modernization

TABLE 3.1 Chinese Interest in Foreign Weapons Systems

Country and Item	Examined	Expressed Real Interest in	Purchased
GREAT BRITAIN:			
Harrier VSTOL aircraft	x	x	--
Spey jet engine	--	--	x
Trident jet	--	--	x
Westland helicopter	x	--	--
Chieftain tank	x	--	--
Rapier AA missile	x	x	--
ASW optical equipment (unknown)	x	x	--
Swingfire AT missile	x	x	--
Radar systems (unknown)	x	--	--
APCs (unknown)	x	x	--
Artillery (unknown)	x	--	--
Red Top AA missile	x	x	--
Light arms	x	--	--
FRANCE:			
Thomson CSF radar system	--	--	x
Super Frelon helicopter	--	--	x
Alouette helicopter	x	x	--
Mirage 2000 fighter aircraft	x	x	--
Crotale AA missile	x	x	x(?)
Roland SA missile ⎱ coproduced ⎰	x	x	--
HOT AT missile ⎰ with ⎱	x	x	x(?)
Milan AT missile ⎰ the FRG ⎱	x	x	x(?)
AMX 30 tank	x	--	--
Berliet APC	x	--	--
Malafon ASW torpedo	x	x	--
Exocet naval missile	x	--	--
Transport aircraft (unknown)	x	x	--
WEST GERMANY (FRG):			
Roland SA missile ⎱ coproduced ⎰	x	x	--
HOT AT missile ⎰ with ⎱	x	x	x(?)
Milan AT missile ⎰ France ⎱	x	x	x(?)
Leopard tank	x	x	--
Messerschmitt helicopter	--	--	x
Marder TPZ-1 APC	x	--	--
Armbrust AT rocket	x	x	--
Mobile artillery (unknown)	x	--	--
Radar systems (unknown)	x	--	--
Light arms (unknown)	x	--	--
ITALY:			
Augusta helicopter	x	--	--
Selenia missile guidance system	x	--	--
Aspide AA missile	x	x	--
Indigo SA missile	x	x	--
Rapid-fire cannons (unknown)	?	x	--
Sonar equipment (unknown)	?	x	--
Naval AA guns (unknown)	?	x	--

(Continued)

TABLE 3.1 (Cont.)

Country and Item	Examined	Expressed Real Interest in	Purchased
SWITZERLAND:			
Oerlikon AA gun	--	--	x
Electronic sensing equipment (unknown)	?	x	--
SWEDEN:			
Viggen fighter aircraft	x	x	--
Submarines (unknown)	?	x	--
YUGOSLAVIA:			
M-980 tank	x	x	--
EGYPT:			
MiG-23 aircraft (Soviet)*	x	--	--
Sagger AT missile (Soviet)*	x	--	--
T-62 tank (Soviet)*	x	--	--
Fire-control radar systems	?	x	--
AUSTRALIA:			
Ikara ASW torpedo	--	x	--
UNITED STATES:			
Lockheed C-130, C-131, C-140 transport aircraft	x	x	--
Lockheed P-3 ASW patrol plane	?	x	--
McDonnell-Douglas electronic gear	?	x	--
Sidewinder AA missile	--	x	--
Sparrow AA missile	--	x	--
TOW AT missile**	x	x	--
F-5 fighter aircraft**	x	x	--
F-16 fighter aircraft	?	x	--
Cobra gunship helicopter**	x	--	--
Bell H-12 helicopter	--	--	x
Sikorsky Model 12 helicopter	--	x	--
Lockheed Tri-Star aircraft	x	x	--
McDonnell-Douglas DC-9, DC-10	x	x	--
Grumman E-2 early-warning aircraft	?	x	--
Ford trucks	x	x	--
Communications gear (unknown)	?	x	--
Laser equipment (unknown)	x	x	--

* Received samples in exchange for repair of jet engines in 1973.

** It is presumed that the Chinese had an opportunity to examine these weapons during the Vietnam War.

TABLE 3.2 Breakdown of China's Interest in Weapons Systems

Items	Number	Percent of Sample
Whole aircraft, engines, spares	22	32.0%
Radar and communication equipment	8	12.1
Tanks and APCs	8	12.1
AA weapons	7	10.6
AT weapons	6	9.0
Naval weapons and missiles	4	6.0
Artillery	3	4.5
ASW equipment	3	4.5
Light arms	2	3.0
Submarines	1	1.5
Missile guidance systems	1	1.5
Trucks	1	1.5
Laser equipment	1	1.5
TOTAL	67	99.8%*

* Discrepancy due to rounding.

outlined in this chapter, foreign exchange constraints, COCOM constraints, and a procurement strategy for acquiring the means of production, I conclude that it is probable that only a few weapons deals will be closed in the 1980s.

To be sure, civilian industrial and scientific development is the greatest asset the PLA could receive at this stage of its protracted quest for a modern national defense. The absorption of foreign technologies will be critically important to the defense sector. The transfer of dual-use technologies will be closely monitored and controlled by COCOM. The full range of these technologies and materials is too voluminous to discuss in detail here, but the categories in which COCOM places them can be outlined.[83]

COCOM

There are three COCOM lists: (1) a munitions list, which includes all military items; (2) an atomic energy list, which includes sources of fissionable materials, nuclear reactors, and their components; and (3) an industrial/commercial list. Most of COCOM's activities relate to the third list as items on the first two are routinely embargoed. The industrial list contains all dual-use items and must be reviewed on a case-by-case basis by the concerned government and COCOM.

The industrial list is further subdivided into three categories: International List 1 (embargoed items), International List 2 (items controlled in quantity), and International List 3 (exchange of information and surveillance items). List 1 contains those items that member nations agree not to sell unless permission is specifically granted for an "exception request." List 2 contains items that may be exported, but only in specified quantities. Licenses to export more than the specified quantity also require an "exception request." List 3 contains items that may be sold, but over which the exporting nations must maintain surveillance of end use. Most of the dual-use items that pose the greatest problems for export controls are contained in List 1, which, in turn, is divided into ten individual groupings. These groupings conform closely to the U.S. Commodity Control List (CCL).

1. Metal-working machinery
2. Chemical and petroleum equipment
3. Electrical and power-generating equipment
4. General industrial equipment
5. Transportation equipment
6. Electronic and precision instruments
7. Metals, minerals, and their manufacture
8. Chemicals and metalloids
9. Petroleum products
10. Rubber and rubber products

These categories are further broken down into infinite detail. The U.S. CCL contains an extensive, itemized sublist of at least thirteen groupings of "critical technologies,"[84] which are evaluated on a number of criteria.[85]

Over the years, the overall trend in COCOM has been toward a liberalization of controls. However, since the Soviet invasion of Afghanistan, the controls have been tightened for the Soviet Union and relaxed for China. In effect, a "China differential" now exists. Certain items that have been denied sale to the Soviet Union, for example a Sperry Univac computer, are now sold to China. U.S. export licenses were granted for $249 million worth of dual-use equipment for the PRC in the first nine months of 1979 alone.[86] The bulk of this figure ($168 million) was for aerospace equipment, aircraft, and spare parts; $52 million was for geophysical technology; and $10.3 million was for electronic computers and equipment.[87] The decision to relax controls for the PRC was a contentious issue during the first two years of the Carter administration,[88] but such a policy was implemented in stages beginning in September 1978.[89] Although still clinging to a policy of no weapons sales to China, the U.S. government was willing to sell "certain kinds" of (nonlethal) military equipment to the Chinese.[90] The Pentagon cited trucks, communications equipment, and early-warning radars as examples. This decision was taken in the wake of the Soviet invasion of Afghanistan, ex-Defense Secretary Brown's trip to China in January 1980, and then-Vice-Premier Geng Biao's follow-up trip to the United States in May 1980. Since these reciprocal high-level visits, increasing numbers of working-level delegations have been exchanged. In September 1980, Dr. William Perry, then-under-secretary of defense for development, research, and engineering, led a twenty-two-member Department of Defense (DOD) delegation of technical experts to China. In an interview at the conclusion of his visit,[91] Dr. Perry said that negotiations between China and private companies in the United States for the purchase of military support equipment were proceeding "at a brisk pace" despite a cutback in China's military budget. He said that the sales were now up to the companies, since the Pentagon had recently cleared "ten or twenty" applications for licenses for sales of such equipment in addition to "four hundred" licenses for dual-use technology items. Perry said the Chinese had again sought permission to buy weapons but that the U.S. government had not changed its restrictions on arms sales. Perry recalled that Geng Biao stated during his visit to Washington that "China looked forward to the time when it could buy American weapons. The Chinese have reitterated [*sic*] those desires on this visit."

Western Options

The question of U.S. arms sales to China is an option that is very much alive for the 1980s, despite repeated public assurances to the contrary. In mid-January 1979, then-President Carter went so far as to send a letter to then-Soviet President Brezhnev reassuring him that the United States would not sell arms to China, but said that the United States "would not interfere" if European governments wished to do so.[92] In the letter, Carter stressed that it was the "sovereign right" of other countries to sell defensive arms and that Beijing also possessed a "sovereign right" to purchase them. This statement was made in response to repeated Soviet warnings/threats to England and France not to sell arms to the Chinese.[93]

To be sure, all governments contemplating arms sales and sophisticated dual-use technology transfers to China must carefully weigh the potential costs on relations with the Soviet Union. The long-term effects of making China "strong and secure"[94] must be thoroughly thought through. There is much to lose, particularly for the West European governments. Even if the West decides to sell major weapons systems to China, the economic constraints and a desire to limit dependency on foreign suppliers may well restrict Chinese buying.

Assistance to the Chinese military certainly is not a zero-sum game. There exist multiple options. At one extreme, there are those people who oppose any sales or transfers on the grounds that they would threaten Taiwan, other noncommunist states in the region,[95] and/or the Soviet Union.[96] The last group argues that such moves would only make the Soviet Union

- more sensitive about threats on its borders,
- more convinced of a U.S.-China-Japan anti-Soviet alignment,
- more dogmatic in dealing with the West,
- more likely to increase defense outlays,
- more prone to military adventurism abroad.

At the other extreme, there are people who are seemingly willing to "open the floodgates" on arms and technology transfers.[97] Such individuals argue that improvement in Chinese defense capabilities would

- restore a regional balance of power in Asia,
- improve the Sino-Soviet military balance,
- cause the Soviet Union to draw down its forces facing NATO, redeploy them to the Far East (which costs much more to maintain), and take seriously the possibility of a two-front conflict,
- provide a potential market of considerable size and serve to bolster domestic production.

In between these two extreme positions lie a range of policy instruments that can be pursued independent of, or in conjunction with, each other. In regard to the hardware issue, Western weapon systems transfers could be targeted specifically at reducing Chinese vulnerability to near-term conventional Soviet attack. Such quick-fix transfers could include anti-tank and anti-air PGMs, anti-submarine detection equipment, early-warning radars, etc. Such equipment is clearly defensive in nature and could not be misconstrued as offensive by the Soviets, Taiwanese, Vietnamese, or others. Offensive weaponry is another matter. Sales of fighters, tanks, APCs, heavy artillery, helicopter gunships, etc., could only be interpreted by China's adversaries as threatening. Remaining are transport and communication equipment, which have already been made available.

All of this consideration of equipment transfers may be moot, since the Chinese evidently have neither the desire nor the foreign exchange necessary to purchase the equipment. As stated earlier, their preferred strategy is to acquire the design technologies and, if possible, the means of production of military equipment. If the West is willing to cooperate in this strategy, both sides must take a very detailed look at matching Chinese needs and absorptive capacity with Western technologies. Such a survey falls outside the scope of this study, but I submit that primary attention be paid to polymer technologies, fabrication of nonferrous metals, high-grade steels, precision machine tools, and a host of electronics: LSI, fiber optics, large-scale computers, and a range of modern telecommunication technologies.

In the early days of the Reagan administration, the United States went an important step further. During his June 1981 visit to Beijing, then-Secretary of State Haig stunned everyone by announcing that the United States had agreed in principle to sell combat weaponry to the Chinese. He said specific arms requests, if they are made by the Chinese, will be considered on a case-by-case basis in consultation with the United States' allies and with Congress. This decision, arrived at after heated National Security Council debates, potentially goes well beyond the Carter administration's policy of selling dual-use technologies and nonlethal military equipment. It was agreed at the time of Haig's visit that PLA Vice-Chief of Staff Liu Huaqing would visit Washington later in the summer with a shopping list. That trip was postponed indefinitely by the Chinese because of the Taiwan arms sale issue. The Chinese believe in issue linkage.

The Taiwan issue has become a major restraint holding back the further progression of Sino-American relations in many other realms as well. This is not the place for an extended discussion of the pros and cons of the Reagan administration's China policy. However, it should be said that the administration evidently views the relationship primarily from a strategic perspective. For example, during his confirmation hearings, Haig stated his belief that a continued effort to normalize relations proceeds from "fundamental strategic reality and is a strategic imperative. It is of overriding importance to international stability and world peace."[98] Taken together with the administration's explicit anti-Soviet bent, this perspective could auger well for increased U.S. assistance to the Chinese military establishment. Haig's successor as secretary of state, George Shultz, has had little to say about China, although undoubtedly his early 1983 visit to Beijing will provide such an opportunity.

Leaving aside the question of weapons sales and military technology transfers, a number of collaborative security measures could be, and in the first two cases have been, undertaken. They include

- the sharing of intelligence data;
- the location of U.S. intelligence facilities in China;

- Western use of Chinese facilities, notably naval and possibly air;
- the stationing of Western military experts in China;
- training of PLA personnel in the West;
- joint maneuvers and exercises;
- joint contingency planning;
- institutionalized regular consultation.

These may seem like extremely unlikely possibilities for the decade of the 1980s, but one must not forget how absurd the current state of Sino-Western relations seemed in the late 1960s or early 1970s.

4. SUMMARY AND OUTLOOK

This chapter has primarily viewed the defense industries in isolation from factors that impact upon them. In reality, they do not operate in a vacuum. Few issues overlap and crosscut so many structural and functional boundaries in the Chinese polity as military modernization. We have noted the problems and choices of industrial investment priorities in the economic realm and the foreign trade decisions related to the procurement of weapon systems and defense technology from abroad. Military modernization is also a complex bureaucratic issue simply because of the extent and overlap of the involved government departments and interest groups. Competition for scarce resources between the military and civilian sectors and among service arms is acute. As we saw in Section 1, military modernization is also subject to shifting political winds. In addition, as a matter of national security, it enters the foreign policy arena insofar as threat perception is concerned.

All of these factors will continue to affect the defense industries in the 1980s. The last factor is perhaps the most imponderable element. Changes in the external environment that increase or decrease the threat to China will directly affect the defense industries. For example, there was an increase in the defense budget following the 1979 Vietnam incursion. Perception of increased threat from the Soviet Union—either directly on the border or via encirclement—would surely lead to increased military outlays (as it did following the 1969 Ussuri clashes) and/or purchase of foreign weapons. Further, failure of the United States to live up to China's expectations as a counter-weight to the Soviets could have the same effect. A basic premise of Deng's calculus for selling his modernization scheme (in which the military ranks last in priority) to the PLA is that improved relations with the United States enhance China's security by tying down Soviet resources elsewhere. On the other hand, a perceived decrease in threat could decrease defense allocation. Although highly improbable, a real relaxation of tensions with the Soviets and/or Vietnamese would bring about such a decrease. Two domestic economic factors might also serve to decrease defense spending. The first would be severe agricultural shortfalls, which would cause China to siphon off funds from other sectors for the purchase of foreign grain. The second factor would be if expected oil revenues do not live up to expectations, causing cutbacks in foreign purchases across the board. Any number of scenarios involving these factors acting in conjunction could fundamentally alter China's modernization priorities and affect allocation to the defense industries.

A host of factors related to technology assimilation will also affect the defense industries in the 1980s. The most fundamental problem will be incorporating new (Western) designs and manufacturing facilities into a preexisting industrial infrastructure of such magnitude and complexity that is still based almost wholly on Soviet designs. Operation and maintenance of these new facilities and equipment require a large pool of highly trained scientists and engineers, not to mention the training needed within the PLA to use such equipment. This training could take place not only abroad, but also inside China. The potential for xenophobic backlash is always lurking beneath the surface of Chinese society. Increased visibility and preferential treatment of foreigners have evidently caused some resentment among the populace.[99]

The most important problem of assimilation is its protracted nature. Will weapon systems and defense technologies be incorporated soon enough to meet pressing security needs? The chances are not good; it could be the late 1980s or even later before the technology of the early and mid-1970s comes on stream and is adequately introduced into the Chinese armed forces.[100] Even then, the qualitative gaps between indigenous output and the state of the art will remain wide (ten years at a minimum). The gap is, of course, widened by the accelerating Soviet-American arms race.

To really close these qualitative gaps requires far more than funding, training of scientists, building the industrial infrastructure, or manufacturing advanced equipment. It requires design innovation. It is the difference between copying and setting the state of the art. Technological innovation is dependent on scientific innovation. It comes from engaging in "basic" scientific research as distinct from "applied" research. Innovation cannot be acquired abroad; it is an indigenous phenomenon. Innovation is not only carried on in the laboratory, but at all levels of society. The current regime is presently engaged in sweeping managerial, institutional, and incentive changes aimed at fostering innovation. These changes may well be the most profound of all factors affecting military modernization well beyond the 1980s.

Notes

1. The best source describing structural changes in the machine building industry is Chu-Yuan Cheng's "Growth and Structural Changes in the Chinese Machine Building Industry, 1952–1966," in *China Quarterly* no. 41 (January–March 1970). This article is drawn from his book *The Machine Building Industry in Communist China* (Chicago: Aldine-Atherton Press, 1971).

2. J. Craig, J. Lewek, and G. Cole, "A Survey of China's Machine Building Industry," in U.S. Congress, Joint Economic Committee, *Chinese Economy Post-Mao*, vol. 1 (Washington, D.C.: Government Printing Office, November 9, 1978), p. 287. Other studies, such as Cheng's, put the number much lower—around forty.

3. Cheng's article, "Growth and Structural Changes," discusses this shift in detail, pp. 29–36.

4. Ibid., p. 28.

5. Craig, Lewek, and Cole, "A Survey of China's Machine Building Industry," p. 287.

6. Bhodan Szuprowicz and Maria Szuprowicz, *Doing Business with the People's Republic of China: Industries and Markets* (New York: John Wiley & Sons, 1978). This book includes, among others, an excellent chapter on machine building. The book is a substantive contribution to the existing body of literature on the Chinese economy. However, there exist several factual mistakes; for example, the incorrect functional ordering of the m.m.b.'s.

7. As calculated by Cheng, "Growth and Structural Changes," p. 55. Calculation of the machine building's share of total industrial output is difficult enough; the proportion of allocation and output of the defense sector is more difficult still. The latter effort points up the avoidable problem of scarcity of sources and reliability of statistical estimates. Further, what is known in the public domain concerning the machine building industries emphasizes civilian machinery; published statistics are consequently weighted in favor of that sector.

8. See, for example, Harold Ford, "Modern Weapons and the Sino-Soviet Estrangement," *China Quarterly* no. 18 (April–June 1969), pp. 160–173.

9. Brief discussions of the NDIO can be found in Harvey Nelsen, *The Chinese Military System* (Boulder, Colo.: Westview Press, 1977), pp. 59–60, and Harlan Jencks, "The Chinese Military Industrial Complex and Defense Modernization," *Asian Survey* (October 1980), p. 976.

10. See Paul H.B. Godwin, *Doctrine, Strategy, and Ethic: The Modernization of the Chinese People's Liberation Army* (Maxwell Air Force Base, Ala.: Documentary Research Branch of Academic Publications, Division of the 3825th Academic Services Group of the Air University, June 1977), p. 18, and David

L. Shambaugh, "Military Modernization and the Politics of Technology Transfer," *Contemporary China* (Fall 1979), pp. 3–13.

11. An excellent examination of the intricacies of Lo's dismissal is Melvin Gurtov and Harry Harding, Jr., *The Purge of Lo Jui-ching: The Politics of Chinese Strategic Planning*, R-548-PR (Santa Monica, Calif.: Rand Corporation, February 1971).

12. Sydney H. Jammes, "The Chinese Defense Burden, 1965–1974," in U.S. Congress, Joint Economic Committee, *China: A Reassessment of the Economy* (Washington, D.C.: Government Printing Office, July 10, 1973), p. 463.

13. Some observers even argue that the Chinese troops provoked the clashes so as to justify accelerated military expenditures to the leadership. A good survey of the existing interpretations and evidence can be found in Kenneth Lieberthal, *Sino-Soviet Conflict in the 1970s: Its Evolution and Implications for the Strategic Triangle*, R-2342-NA (Santa Monica, Calif.: Rand Corporation, July 1978), pp. 5–8.

14. Jammes, "The Chinese Defense Burden," p. 462.

15. U.S. Central Intelligence Agency, *Policy Issues in the Purge of Lin Piao*, report released to the public as a result of the Freedom of Information Act (Washington, D.C., June 20, 1978), pp. 41–42.

16. See, for example, Thomas Gottlieb, *Chinese Foreign Policy Factionalism and the Origins of the Strategic Triangle*, R-1902-NA (Santa Monica, Calif.: Rand Corporation, November 1977), and U.S. Central Intelligence Agency, *Policy Issues*.

17. PLA influence in national level politics grew steadily from the "Learn from the PLA" campaign of 1964 to restoration of order following the 1967 Wuhan Incident and reconstitution of "revolutionary committees" after the Cultural Revolution. PLA influence in elite-level politics reached its zenith in 1969. A civil-military breakdown of the Ninth Central Committee (1969) shows that 45 percent of its composition were military figures—the highest proportion ever. To be sure, many of China's first-generation political elite served in one of the field armies before 1949 and retained some military functional roles after liberation. The 45 percent figure includes those who "wear two hats" as calculated by the CIA in *A Look at the Eleventh Central Committee* (Washington, D.C., October 1977).

18. Soviet sources have told this writer that Lin and others aboard were found shot in the head, suggesting that they had been executed in China, put on the plane, and the plane flown north to give the impression that Lin was in cahoots with the Russians. The trial of the Gang of Four and the "Lin Biao clique" shed little new light on this still inexplicable event.

19. For a discussion of the politicization of the PLA and the CCP's ability to exploit it for purposes of control see, for example, David L. Shambaugh, "The Role of the People's Liberation Army in Chinese Politics," in *Spring–Autumn Papers* (Center for Chinese Studies and the Center for Japanese Studies, University of Michigan) 3:1 (1981), pp. 45–56.

20. For an intricate discussion of this and other allegorical debates during the period, see Kenneth Lieberthal, "The Foreign Policy Debate in Peking

as Seen Through Allegorical Articles 1973–1976," *China Quarterly* no. 71 (September 1977), pp. 528–554.

21. Craig, Lewek, and Cole, "A Survey of China's Machine Building Industry," p. 288.

22. An excellent review of the Spey case, the aircraft industry, and China's approach to technology acquisition can be found in Hans Heymann, *China's Approach to Technology Acquisition: Part I—The Aircraft Industry* (Santa Monica, Calif.: Rand Corporation, 1975). Also see Jonathan Pollack, *Defense Modernization in the People's Republic of China,* N-121-1-AF (Santa Monica, Calif.: Rand Corporation, October 1979).

23. A review of the contrasting positions taken in the media and the conferences can be found in Shambaugh, "Military Modernization," and Paul H.B. Godwin, "China's Defense Dilemma: The Modernization Crisis of 1976 and 1977," *Contemporary China* (Fall 1978), pp. 63–85.

24. See, for example, "Wang Zhen Attends National Defense Industries Meeting," Foreign Broadcast Information Service, *China* (henceforth FBIS-China), January 22, 1980, p. L1.

25. Xu Xiangqian, "Strive to Achieve Modernization in National Defense," FBIS-China, October 18, 1979, pp. L12–19.

26. A good discussion of the problems of calculating the Chinese defense budget can be found in Angus Fraser, "Military Modernization in China," *Problems of Communism* 28 (September–December 1979), pp. 46–47. The CIA's methods of calculation are best described in U.S. Central Intelligence Agency, *Chinese Defense Spending, 1965–79,* Research Paper SR80-10091 (Washington, D.C.: National Foreign Assessment Center, July 1980).

27. Zhang Jingfu, "Report on the Fiscal State Accounts for 1978 and the Draft Budget for 1979," *Beijing Review* no. 29 (July 1979), pp. 18–23. This figure, it should be noted, is a 20 percent increase over 1978. The budget for the fiscal years of 1980–1983 has also been released. See, for example, "Chinese Increase Military's Budget," *New York Times,* May 6, 1982.

28. U.S. Central Intelligence Agency, *Chinese Defense Spending 1965–79,* pp. 3–5.

29. Craig, Lewek, and Cole, "A Survey of China's Machine Building Industry," provides an excellent analysis of this industry.

30. A very thorough documentation of Soviet assistance to the Chinese nuclear program can be found in Paul H.B. Godwin, *The Chinese Tactical Air Forces and Strategic Weapons Program: Development, Doctrine, and Strategy* (Maxwell Air Force Base, Ala.: Air University, Documentary Research Division, 1978), pp. 6–13.

31. Jencks, "The Chinese Military Industrial Complex," p. 966.

32. Good sources for a much more thorough description of China's aircraft industry are Bill Sweetman, "The Modernization of China's Air Force," in Ray Bonds, ed., *The Chinese War Machine* (New York: Crescent Books, 1979), pp. 122–147; Appendix Z in U.S. Defense Intelligence Agency, *The Chinese Armed Forces Today* (Englewood Cliffs, N.J.: Prentice-Hall, 1979); Heymann, *China's Approach to Technology Acquisition;* Fraser, "Military Mod-

ernization in China"; *Jane's Fighting Ships* (London: Macdonald and Jane's Publishers, 1979); and International Institute for Strategic Studies, *The Military Balance* (London: Adlard & Son, Bartholomew Press, 1979). Information and figures in this section are largely derived from these sources.

33. See testimony of Lt. General Eugene F. Tighe, Jr., before the Subcommittee on Priorities in Government, July 9, 1979, U.S. Congress, Joint Economic Committee, *Allocation of Resources in the Soviet Union and China— 1979* (Washington, D.C.: Government Printing Office, 1980).

34. Jonathan Pollack, "The Logic of Chinese Military Strategy," *Bulletin of Atomic Scientists* (January 1979), p. 29.

35. "China's Defense Industries," in International Institute for Strategic Studies, *Strategic Survey 1979* (London: Neil Moore Associates, 1980), pp. 67–72.

36. Szuprowicz and Szuprowicz, *Doing Business*, p. 256. Pages 256–273 contain a quite detailed description of China's electronics industry.

37. Bhodan Szuprowicz, "Electronics in China," *China Business Review* (May–June 1976), p. 22.

38. The author can testify to this difficulty from first hand experience in the U.S. government, but also see "How RCA Got Offer to Build a TV Plant in China," *Christian Science Monitor*, October 25, 1978.

39. U.S. Congress, Office of Technology Assessment, *Technology and East-West Trade* (Washington, D.C.: Government Printing Office, 1979), p. 275.

40. Ibid.

41. "Known PRC Computers," *China Business Review* 7:5 (September–October 1980), pp. 26–27.

42. Ibid.

43. Ibid.

44. Ibid.

45. "U.S. Plans to Sell a Satellite Ground Station to China," *New York Times*, January 9, 1980, p. A9.

46. "China's Electronics Industry—Thirty Years of Development," FBIS-China, January 25, 1980, p. L3.

47. The following is compiled from International Institute for Strategic Studies, *The Military Balance 1979* and Bonds, ed., *Chinese War Machine*, pp. 119–120.

48. Fraser, "Military Modernization in China," p. 49.

49. Reuters reported the conclusion of a package deal with France worth $700 million in 1978 (see "Agreement on Sale of Missiles to China Confirmed by France," *Washington Post*, October 22, 1978). It should be noted that this report has not been confirmed by other sources.

50. I am indebted to Harlan Jencks and Paul Godwin for explaining the evolution of the following vehicles and setting me straight on types in current production and deployment.

51. Fraser, "Military Modernization in China," p. 39.

52. Bonds, ed., *Chinese War Machine*, p. 120.

53. General David C. Jones, *United States Military Posture for Fiscal Year 1980—An Overview* (Washington, D.C.: Department of Defense, n.d.), p. 60, as cited by Fraser, "Military Modernization in China," p. 39.

54. "Tribute to an Imperial Five-Jewelled Eunuch: The PLA Navy," *Far Eastern Economic Review* 8 (February 1980), p. 45.

55. More detailed descriptions of these crafts are given in Bonds, ed., *Chinese War Machine*, pp. 119–121. The numbers in circulation are given in International Institute for Strategic Studies, *The Military Balance 1979*, p. 61.

56. "Tribute to an Imperial Five-Jewelled Eunuch," p. 45.

57. *Allocation of Resources in China and the Soviet Union 1977* (Washington, D.C.: Government Printing Office, 1977), p. 92.

58. Nelsen, *Chinese Military System*, pp. 3, 73.

59. The following is derived from International Institute for Strategic Studies, *The Military Balance;* Fraser, "Military Modernization in China"; Bonds, ed., *Chinese War Machine;* and U.S. Defense Intelligence Agency, *The Chinese Armed Forces Today.*

60. International Institute for Strategic Studies, *The Military Balance 1979*, p. 60.

61. See, for example, FBIS-China, March 3, 1978, June 1, 1978, and June 20, 1978.

62. "Decisions Announced at the Fifth NPC Standing Committee Session," FBIS-China, September 14, 1980, p. L1.

63. International Institute for Strategic Studies, *Strategic Survey 1979*, p. 69.

64. *China Business Review* 7:4 (July–August 1980), p. 25.

65. A good, although hypothetical, discussion of the NDSTC's functioning can be found in Jencks, "The Chinese Military Industrial Complex," p. 978.

66. "NPC Decision on Machine Building Industry Commission," FBIS-China, February 12, 1980, p. L10.

67. "Hebei Radio Editor on National Defense Industries," Hebei Provincial Service, FBIS-China, January 9, 1980, p. R1.

68. Zhao Ziyang, "Study New Conditions and Implement the Principle of Readjustment in an All-Round Way," *Hongqi*, no. 1 (January 1, 1980), FBIS-China, January 18, 1980, p. L11.

69. "First Congress of Chinese Nuclear Society Opens in Beijing," FBIS-China, February 22, 1980, p. L2.

70. "Military Industry Manufactures Products for Civilian Use," FBIS-China, February 29, 1980, p. L7.

71. "Yao Yilin Reports on Economic Status, Policies," FBIS-China, September 2, 1980, p. L8.

72. "Defense Industry Conference Urges Civilian Goods Production," FBIS-China, November 13, 1979, p. L18.

73. Ibid., p. L17.

74. Ibid.

75. See, for example, "Ministry Issues Circular on Army-Support Campaign," FBIS-China, February 21, 1980, p. L6; "Lei Feng Campaign Spreads Throughout Country," FBIS-China, March 10, 1981, p. L32.

76. "Beijing Tea Party Honors National Defense Scientists," FBIS-China, February 21, 1980, p. L1.

77. "Yu Qiuli Presents Awards for Quality Military Products," FBIS-China, December 27, 1979, p. L14.

78. "PLA Science, Technology University Promotes Personnel," FBIS-China, February 1, 1980, p. L6.

79. "China, History of," *Encyclopedia Britannica,* 15th ed. (Chicago: William Benton and Helen Hemingway Benton, 1975), p. 361.

80. The latter notion is best argued by Professor Lucien Pye in "Armies in the Process of Political Modernization," in John J. Johnson, ed., *The Role of the Military in Underdeveloped Countries* (Princeton, N.J.: Princeton University Press (1962), pp. 69–89.

81. See, for example, Pollack, *Defense Modernization,* p. 6.

82. A U.S. government source told the author that from 1976 to 1978, approximately 600 military-related delegations (4,000 to 5,000 people) visited Western Europe and the United States.

83. The following information is derived from U.S. Congress, *Technology and East-West Trade,* pp. 155–160.

84. The actual technologies are contained on this list. Although the list itself is secret, an excellent approximation can be found in two sources: *U.S. Technology and Export Controls* (Washington, D.C.: Machinery and Allied Products Institute, 1978), pp. 72–76, and *Phase II Progress Report for Identification of Strategically Significant Technologies* (Columbus, Ohio: Battelle Columbus Laboratories, 1977).

85. U.S. Congress, *Technology and East-West Trade,* p. 157.

86. "Chinese Getting More Dual-Use U.S. Equipment," *Washington Post,* January 16, 1980. Also see Karen Berney, "Dual-Use Technology Sales," *China Business Review* 7:4 (July–August 1980), pp. 23–29.

87. "Chinese Getting More Dual-Use Equipment."

88. See, for example, "U.S. Aides Split on Defense Technology for China," *New York Times,* January 4, 1978.

89. See, for example, "Brown Sets New Technology Policy—Expected to Favor China's Needs," *New York Times,* September 10, 1978.

90. See, for example, "Pentagon Willing to Sell Chinese Some Military Equipment," *Washington Post,* January 24, 1980, and "U.S., In Rebuff to Soviet, Announces It Will Sell China Military Support Equipment," *New York Times,* January 24, 1980.

91. "China Agrees to Sell U.S. Three Metals Needed for Making Airplanes," *New York Times,* September 10, 1980.

92. "Carter Tells Brezhnev U.S. Won't Sell China Arms," *New York Times,* January 25, 1979.

93. See, for example, "Soviets Warn Not to Sell Peking Arms," *Washington Post,* October 27, 1978, and "Brezhnev Warns Britain on Sales of Jets to China," *Washington Post,* November 24, 1978.

94. The Carter administration used this phrase often in frequent pronouncements concerning China.

95. Ray Cline, executive director of the Georgetown University Center for Strategic and International Studies, is the chief representative of this position.

96. Former Secretary of State Cyrus Vance might be associated with this position.

97. See, for example, Michael Pillsbury, "U.S.-China Military Ties?" *Foreign Policy* no. 20 (Fall 1975), pp. 50–64.

98. "President Reassures China on Ties as Signs of Strain Begin to Emerge," *New York Times,* March 21, 1981.

99. See, for example, "Foreigners Emerge as a Privileged Class," *Washington Post,* March 9, 1980.

100. Pollack, *Defense Modernization,* p. 18.

Part 3

Leadership and Management

4
The Rectification of "Work Style": Command and Management Problems

Richard J. Latham

Introduction

Few people would take exception with the observation that from 1966 to 1976, the People's Liberation Army endured the most tumultuous years of its history. Notwithstanding some improvement in tactical and strategic weapon systems during the period, it was a decade of political chaos, dissipated defense resources, and declining morale and discipline in the army. In most instances, the damaging experiences that beset the army were caused by political events that were only remotely related to fundamental military matters. The most important were the Cultural Revolution (1966–1969) and its aftermath, the Lin Biao affair and the Gang of Four episode. So thoroughly debilitating were these political events that China's defense establishment stagnated, along with most of Chinese society, for more than a decade. Consequently, as the PLA addresses its "army building" tasks in the 1980s, undoing the devastation of more than ten years will rank near the top of the list. The modernization of weaponry; the upgrading of training; the development of new tactics, strategies, and doctrine; and the reestablishment of professional military education will all require priority consideration.

To the above list we must add a less frequently mentioned but nevertheless important task: the rectification or reformation of leadership practices in the PLA, or, to use the Chinese phrase, "work

The views expressed in this paper are those of the author and should not be regarded as an official statement of the United States Air Force, Air Force Academy, or Department of Defense.

style."[1] Improving the ways that cadres in the Chinese Communist Party (CCP) perform their assignments has been a persistent objective of the CCP's central leadership since the early 1950s. For example, during the "three anti" (i.e., corruption, bureaucratic behavior, and waste) and the "five anti" (i.e., bribery, tax evasion, theft of state property, cheating on government contracts, and stealing state economic information) campaigns of 1951–1952, managerial practices among CCP cadres, state bureaucracies, and bourgeois businessmen were frequently criticized.[2] Prior to 1979, however, there were rarely any similar references to leadership deficiencies in the PLA. To the extent that army leaders did address the issue, there was no sense of urgency of feeling that there were widespread lapses in the quality of military leadership. One possible explanation is that the PLA's work style was comparatively less encumbered by bureaucratic practices than the CCP's during the 1950s and 1960s. A more plausible explanation might be that the exigencies of national security (e.g., the Korean War, the Taiwan Strait crisis, the subjugation of Tibet, the Indian Border War, the Vietnam War, and eventually, tensions along the Sino-Soviet border) masked the existence, or at least deferred a discussion, of some problems dealing with work style in the army during those years. Chinese leaders now admit that the quality of their work style or leadership during the 1970s fell below the levels that were achieved in the 1950s and 1960s. Reestablishing those levels of professional competence and integrity, therefore, must be included in the broad task of military modernization in the last quarter of the twentieth century.

Party and army cadres alike have voiced growing concern since 1979 that many of the worst practices associated with bureaucracies may have become a part of the PLA's work style. This concern, in turn, has led to a fear that the PLA will be unable to modernize itself technologically if its cadres (officers) continue to be "ossified" and tolerate among themselves selfishness, slackness, corruption, and perfunctory performances.[3] A second fear is that the development of a privileged elite in the PLA will alienate public support and undermine unity, morale, and efficiency within the army itself. The resolution of these problems, according to *Red Flag*, the CCP's theoretical journal, is "an urgent task on the military front" that cannot be delayed.[4]

Invariably, discussions involving China's defense modernization plans focus on hardware. PLA leadership, however, has unobtrusively stressed a fundamental overhaul or "rectification" of leadership performance. In making it clear that the leadership problem is of major importance, PLA officials have argued that the effective use of modern weapons cannot be achieved until the people who will operate such weapons are also modernized. The clearest statement in recent times on this subject was made by Xu Xiangqian, then minister of national defense and vice-chairman of the Military Commission of the CCP Central Committee. Writing in the October 1979 issue of *Red Flag*, Xu said, "To modernize our national defense *we need not only modern weapons but also people, especially cadres,* who are devoted to the socialist cause and are versed in modern weapons and operational methods."[5] He added, moreover, that the required modern weaponry must be "combined with men who have advanced modern military thinking."[6]

On August 1, 1979, the *Liberation Army Daily*, the official Party newspaper of the PLA, addressed the same subject. Military modernization, the article argued, "consists of the issues of weaponry and men's political consciousness and military accomplishments." The key issue, according to the article, "is that the command level of our commanders . . . still cannot keep abreast of the requirements of modern warfare."[7] In Xu Xiangqian's assessment of the quality of command levels or leadership in the army, he raised the following question: "How high are our army's tactical and technical levels, its levels of organization, command and management and its scientific and cultural levels? We should admit that our army cannot meet with the demands of a modern war. . . . Even if our army had advanced weapons, it cannot use them and bring them into full play."[8] Xu's answer to his own question clearly indicates that in the areas of command ability or leadership, as well as in combat skills, the army is in need of substantial improvement. Wei Guoqing, director of the PLA General Political Department, voiced a similar conclusion when he asserted that to solve what he called the "thinking and understanding" problems in the PLA, "it is necessary to begin with the leadership."[9]

Deng Xiaoping, when he was both vice-chairman of the CCP and chief of the PLA General Staff, argued that the present deficiencies in PLA leadership stem from the corruptive years—the 1970s.[10] Quite apart from the political ambitions and schemes of such individuals as Lin Biao and the members of the Gang of Four, the key source of problems was the Cultural Revolution, which diverted the army from performing its primary missions for the better part of a decade. Forced into a caretaker role for civilian institutions, army leaders were exposed to new arenas of power, resources, and privileges.[11] The politically charged climate of that period left little time or opportunity for strictly military considerations of national security affairs. From the standpoint of developing or perpetuating professional military ethics, values, traditions, or doctrines, the 1970s were lost years. Instead, radical politics dominated the period. There was little the professional soldier could take from his responsibilities in the 1970s that could be transferred to normal military work. In many instances, the professional soldier was supplanted by the politicized soldier who, it now seems, was good at neither politics nor defense matters. The net result for the PLA was corruptive: Military skills deteriorated, command levels fell, privileged elites increased, and the army's once-honorable relationship with China's masses was tarnished.

In the remainder of this chapter, I will examine in more detail the problem of command and management as raised by Xu Xiangqian. The Chinese press and Party statements, which have been surprisingly informative regarding this issue, have usually discussed the problem in terms of cadre work style, "new privileged elites," and "army-people solidarity." I will use those categories or themes to analyze the command problems the PLA faces, as well as some of the solutions that have been pursued.

Work Styles in the PLA

In September 1979, the modern drama troop of the Nanjing PLA units performed *Forward! Forward!* in Beijing. The central figure in this stage play was a former heroic division commander. When faced with the tasks of modernization, however, his thinking became "ossified," and he hesitated to move forward.[12] Also playing in Beijing at the same time was *The Future Is Making a Call,* a controversial play that dealt with Yu Guanqun, the manager of the Number 207 military armament branch factory. Yu, who was also the secretary of the factory's Party committee, eventually was removed from office because he "lost his revolutionary zeal," and through his dullness, caution, and uninformed and inflexible approach to management, jeopardized important national defense projects. In short, he was ossified.[13]

The characterizations of Yu and the old division commander epitomized the work style the PLA has been trying to eradicate. The ideal leader, senior army officers have contended, should be forward looking; aggressive; creative; well read in technical, professional, and political fields; and flexible. Such qualities apparently have been comparatively rare in the PLA. Since 1979, Chinese military leaders have frequently deplored this disparity between the ideal and actual while trying to meet "army building" goals. While addressing a meeting of the PLA navy's Enlarged Standing Committee in August 1979, Deng Xiaoping stated that during the 1970s, "the party's work style was destroyed, and the army's style and social atmosphere were corrupted."[14] When Xi Zhongxun, first secretary of the Guangdong Provincial CCP Committee, spoke at a plenary session of the Party

Committee of the Guangdong Provincial Military District that same month, he also underscored the harm that had been done to leadership in the army. One of the problems Xi saw in the Guangdong Military District was the poor implementation of democratic centralism. Commanders tended to be patriarchal, and they either discouraged or failed to encourage inputs from the lower ranks. Xu also found commanders unwilling to use the standard Party techniques of criticism and self-criticism to identify and correct mistakes. PLA leading cadres were also faulted for their unwillingness to persevere in' times of adversity, for showing favoritism in appointing friends to posts, and for using their power to pursue private interests.[15]

A similar, yet more sharply critical, description of self-serving cadres was given in mid-1979 by Ma Wenrui, first secretary of the Jilin Provincial Military District Party Committee and concurrently the first secretary of the Jilin Provincial Party Committee.

At present, some cadres, including a number of veteran comrades, think less about the affairs and future of the party and the state and care little for the sufferings of the masses. Some have strong desires for position and fame and lack a sense of organization and discipline. When assignments are being made, some often complain that their "official titles" are not high enough and are always rank conscious. Some always seek pleasure and comfort while fearing hardship. Their revolutionary will is weak, and they lack the kind of enthusiasm they displayed in making the revolution years ago. They carry out their work perfunctorily and wearily. They love to assume official airs in speech and action. Some even openly resist the correct instructions of their superiors.[16]

An equally severe indictment of leadership style was printed in *People's Daily*. The problem, according to the CCP's official newspaper, clearly was of national proportions. Some cadres, the article read,

. . . study what is mentioned in "The Dream of the Red Chamber" about the amulet symbolic of official protection and the art of finding a patron to advance one's own career or protect one in case of trouble. Some people get involved with investigation and study. However, the object of their investigation and study is not the causes of misery for the masses or the problems encountered in work, but how things go with "those above" and their tastes and preferences, so that reports submitted will be in line with the proper "spirit" and the right kinds of gifts can be arranged. Such people fawn upon superiors and impose on inferiors. They excel in nothing, but do everything through coercion. They do nothing but excel in bragging. They are dull and insensitive in socialist construction but are all things to all men in government circles. What is left to recommend them as Communist Party members? Some people abuse their authority, violating law and defying discipline, misspending money and launching projects in a big way. Their extravagant tastes, their life of luxury and their fondness for showing off could not go uncriticized even in a feudal society.[17]

Specific criticisms of "unhealthy" work styles in the PLA can be divided into two categories: leadership and administration. The most frequent leadership problem has involved commanders or leading cadres who do not lead, but "order" their units from their desks.[18] This, of course, has been a pervasive problem in all areas of Chinese society for years. It is a more acute problem for the PLA because the damage may not be evident until army units are actually in combat. Such commanders are portrayed as soldiers who are not so much concerned with the primary affairs of defense as they are with administrative details, staff meetings, politics, and their personal comforts and prerogatives. To some extent, China's desk-bound officers are victims as well as villains. A professional soldier, for example, is not merely a career employee who may be only concerned with security and routine tasks. The career military officer, to the contrary, is motivated by values and beliefs that involve certain standards of excellence, skills, professional knowledge, and dedication to the mission of his service. For much of the last ten to fifteen years—almost a full career in some Western militaries—China's army has been part of political and social movements that generally have been hostile to the development of distinct military values. The ethic that the professional Party cadres have developed in its stead is suffused with undertones of supervision, administration, and politics. For more than a decade, therefore, senior military leaders have been burdened with administrative jobs and have been unable to return to assignments that involve "command" responsibilities.

To solve this problem, commanders have been encouraged to develop and maintain close links or channels of communication with their subordinates, to make on-the-spot inspections, and to work and live with their men. These solutions, however, have often been directed at only part of the general problem of command and leadership. The process of communication in the army, as well as the Party, has always relied on the principle of democratic centralism. The democratic element of the process has provided inputs and feedback from below; centralism has consisted of orders and directives from the top to subordinate units. Commanders have been ordered to include democracy in the army's communication processes,[19] but many individuals have been fearful that by "starting up the machinery," democracy in the army and Party will get out of hand.[20]

Inspections are a routine part of military activities, and their purpose is to ensure high standards of readiness, proficiency, and uniformity. Apparently, inspections have not been carried out by some army commanders. As a result, they have been told to leave their offices, "go deep into the ranks" of their units, and determine what is really going on. Charges of falsified reports and perfunctory performances of responsibilities have led to the conclusion in some quarters that some army cadres missed the actual intent of inspections. During the 1979 year-end inspection, the PLA went to great lengths to specify what should be inspected and why the inspection was necessary.[21] Finally, the requirement to work and live with or near the unit an officer commands seems to be a simple requirement, but some PLA leaders have ensconced themselves in civilian housing away from the military installations they have been responsible for.

Xiao Ke, commander and first political commissar of the PLA Military Academy, has taken to task some officers who are beset by the "whatever mentality." According to Xiao, they are "afraid of so-called 'forbidden areas,' or 'What was written in books must not be changed or expanded; and what was not written in books must not be said or thought. The result was nothing of the past could be changed and everything had to be done in the same way it was done in the past.' "[22] Officers who have engaged in this kind of thinking, Xiao Ke has argued, are tied to protomilitary doctrines that are thirty to fifty years old. Modern military commanders, on the other hand, should be looking creatively at the future and contributing to new military practices and tactics.

Xiao Ke also has attacked a xenophobic or ideological disdain for foreign military experiences. At the PLA Military Academy, Xiao has advised senior officers to discontinue the "closed-door policy of military affairs," which holds that all military experience, doctrine, or programs must be based on Chinese or Marxist experience, while foreign contributions, particularly those of enemy nations, must be disregarded.[23]

In the army as well as the Party, some officials have pressed the issue of promoting "new successors" to occupy the positions of retiring commanders. In November 1979, Wang Enmao, first secretary of the Jilin Provincial Military District Party Committee, addressed the problem and stressed training as well as selection of young cadres. The new successors, he said, ideally should be young, but must also meet certain requirements. In all cases, he added, "We should not select those cadres who talk well, but those who perform well."[24]

Leading cadres in the PLA have also been criticized for being poorly read and informed. "Many of our leading cadres have not undergone systematic training," claimed Zhang Tingfa, a member of the CCP's Politburo and commander of the PLA air force, "and have only scant knowledge about many things. They should be determined to consciously change the situation of 'jack of all trades and master of none.' "[25] Military officers are now advised to be an expert in one field and be well informed in several other areas. Zhang also has told members of the PLA air force's Party Committee that it was the responsibility of each committee member to oppose in the air force an attitude of "muddling along in one's life without studying books or reading papers."[26] In regard to cadres who had read books, the PLA General Staff Department chided some for "mechanically copying the books and turning them into dogma."[27] Wei Guoqing, director of the PLA General Political Department, pointed out that "cadres at all levels, particularly senior leading cadres, should study more of the basic Marxist theories more profoundly."[28] Even though Zhang Tingfa has emphasized the importance of improving general leadership skills, he, too, has deplored the lack of a basic understanding of Marxism among many leading Party members in the air force.[29]

The work styles of the PLA's political officers also have been attacked. Nothing short of a large-scale reform of political education was called for following the 1979 All-Army Political Work Conference.[30] The context of the reforms suggested that political work had become an empty ritual. Political commissars were told to avoid giving boring or trite speeches, to commence "systematic and comprehensive" education in light of reality, to develop a "unified plan for study," to "no longer merely rely on the lectures of political cadres," and to help cadres and soldiers "correctly handle such problems as the future, honor and disgrace, suffering and joy, life and death, love and marriage and family life." During political meetings, political officers were told to "include problems the fighters are concerned about and bring controversial questions into special topics." Even "electronic teaching by television" was advocated.[31] Some political officers also have been bound to their desks. The commander of a unit of the South China Sea Fleet discovered that some political instructors in his unit "did not know how to do ideological-political work at sea."[32]

Some of the strongest criticism concerning work style in the army was reserved for the performances of PLA cadres as administrators. The PLA's air force commander, Zhang Tingfa, was particularly critical of bureaucratic practices in the air force—more so than the commanders of other major PLA components. As early as March 1978, the PLA air force launched a sixteen-day campaign for "three investigations, three rectifications." The three investigations concerned fighting will, discipline, and work and study. The rectification program was clearly aimed at administrative work styles and was designed to get rid of "softness, laziness and laxness," to eradicate bureaucratism, and to improve writing styles.[33] In explaining the thrust of the air force's campaign, the *Liberation Army Daily* revealingly described the shortcomings and practices of some officers:

—In the rectification to get rid of softness, laziness and laxness, primary attention should be given to eliminating such questions as putting fear before everything else, departing from principles, not reading books and newspapers, not thinking, not going down to grassroots units and creating disunity among the comrades.

—Rectification to liquidate bureaucratism means, basically, to do away with such work styles as acting as bureaucrats and overlords, who neither investigate nor study, nor understand the situation at lower levels, nor attend to the work themselves, who cannot go out to work without a cane, who cannot make reports without using a notebook and who cannot speak without written scripts.

—With regard to the rectification of writing style, the main thing to do is eliminate the pernicious influence of the stereotyped writing of the gang of four and eliminate such bad styles as failing to point out, analyze and solve problems in making speeches, giving instructions or writing reports. Primary efforts should also be made to do away with empty talk, bragging and hackneyed phrases. Formalism, red tape, exaggeration and deception should be eliminated as well.[34]

To assess the successes of the PLA's efforts to rectify work styles during 1979, the CCP's Military Commission issued the "Circular on Year-end Education Review." This document, which outlined the scope and methods of the review, applied primarily to PLA training units, but all other branches of the PLA followed the guidance contained in the circular. The emphasis of the review was on the "commanding and directing ability of the reviewed units," an assessment of the extent to which PLA personnel were "studying science, culture and modern warfare," and the improvement of political work.[35] Although no formal results of the review had been publicized by early 1980, there was evidence in 1979 that some units were acting to improve their performances in the areas of work style and to acquire technical knowledge related to defense matters.[36] Much less was said, however, about political education and training.

The PLA air force, as discussed already, took the lead in calling for better command and management practices. In two areas, at least, their remedial measures were discussed publicly. First, the number of coordination and staff meetings was cut to allow more time to accomplish primary mission assignments. Second, the volume of paperwork was reduced. In the PLA's air force Command Headquarters, internal publications were cut from thirty-five to seven in one year. Confidential documents were reduced by 48 percent in the Engineering Department and 36.2 percent in the Command Headquarters.[37] There was no mention of military programs specifically designed to improve individual command or management techniques, although the CCP as a whole conducted extensive management training classes in mid-1979.[38]

In 1979, some PLA units began taking action to introduce leading cadres, normally at or above the division level, to technical information related to national security affairs. Presumably, a "Notice on Conducting Education of Science and Culture Throughout the Units," issued early in 1979, was the driving force.[39] The PLA air force soon announced it would publish 8 books on military science "essential to the modernization of the PLA Air Force."[40] Later in the year, the PLA Fighters Publishing House announced plans to publish approximately 100 books in a series dealing with modern military techniques and the history of warfare.[41] PLA units in Nanjing, however, were the most active. They began a system of devoting two afternoons each week to the study of defense science and technology, tactics, and "conditions of foreign armed forces."[42] The PLA General Staff Department held a short series of "Lecture Classes on Modern Science and Technology and Knowledge of Modern Warfare" for senior- and middle-level cadres throughout the PLA, the National Defense Science and Technology Commission, and the National Defense Industries Office. The classes apparently did not cover the subject matter in great detail, since cadres were encouraged "to improve themselves through self-study" following the conclusion of the lecture series.[43] No specific actions by political commissars to improve political training were mentioned in the Chinese press, although the 1979 All-Army Political Work Conference called for a thorough reform of political training. Zhang Tingfa, in remarks to the PLA air force's CCP Standing Committee, did stress the need to conduct systematic education in "basic knowledge about the party" among Party members in the air force.[44]

To summarize, the movement to rectify the work style of the PLA primarily has been concerned with leadership and administrative performances. In both categories, senior commanders have criticized the PLA's corps of leading cadres for tolerating too much "softness, laziness, and laxness" among themselves and for being poorly informed about their profession and the Party. Officers have been encouraged, moreover, to be forward looking, progressive, actively involved in the military profession, and well informed about issues and technical matters that have a bearing on national security.

Privileged Elites in the PLA

"Bourgeois rights" have always been a particularly troublesome problem for communist societies. On the one hand, Marxist ideology has condemned bourgeois rights and has called for their elimination. On the other hand, subsequent practitioners of Marxism have confessed that bourgeois rights can only be *restricted* during the historical period of socialism; eradication can only come during full communism. Thus, special privileges, or bourgeois rights, must be accepted as inevitable, although reprehensible, as long as communist countries still practice socialism. In China and the Soviet Union today, bourgeois rights involve the distribution of the social wealth on the basis of "to each according to his work." This phrase is, of course, that the distribution of wealth will be greater for some than for others, because the contributions of some workers may be quantitatively or qualitatively greater than those of others. According to Leon Trotsky's *The Revolution Betrayed,* the beneficiaries of this redistribution of the wealth under socialism have become a "new privileged class" within the Communist Party. This class of ruling elites has been able to seize and perpetuate privileges through the monopoly of administrative or bureaucratic work. Being responsible for the general redistribution of wealth for the state, the members of this privileged elite have been in positions to ensure that they receive appropriate, and even excessive, shares of the wealth of the state.[45]

By 1958, doctrinaire Chinese Marxists believed they could succeed where the Soviets had failed in eliminating bourgeois rights. A variety of radical social and economic programs were proposed. The commune system was the key program for implementing radical change. The ultimate objective was the destruction of the wage-scale system, which the Chinese Marxists believed perpetuated inequality in the distribution of wealth. Zhang Chunchiao, then chief of the Propaganda Department of the Shanghai Municipal CCP Committee, led the assault. His article, "To Abolish Bourgeois Rights," which was printed in *People's Daily* (October 13, 1958), was a radical attack on China's wage system.[46] Although China's advocates of radical change were unsuccessful in their efforts to eliminate bourgeois rights and the wage-scale system, they were able to make the criticism of bourgeois privileges part of the fabric of Chinese politics. In recent years, so-called radicals and moderates alike have voiced concern about the emergence of China's own "new privileged class." Speaking to the second session of the Fifth National People's Congress, Premier Hua Guofeng observed that "new exploiters" within the Party itself were neither small in number nor lacking in ability to maintain their vested interests.[47] Hua acknowledged that organizational readjustments in the Party, government, and army had placed leadership in the hands of cadres whom the people could trust. He added, however:

> there are some people who think that obligations and discipline are laid down for the common people, while cadres and high ranking [officials] only have rights without obligations and need not observe discipline. . . . Malpractices left over mainly by the feudal order, such as the pursuit of privileges, "backdoor dealings" and suppression of democratic rights, still remain today to a considerable extent.[48]

Most recently, policies have emphasized the need to restrict rather than eliminate the spread of bourgeois privileges.[49] It is, however, an uneasy compromise. There are no clear distinctions between acceptable shares of the social wealth and unacceptable abuses of privilege. On the one hand, cadres have been admonished to live simple, unpretentious lives. On the other hand, even critics of bourgeois rights have implicitly acknowledged that cadres, particularly leading cadres, are entitled to "certain special working conditions" and "some proper attention" in view of the value of the work they perform. Zhang Tingfa called it "good treatment."[50]

The problem of a privileged elite is particularly vexing for the PLA, notwithstanding the elimination of official rank designations in May 1965. First, abuses by PLA cadres effect morale within the army, especially among the enlisted soldiers and in the lower ranks. The existence of a privileged elite, it has been argued, destroyed the army's "fighting spirit."[51] Second, the presence of "new exploiters" in the army led to acrimonious relations between army cadres and local Party officials. For example, officials of the Wan County Military Subdistrict in Sichuan Province suggested they would find it difficult to do their part in supporting the government and the army if the army refused to vacate buildings and return appliances that were illegally taken by the army during and after the Cultural Revolution. Once the dispute was made public, the army not only agreed to return the buildings and appliances in question, but offered to pay rent for the period that the army used the property.[52] Finally, the PLA must worry about its image among the rank and file of the CCP. Although the frequency of abused privileges may not be any greater in the army than among civilian Party cadres, the army is more vulnerable to criticism. The

PLA not only is an exceptionally visible part of modern Chinese society, but it is allowed certain privileges (i.e., legal preferential treatment). Violations of Party discipline, therefore, are more visible and susceptible to criticism by civilians and Party colleagues who have complained that the military already has more privileges than it should have. Although instances of excessive privileges may have little effect on the decisions of the Politburo or the Central Committee's Military Commission, they most certainly will have a harmful impact on local levels where PLA units routinely depend on local production units for certain foods, commercial commodity distribution, public services, and housing construction.[53]

Criticism of the new exploiters in the army has generally fallen into three categories: the pursuit of special privileges, corrupt or illegal practices, and "showing favoritism." Such practices have long been criticized in the CCP and state bureaucracy; hence they are not exclusively military problems. In fact, one point of significance in the discussion of bourgeois rights in the army is that it has taken so long for criticism of this nature to develop in the PLA.

The Pursuit of Special Privileges

We can be certain that PLA leaders have always enjoyed some kinds of privileges. In recent years, however, Party and public attention has focused on army cadres who have solicited or accepted special privileges that exceeded the ill-defined limits of Party propriety. Two areas in particular have drawn considerable attention: housing and transportation.

China's housing shortage has been widely discussed in the official press.[54] Residential housing has been at a premium in most areas for several years, and office space currently is limited in major cities. Authorities recently curtailed the issuance of building permits for office buildings in Beijing to divert more resources into the construction of residential housing.[55] It is understandable, therefore, that comfortable housing or office facilities have become a much-sought-after privilege. Military leaders, largely as a result of the PLA's monopoly of coercive force, frequently have been criticized on this point. Wall posters in Beijing, for example, alleged that Wang Dongxing, Mao's personal bodyguard and former head of PLA Unit 8341—the CCP Central Committee's garrison force—spent millions of yuan on a residence in Zhongnanhai.[56] The case of Zheng Xuyu, however, has drawn far more public attention.

Zheng, a Hebei Military District adviser, occupied the private residence of the renowned Beijing opera actor, Hao Shouchen. Zheng moved from his original military quarters (ten one-story houses totaling

110 square meters) in 1968 to Hao's "small courtyard" (twenty-three one-story houses totaling 393 square meters and ten adjacent houses totaling 90 square meters). The PLA housing office had temporarily taken over the buildings that same year. In 1972, central government authorities ordered that all local housing, particularly civilian houses occupied by the military, be returned to the local authorities. Zheng unwillingly agreed to move if adequate replacement housing was provided. Although the Beijing Municipal Housing Department offered fifteen one-story buildings that were occupied already by six households, Zheng rejected the offer as being unsatisfactory and began to withhold his rent payments. Finally in 1979, strong pressure from the Office of Policy Implementation for Housing in Beijing and Beijing military authorities compelled Zheng to move by the end of the year. Surprisingly, the central issue in the Zheng Xuyu incident was not his right to have a large residence. The housing authorities, after all, were prepared to offer his family (wife, son, daughter-in-law, and two grandchildren) a courtyard that was already occupied by six families. The real issue was that Zheng used his elite position to stand above any responsibility to obey Party, state, or military regulations.[57]

In another case, the self-serving actions of an unidentified general were recounted in a long poem published in Shanghai's *Wenhui bao.* In Ye Wenfu's "General, You Must Not Do This," the poet attacked a "senior general" who admittedly had been "ruthlessly persecuted by the 'gang of four.'" After being reinstated in his leadership posts, however, the general ordered the dismantling of a nursery school to make way for the construction of his house, which eventually included modern fixtures that cost several thousand yuan worth of foreign exchange. In his poem, Ye lashed out bitterly, yet sadly at times, at the old hero who once was a revolutionary who contributed much to a new China but since being rehabilitated, had "established" himself in the "new privileged class." Ye saw the old general and all other privileged elites as arrogant traitors who replaced their revolutionary vigor with disdain for China's masses. "You, General," have regarded the sacrifices and burdens of the people as "Droplets of oil and spittle / Flung from your fingertips / As a result of your belch."[58]

The use of government and military vehicles for private purposes also has been cited as an abused practice among military cadres. Given the general shortage of automobiles in China, the access to fleets of vehicles has been a tempting privilege in the army. To avoid charges of misusing military equipment and to set an example for other cadres, the commander of the Guizhou Military District, Hu Binfu, as well as his immediate colleagues, began paying their own transportation expenses in 1977. They also prohibited family members from using "private cars" and reduced to a minimum their own use of such vehicles.[59] Hu's circumspect behavior is contrasted with that of Zhang Huaiying in Shanxi Province. Zhang retained two vehicles for his personal use—a sedan and a jeep—and frequently dispatched special vehicles to his native town to deliver gifts to family and friends. Zhang also did little to cement relationships with local Party cadres when he evicted seven secretaries of a prefectural CCP Standing Committee from their houses to make room for his own family.[60] In Yunnan Province, PLA personnel were ordered to "pay fees in accordance with the proscribed norms" if an official vehicle was used for private business.[61]

Corrupt and Illegal Practices

In some respects, corrupt or illegal actions are merely extensions of special privileges but there are differences. Those people who seek special privileges are usually guilty of poor judgment or "mistakes" that are punishable by intra-Party or army discipline. Corruption, however, has usually involved criminal actions. Cadres often have avoided criminal prosecution during the last ten to fifteen years because there were no regular civil courts or codified laws that could be used to indict offenders. Consequently, leading cadres often avoided punishment through "connections." At worst, they were required to write self-criticisms. With the exception of some unusual cases,[62] most instances of bourgeois privilege that have involved fraud or criminal acts have consisted of petty embezzlement or theft. These crimes have included receiving and soliciting gifts in return for favors, using public funds to give dinners or send gifts to friends and superior officers, and receiving "backdoor benefits" or kickbacks.[63] Some cadres have also accepted or solicited reduced prices on factory goods or unauthorized samples. In some instances, public funds were used to provide entertainment, such as free movies, for participants at work conferences.[64]

The greatest potential for abuse and, ultimately, public disclosure of illegal actions has involved the PLA's relationships with civilian production units such as factories and communes. Because regulations require that production units provide certain goods and services for the army, there is a complex system of commercial links between the army and commercial enterprises. Although the PLA is generally careful to avoid the image of a warlord army, there are occasional violations of acceptable conduct. In 1979, for example, the deputy head of a PLA logistics unit in the Beijing Military Area Command placed an order for five hunting rifles with a repair factory of the Batong Coal Mining Bureau. Since the factory did not have the tools to do the job, several thousand yuan were to be spent to retool. Some workers protested what they believed was an illegal request. Others cautioned, "The man is a big shot. Dare you disobey?" In this instance, an investigation ensued, the order was canceled, and the official was required to make a self-criticism.[65]

Showing Favoritism

Privileged elites also have been criticized in China's press for extending privileges, benefits, or favors to family members, friends, "comrades-in-arms, colleagues, old subordinates, old superiors or their relatives' children."[66] Other abuses in this category have included letting "factional views" determine who will be promoted, rewarded, punished, or commended;[67] allowing cadres to receive less severe punishments than fighters for the same violations; excessively tolerating, accommodating, or shielding the mistakes or crimes of some army cadres who were personal friends, faction members, or relatives; and "bending the law for the benefit of relatives or friends" when crimes have been committed or when such action would allow them to enjoy privileges they normally would not be entitled to.[68] *Liberation Army Daily* has stressed that these "abnormalities . . . in inner-party democratic life . . . and inner-party common practice" have greatly influenced the lower levels and have harmed the army's work style, morale, and confidence.[69]

Army-People Solidarity

Late each year, normally just before the New Year, the Ministry of Civil Affairs and the PLA's General Political Department launch an annual "Support the Army, Cherish the People" movement. Sometimes called the "Army-People Solidarity drive," it lasts until approximately the spring festival. Each department has routinely issued circulars that call "for efforts to carry out extensive and indepth activities to support the army and give preferential treatment to families of army men and to support the government and cherish the people."[70] Until 1979, the annual event was fairly ritualized and rarely provided any insights into relationships between the army and Chinese society as a whole. Army units usually stepped up "fraternal" visits to neighboring production brigades, army medical teams visited the masses, and the official press devoted considerable coverage to the "fine traditions" that existed between the army and the people. In many respects, this annual movement has been a memorial to China's early revolutionary days when the army was inescapably close to the peasants, depended on the peasants for provisions, and repaid their debt with honesty, disciplined behavior, and labor.

The image of amicable PLA-civilian relations had worn thin by 1979. Indeed, a serious divergence of views became evident as the 1979 Army-People Solidarity movement unfolded. An accumulation of more than ten years of bickering and mutual recrimination began to surface. Although blame for the deteriorated relationship was regularly attributed to Lin Biao and the Gang of Four, the Cultural Revolution and its aftereffects seemed to be more appropriate explanations. It seems that the chaos, political disintegration, political abuses, and deterioration of PLA discipline during and after the Cultural Revolution have not been easily forgotten by some civilians who developed resentment for the army. In early 1980, for example, Party officials in Heilongjiang Province asked civilians to put aside bad experiences and to "approach this problem from all angles and look at it from a historical point of view."[71] Civilians who had been involved with the PLA were asked to realize that any mistakes made by the PLA were committed through inexperience or "incorrect instructions from some leaders." At the heart of the current antagonisms is the implied, if not actual, claim that privileged elites in the army are far from interested in "cherishing the people." Consequently, some civilian cadres have questioned the need to give preferential treatment to the army or the families of PLA servicemen.

In January 1979, the *People's Daily* carried a frank discussion of the problem. In the editorial, the author asked for more understanding and less complaining between the army and local authorities: "Some comrades' idea of supporting the army and giving preferential treatment to families of armymen and supporting the government and cherishing the people has weakened. At present, some people often see only the shortcomings and problems of the army or the localities. . . . Various localities and PLA units must try to understand and help . . . instead of complaining and blaming each other."[72] The resentment between the two groups has been so extensive that Chinese officials have found it necessary to initiate activities and programs specifically "to educate the cadres and the people to treasure their army as they treasure their own eyes."[73]

The PLA is particularly sensitive to its relationship with the civilian Chinese population for several reasons. First, the PLA must struggle against the memory of a not-too-distant era of warlords and armed bandits who pillaged much of the Chinese countryside. Lapses of discipline by the army could all too easily prompt unfavorable allusions to modern warlords and bandits. Second, the provisioning of the PLA is highly dependent upon local support. "Preferential treatment" for the PLA has included giving the army priority consideration, in accordance with regulations, for supplies, parts, repairs of equipment, and public services.[74] Disaffected or angry communities near military installations could impede some defense activities by withholding cooperation or bureaucratically delaying deliveries of goods and services.

Third, veterans from the war of liberation and the Korean War are now reaching maximum retirement age, and the PLA is facing, for the first time, the difficulties of dealing with a large body of retired servicemen.[75] Since retirement pensions are not large, suitable civilian employment has become an important issue for veterans. Technically trained veterans have had fewer problems than others, but acute unemployment conditions have made job placement difficult at best. Civilian communities, already unhappy about the requirement to give preferential treatment to the dependents of PLA servicemen, have also been asked to give veterans favorable consideration ahead of local people. Finally, an official insistence that democracy as well as centralism be practiced within the Party has increased the chances of unprecedented public awareness of problems involving the army. Such disclosures, therefore, could feed discontent or embarrass officials. Consequently, in 1979 and 1980, the PLA began taking a variety of measures to defuse conditions that could impair amicable and productive interaction between the army and local communities and ultimately jeopardize modernization of the army in the 1980s.

Combating the Warlord Image

In October 1979, the PLA's occupation of university facilities in Beijing made international headlines. One disgruntled Chinese professor was reported to have said, "It's too much. How could the People's Liberation Army turn into warlords?"[76] The unfavorable, and perhaps not altogether deserved, remark was in reference to the continued occupation of parts of the People's University by elements of the PLA's Second Artillery. During the Cultural Revolution, the Second Artillery originally entered the university facilities to preserve public order. With the closure of the university from 1969 to 1979, the PLA's occupation of the campus became an unanticipated convenience in the face of increasingly scarce office and housing space. Despite 1972 directives from the central government requiring the PLA to vacate civilian facilities, compliance was uneven, especially when it appeared that vacated buildings would go unused. Such was the case of the People's University, which did not reopen until 1979. Although part of the campus was returned to the university for its use, the Second Artillery retained control of about two-thirds of the campus. Consequently, in October 1979, students and faculty members held a three-day boycott to protest the continued use of the campus by the PLA. Sensitive to the impact of adverse public opinion, the army agreed to leave in stages. A spokesman for the Second Artillery observed that they had underestimated the difficulties to the university and had paid too much attention to their own problems.[77]

The incident at the People's University was symptomatic of more widespread practices involving the PLA. In Liaoning Province, for example, the army was instructed to return land to which it was not entitled to communes and brigades. Additionally, army units were ordered to protect grassland resources and were strictly forbidden to reclaim wilderness lands.[78] In Hebei Province, the Provincial Military District adviser had illegally continued to live in the private house of a civilian since 1968. After more than eight years of appeals, the offender was finally persuaded to vacate the premises.[79] Elsewhere, PLA cadres have been advised to settle promptly matters of "real estate ownership."[80]

The use of scarce housing and office space has been a particularly acute "contradiction" between the PLA and civilian communities. With a universally acknowledged shortage of investment in housing and services—such as water supply and sewage disposal systems, power, heat, and telecommunications[81]—the PLA has had to balance critical public opinion and discontent within the army where housing also is in short supply. With the exception of some flagrant cases of excessive bourgeois rights, the PLA's normal response has been to vacate civilian premises and ask servicemen and their families to sacrifice their comfort for the benefit of the masses. One of the air force's model divisions was cited on several occasions because its cadres "found pleasure in living in their small and simple rooms" and were willing to share "weal and woe."[82] Other Party and PLA cadres have been admonished to follow the example of this PLA unit and to regard their accommodations, however humble, as far more comfortable than the tamped-earth houses of Daqing or Chairman Mao's cave dwelling in Yenan.[83] By forgoing some housing comforts, the PLA has hoped to score more enduring gains with civilian communities.

Preferential Treatment

A constant irritant between the army and adjoining communities has been the policy of "preferential treatment." In accordance with state regulations, communities near military installations have been required to provide priority consideration for the PLA in two ways. First, local state purchasing bureaus and commodity distributing agencies have provided the army with certain kinds of supplies, goods, and public services. Preferential treatment has ensured that the military has been given priority when there are competing orders among state agencies. Minimum-quality standards also are assured. Although such treatment is required by law, local Party officials and cadres apparently have not always been responsive, especially if they felt the PLA was making excessive demands or was disregarding local conditions or regulations.

The second form of preferential treatment has involved individuals: PLA servicemen, their dependents, veterans, demobilized servicemen (i.e., personnel mustered out of the PLA prior to retirement), disabled servicemen, and heroes. Providing special treatment in such areas as housing, employment, and schooling for these people has been a much more sensitive issue than the priority consideration given to impersonal defense institutions. Because military people are regarded as outsiders or temporary residents, the injunction to help them often has given rise to conflicts. With local communities already hard pressed to satisfy the demands of permanent residents, their responsiveness to military requests sometimes has been less than wholehearted. For example, *Nanfang Daily* published an article that revealed that the mere mention of soldiers as part of the old three-in-one combination of "workers, peasants, and soldiers" gave rise to feelings of antagonism: "Currently, whenever the workers, peasants and soldiers are mentioned, some people immediately feel resentful. People are reluctant to represent the workers, peasants and soldiers, nor are they eager to meet their needs and they even go so far as 'shutting them outside.' "[84] Thus, when cases of abused privileges by army personnel—real, inflated, or imagined—have come to light, they have resulted in the local authorities occasionally becoming somewhat intractable in their willingness to support the army's requests.

The antagonisms between military and civilian groups regarding "preferential treatment" and "cherishing the people" can be seen in a joint pledge prepared by the Nanjing PLA units and the Xuzhou Prefectural Administration Office for the 1979–1980 campaign to cement army-people solidarity. The army agreed, for example, and thereby implied some degree of previous negligence, to respect local Party committees and governments; to implement local government regulations; to encourage cadres and fighters (enlisted personnel) to observe Party and state laws; to work toward a decrease in problems arising between the military and the local people; to settle disagreements regarding ownership of real estate; to improve the supervision of the drivers of military vehicles, thereby improving traffic safety; and to prevent civilian accidents resulting from military exercises outside military installations. In a more positive vein, the PLA units pledged to assist with agricultural projects (local production units would have to pay for the gasoline used by army vehicles), health care, and public security; to provide labor for public works; and to support the four modernizations. The pledge of the civilian authorities, on the other hand, was also revealing. Xuzhou officials promised to improve their efforts to "give priority to guaranteeing the supply of grain, nonstaple foods, and vegetables needed by the military according to state regulations and actual local conditions"; to "protect the marriages of armymen and . . . [to] punish according to the law criminal acts undermining marriages involving armymen"; to implement policies regarding the placement and preferential treatment of retired and demobilized soldiers; and to give priority treatment to the jobs of the armymen's family members and their children's education and employment, in accordance with party policies.[85]

To ease the burden of preferential treatment on local communities, some PLA units have taken measures to provide jobs for their own dependents. The air force's General Headquarters has taken steps to create jobs for children of cadres. These jobs have included making and reupholstering sofas, repairing motor vehicles, fixing barracks appliances, and printing publications.[86] The PLA navy has undertaken similar programs.[87]

Meeting Veterans' Needs

As the PRC enters its fourth decade, the financial and social needs of large numbers of retired servicemen have become an important issue. Many veterans from the late 1940s and 1950s, who contributed thirty to forty years of military service, are now retired or have reached the age of retirement. As the size and the standards of efficiency of the PLA's manpower structure have changed, especially during the 1970s, many other servicemen were demobilized, or discharged, before completing full careers. Hence in 1979 and 1980, veterans and demobilized soldiers began to make strong demands on the government concerning employment and security following separation from the army. Technically, veterans' affairs are largely the responsibility of the Ministry of Civil Affairs, but the Ministry of National Defense has maintained an important interest in the treatment of retired and demobilized personnel. A vocal and dissatisfied body of ex-PLA soldiers has developed in some urban areas, especially Beijing.

Demobilized soldiers were the first to publicize forcefully their grievances for jobs, security in retirement, and social status. In 1979, representatives of more than 400,000 PLA military cadres who were demobilized in the 1970s began to air their complaints on wall posters in Beijing. "Representatives of the Demobilized Cadres of the Three Services of the PLA in All Provinces, Municipalities, and Autonomous Regions" argued that they not only "lost their cadre status on being demobilized," but "we returned home poor and politically suspect. Some of us became beggars and others committed suicide."[88] The protesters argued that the restructuring of the army in 1968 and 1969, which caused a large-scale demobilization of cadres and soldiers, has been recognized as an illegal act. The PLA's General Office for Political Affairs, they continued, has done little to rectify the injustices suffered by those who were improperly demobilized. The goals of the demobilized cadres were reinstatement in the army; if that could not be done, they demanded assistance in obtaining suitable employment with commensurate status among civilians.[89]

Enlisted personnel—retired or demobilized—have fared no better. In May 1979, they used wall-poster cartoons in Beijing to express their complaints. According to their posters, the 1958 Military Service Law, which they viewed as a contract that specified the obligations of the state and the soldiers, was "demolished" in 1961, 1965, and again after 1967. Chen Boda, Mao Zedong's former ideologist, was blamed for tampering with the law. In one cartoon, Chen was shown standing in front of a severed bridge that symbolized the 1958 Military Service Law and shouting, "You repair; I demolish."[90] The protesters alleged that the government had not protected two inherent assurances in the 1958 law: retired or demobilized servicemen could return to their pre–military service production units, and they could return to cities if they had entered the PLA from an urban area.

Many servicemen who enlisted in the 1950s, according to the wall posters, were unhappy that they were not allowed to return to their production units because their former jobs were no longer available. Although some veterans had been absent from their civilian production units for more than twenty years, they still maintained that the 1958 law applied to them as much as it did to demobilized soldiers who had served for only three or four years. A government official in one cartoon claimed, "It is absolutely impossible to give you work." The veterans' bitterness was summed up in the charge that "Everybody else has been rehabilitated except us."[91] Other servicemen, specifically those who had been recruited from urban areas—and perhaps some who had come to enjoy the amenities of city life—protested their postmilitary assignments to China's rural areas. Their advocates argued that "when they were demobilized they were sent 'by force' to live in the countryside where they were sometimes considered as 'criminals' or political offenders by the peasants who did not understand why they should have been sent to the countryside."[92]

PLA officials have responded weakly to the petitions of veterans and demobilized soldiers. The reason, no doubt, is that the army is powerless to attenuate certain problems (e.g., employment, housing, preferred geographic location) that are as endemic among China's civilians as they are among former servicemen. PLA leaders, nonetheless, have routinely visited veterans' groups, have voiced sympathy for their problems, have praised their contributions, and have persistently pressed the Ministry of Civil Affairs and local governments to assist ex-PLA members and provide them preferential treatment. For example, Wang Enmao, the Jilin Provincial Party secretary, spoke in August 1979 to a forum of veteran Red Army men and retired cadres in Changchun. Wang assured the former servicemen that "the party and the people will never forget [you] . . . veteran cadres who have contributed to the cause of the revolution."[93] At a similar meeting held in Xinjiang, various groups of ex-PLA personnel were brought together in a formal organization: the Third Xinjiang Regional Congress of Family Members of Martyrs and Deceased Armymen, Disabled Armymen, Demobilized and Retired Soldiers, and Those Transferred to Civilian Jobs from Active Service. Only the greeting message from the Ministry of Civil Affairs suggested that the November 1979 Congress might have addressed the sensitive issue of veterans' problems.[94]

The effective handling of veterans' needs has been complicated by widespread civilian unemployment and underemployment, decentralized control of large areas of potential employment, and uneven civilian responsiveness or ability to help former PLA soldiers. Even such Western schemes as "transition training" and job fairs would be of little value since the problem normally is not necessarily one of job skills, but the mere existence of any kind of work.[95] Hence, with no apparent nationwide programs to assist unemployed veterans or demobilized soldiers, they must return to former homes, or even new locations, and compete with large numbers of local unemployed youths in areas where parochial interests and strong local pressures dominate local actions.

The retirement and replacement system devised in the city of Yanji, Jilin Province, illustrates the difficulties involved in placing former servicemen. According to Yanji officials, there has been no unified system for recruitment of personnel in the "neighborhood industries and production and service trades." Consequently, during the late 1960s and 1970s, "each neighborhood set up its own factories and its own way of recruiting personnel and drawing up the work plans. . . . A number of housewives and idle people undertook the work." By the late 1970s, "vigorous young people had nothing to do while the old, weak, sick, and disabled had to go to work." Neighborhood Party committees, therefore, drafted specific retirement and replacement measures. In almost half the instances where vacancies were created through retirement, the vacancies were filled by sons and daughters of those people who had retired.[96] Understandably, returning veterans and demobilized servicemen have had difficulty penetrating such restricted economic and social networks.

Conclusion

Some of the PLA's current command and management problems involving work style, privileged elites, and army-community relations have always existed. If we are to believe the statements of PLA leaders and high Party officials who have been quoted in the Chinese press, then the quality and integrity of leadership in the PLA is, in fact, in need of extensive rectification and reform. Some Chinese leaders have regarded this as "the modernization of people." The CCP Committee of the Chengdu PLA units assessed the breadth of the problem as follows:

> We are faced with mountains of problems, difficulties, and troubles. The international scene is also not tranquil. Some comrades lack a correct understanding of the twists and turns and difficulties on the road to advancement. Hence, they lack sufficient confidence in accomplishing the four modernizations. Some doubt the superiority of the socialist system. Some are worried that we will again embark on a tortuous road in carrying out the three years of readjustment.[97]

In modernizing personnel and negotiating the twists, turns, and difficulties of change, the leaders of that effort most confront the problem of entrenched practices and the fear of change in the PLA itself. Party and PLA cadres alike have been often required to advance along a tortuous road, and many have become exceptionally cautious or cynical regarding new policies and programs.

Army and Party cadres have expressed their confidence that the damage caused during the ten years of chaos can be repaired. One official proudly observed that "Our bringing into the open the various demonstrations of unhealthy party style shows precisely that we are confident in and capable of correcting party style."[98] Solutions will not easily be realized. To improve work styles, for example, the army has viewed education and training as the solution. But unless the PLA's education programs are carried out more extensively than the training seminars and conferences that have already been held, it is doubtful there will be a measurable improvement in command levels for many years. Many of the training and education programs for cadres thus far appear to have been too short and superficial to have had any important impact on leadership and management skills. The socialization and training of servicemen before they join the PLA, therefore, may be more important than the leadership training they receive after they enter the army.

Restricting the spread of bourgeois rights among privileged elites is certain to be one of the most difficult problems the PLA must confront. Cadres have been asked to eschew comfort and personal pleasures, yet the CCP has implicitly encouraged an unequal distribution of the social wealth by supporting such practices as job titles, economic incentives, and the wage-scale system. An important question is whether or not the army will be able to successfully cultivate high ethical standards of its own if the CCP is unable to tighten Party discipline across the board. At a minimum, the CCP will have to define more clearly what is acceptable treatment of cadres, albeit bourgeois in nature, and what is a criminal offense according to civil statutes. As long as flagrantly dishonest actions can be subject to intra-Party discipline rather than to civil laws, cadres are likely to regard the risks and penalties as comparatively light.[99]

If the army continues to redress the mistakes that were made in the 1970s, such as returning real estate to private individuals and civilian production units, most major irritants will be removed or forgotten. There will always be, however, certain unavoidable tensions between army installations and surrounding communities that can be attenuated, at least, by a continuation of the annual Army-People Solidarity drives. Preferential treatment for families of servicemen, veterans, and demobilized soldiers will continue to be a sore point between the PLA and local officials. Some PLA air force and navy units have found solutions by creating jobs for their own dependents. By establishing these programs to meet some of the needs of PLA servicemen and their families, the army may be able to reduce its economic and social dependence on local communities. At the same time, however, such self-help efforts could lead to a more insular existence for army personnel and more misunderstandings between army installations and neighboring civilian communities. In the area of similar government-sponsored programs for retired or demobilized soldiers, the PLA and central government authorities seem to have responded weakly. Former PLA members who are vocally dissatisfied understandably will do little to boost sagging morale.

The command and management problems the PLA will face in the 1980s are not insurmountable, but they are imposing. How successfully the army deals with its problems of leadership style, privileged elites, and community relations will depend on the tenacity and vision of present leaders such as Zhang Tingfa, a frequent critic of incompetence and stodgy management practices in the military. The Achilles' heel, however, will be the senior cadres who are expected to set examples. In many instances, the leading cadres are the solution as well as the problem.

Notes

1. Li Ming-hua, "The CCP Leadership and Party Works in 1975," *Issues and Studies* 13:2 (February 1976), pp. 67–78; Fan Ching-yuan, "Problems of Military Leadership in Mainland China," *Issues and Studies* 14:11 (November 1978), pp. 27–48. For a recent discussion about the problem of leadership in the Chinese Communist Party, see Li Honglin, "The Kind of Party Leadership We Uphold," *Renmin ribao* (henceforth *People's Daily*), October 5, 1979, p. 3, reported in Foreign Broadcast Information Service, *Daily Report*, 1:201 (henceforth FBIS-CHI), October 16, 1979, pp. L7–6.

2. John Gardner, "The Wu-fan Campaign in Shanghai: A Study in the Consolidation of Urban Control," in A. Doak Barnett, ed., *Chinese Communist Politics in Action* (Seattle: University of Washington Press, 1969), pp. 477–539.

3. "Liaoning Ribao Discusses Rectifying Party Style," Shenyang, Liaoning Provincial Service, May 31, 1979, in FBIS-CHI, June 6, 1979, pp. S6–7.

4. Xiao Hua, "Bring the Powerful Force of Political Work into Play in the Modernization of the Armed Forces," *Hongqi* (henceforth *Red Flag*) no. 6 (June 2, 1979), pp. 32–38, in FBIS-CHI, June 27, 1979, pp. L21–30.

5. Xu Xiangqian, "Strive to Achieve Modernization in National Defense— In Celebration of the 30th Anniversary of the Founding of the People's Republic of China," *Red Flag* no. 10 (October 2, 1979), in FBIS-CHI, October 18, 1979, p. L14; italics added.

6. Ibid., p. L15.

7. "Raise Our Army's Combat Capabilities to the Modern Level," Beijing, New China News Agency (henceforth NCNA), August 1, 1979, in FBIS-CHI, August 2, 1979, p. L3.

8. Xu Xiangqian, in FBIS-CHI, p. L16.

9. "Wei Guoqing on Unifying Thinking, Action of PLA Units," NCNA, July 30, 1979, in FBIS-CHI, July 31, 1979, p. L20.

10. "Deng Xiaoping Addresses Navy Party Committee Meeting," NCNA, August 17, 1979, in FBIS-CHI, August 20, 1979, p. L2.

11. See Parris Chang, "The Changing Pattern of Military Participation in Chinese Politics," *Orbis* 16:2 (Fall 1972), pp. 780–802; Jurgen Domes, "Generals and Red Guards," *Asia Quarterly*, pt. 1, no. 1 (1971), pp. 3–31, and pt. 2, no. 2 (1971), pp. 123–160; John Gittings, "Army Party Relations in the Context of the Cultural Revolution," in John Wilson Lewis, ed., *Party Leadership and Revolutionary Power in China* (London: Cambridge University Press, 1970), pp. 373–403; Ellis Joffe, "The Chinese Army in the Cultural Revolution:

The Politics of Intervention," *Current Scene* 8:18 (December 7, 1970), pp. 1–25.

12. "New Drama Depicts Struggle in PLA," NCNA, September 3, 1979, in FBIS-CHI, September 4, 1979, pp. L12–13.

13. Han Wuyan, "Should Yu Guanqun Be Dismissed from His Post?—Notes on the Stage Play 'The Future Is Making a Call,'" NCNA, August 29, 1979, in FBIS-CHI, September 4, 1979, pp. L13–14; also FBIS-CHI, September 10, 1979, pp. L17–20. A similar theme is also found in Jiang Zilong's *Plant Director Qiao Assumes Office* (see Ding Zhenhai and Zhu Bing, "A Good Work Promoting the Four Modernizations—Also Commenting on 'Plant Director Qiao Assumes Office' and Debating with Comrade Zhao Ke," *People's Daily*, October 18, 1979, p. 3, in FBIS-CHI, November 7, 1979, pp. L20–23).

14. "Deng Xiaoping," in FBIS-CHI, p. L2.

15. "Xi Zhongxun Attends Guangdong PLA Party Meeting," Guangzhou, Guangdong Provincial Service, August 12, 1979, in FBIS-CHI, p. P5.

16. "Shanxi First Secretary Stresses Need to Improve Party Style," NCNA, June 6, 1979, in FBIS-CHI, June 7, 1979, p. T4.

17. Contributing commentator, "Fine Work Style of Party Is a Fundamental Condition for the Party to Lead the People in Achieving the Four Modernizations," *People's Daily*, July 1, 1979, p. 1, in FBIS-CHI, July 9, 1979, p. L24.

18. "PLA's South China Fleet Unit Improves," NCNA, May 22, 1979, in FBIS-CHI, May 23, 1979, p. L13.

19. "Zheng Siyu Addresses Party Session of Jinan PLA Units," NCNA, August 21, 1979, in FBIS-CHI, August 24, 1979, p. O3.

20. "PLA Air Force Commander Discusses Criterion of Truth," NCNA, September 7, 1979, in FBIS-CHI, September 11, 1979, p. L16.

21. "PLA Units Conduct Year-end Review of Training, Education," NCNA, November 7, 1979, in FBIS-CHI, November 9, 1979, pp. L13–14.

22. "Military Academy President Stresses Emancipating the Mind," NCNA, September 9, 1979, in FBIS-CHI, September 10, 1979, p. L13. The "whatever" label is derived from the "whatever faction." In 1978 and 1979, this faction within the CCP is said to have argued that whatever Chairman Mao wrote or said represented the final word on the subject. Deng Xiaoping told a Japanese reporter that there were two "whatever factions." One group believed that whatever Chairman Mao said must be done, and the other group maintained that whatever Mao did not say something about could be done.

23. Ibid.

24. "Wang Enmao Addresses Issue of Selecting Young Army Cadres," Changchun, Jilin Provincial Service, November 12, 1979, in FBIS-CHI, November 15, 1979, p. S2.

25. "PLA Air Force," in FBIS-CHI, p. L18.

26. "PLA's Zhang Tingfa Calls for Improving Party Work Style," NCNA, June 2, 1979, in FBIS-CHI, June 4, 1979, p. L14.

27. "PLA General Staff Holds Class for High-ranking Cadres," NCNA, November 11, 1979, in FBIS-CHI, November 13, 1979, p. L19.

28. "Wei Guoqing," in FBIS-CHI, p. L19; "Zheng Siyu," in FBIS-CHI, p. O2.

29. "PLA's Zhang Tingfa," in FBIS-CHI, p. L15.

30. Xiao Hua, in FBIS-CHI, pp. L21–30; also "Shenyang PLA Units Hold Political Work Forum," Shenyang, Liaoning Provincial Service, August 23, 1979, in FBIS-CHI, August 28, 1979, p. S3.

31. Xiao Hua, in FBIS-CHI, p. L26.

32. "PLA's South China Fleet," in FBIS-CHI, p. L13.

33. "Air Force Organ Conducts 'Three Investigations, Rectifications,' " Beijing Domestic Service, March 13, 1978, in FBIS-CHI, March 16, 1978, p. E6.

34. Ibid., p. E7.

35. "PLA units," in FBIS-CHI, p. L14.

36. "Air Force Commander Stresses Stability, Unity," NCNA, December 14, 1979, in FBIS-CHI, December 20, 1979, pp. L5–7.

37. "Air Force Leading Organs Adopt Measures to Simplify Communication Procedures," *People's Daily*, May 2, 1979, p. 4, in FBIS-CHI, May 7, 1979, pp. L18–19.

38. A typical example is found in "Jilin Opens Cadre Training Course 20 May [1979]," Changchun, Jilin Provincial Service, May 21, 1979, in FBIS-CHI, May 24, 1979, p. S1.

39. "PLA General Staff Department Holds Lectures on Modern Warfare," NCNA, July 28, 1979, in FBIS-CHI, July 30, 1979, p. L18.

40. "Military Science Books," NCNA, February 2, 1979, in FBIS-CHI, February 15, 1979, p. E9.

41. "New PLA Publication," NCNA, October 21, 1979, in FBIS-CHI, November 16, 1979, p. L8.

42. "Nanjing PLA Leaders Attend Lecture on Electronic Computers," Nanjing, Jiangsu Provincial Service, September 6, 1979, in FBIS-CHI, September 11, 1979, p. O6.

43. "PLA General Staff Department," in FBIS-CHI, p. L18.

44. "PLA's Zhang Tingfa," in FBIS-CHI, p. L15.

45. Leon Trotsky, *The Revolution Betrayed* (New York: Merit Publishers, 1965); also Ch'iu K'ung-yuan, " 'Bourgeois Rights' and the People's Livelihood in Mainland China," *Issues and Studies* 13:8 (August 1977), pp. 7–25.

46. Ch'iu K'ung-yuan, " 'Bourgeois Rights,' " p. 13.

47. Ji Xin, "The Class Situation and Principal Contradictions in Mainland China—An Important Theoretical Issue at the Second Session of the Fifth NPC," *Qishi niandai* [The seventies] (August 1979), pp. 26–33, translated in FBIS-CHI, August 13, 1979, p. U4.

48. Ibid., p. U3.

49. Reference Material Section, Tientsin Institute of Historical Research and Editorial Department, "Questions Relating to the Struggle Between the Two Classes and the Two Lines and Restriction of Bourgeois Rights Since the Founding of the People's Republic of China," *Tientsin Normal College Journal* no. 3 (May 25, 1975). *Qishi niandai* [The seventies], a left-wing Hong

Kong publication, has speculated that authorities in Beijing are intimidated by the pervasiveness of bourgeois privileges, hence they "lack adequate resolve to straighten things out" (see Ji Xin, "Around the Fourth Plenary Session of the CCP Central Committee," *Qishi niandai* no. 11 [November 1979], pp. 14–23, translated in FBIS-CHI, November 21, 1979, p. U19).

50. Da Chang, "Leading Cadres Should Take the Lead in Working Hard and Living a Simple Life," *People's Daily*, April 18, 1979, in FBIS-CHI, April 20, 1979, p. L7.

51. "A Tendency Which Should Not Be Neglected," *People's Daily*, December 14, 1979, p. 3, in FBIS-CHI, December 19, 1979, p. L7.

52. "PLA Units Return Occupied Houses in Sichuan to Owners," Beijing Domestic Service, November 28, 1979, in FBIS-CHI, December 4, 1979, p. Q1.

53. "Song Ping Addresses Gansu Army-Government-People Forum," Lanzhou, Gansu Provincial Service, January 16, 1980, in FBIS-CHI, January 17, 1980, p. T1.

54. "Guangming Daily Urges End to Housing Shortage," NCNA, November 17, 1979, in FBIS-CHI, November 20, 1979, p. L5.

55. "State Council Orders Reduced Building Construction," FBIS-CHI, January 17, 1980, p. L4.

56. Xia Yan, "Inside and Outside the Red Wall in Zhongnanhai," *Jing Bao* [Hong Kong] no. 18 (January 10, 1979), translated in FBIS-CHI, January 16, 1979, pp. N1–5; Chen Ji, "Changes in the Status of CCP Leaders as Seen from Titles Used in Propaganda," *Zheng ming* no. 16 (February 1979), pp. 9–10, translated in FBIS-CHI, January 30, 1979, pp. N3–4.

57. "People's Daily Criticizes PLA Adviser's Occupying Private Quarters," NCNA, April 22, 1979, in FBIS-CHI, April 25, 1979, pp. L15–18.

58. Ye Wenfu, "General, You Must Not Do This,' *Shi kan* [Poetry] no. 8 (August 1979), reprinted in *Wenhui bao* (Shanghai), September 8, 1979, p. 3, translated in FBIS-CHI, October 24, 1979, pp. L14–19.

59. "Economy Measures Emphasized by Guizhou Military Leaders," Guiyang, Guizhou Provincial Service, December 12, 1979, in FBIS-CHI, December 21, 1979, p. Q1.

60. "People's Daily Letter on Shaanxi Prefecture Cadres' Privileges," NCNA, September 27, 1979, in FBIS-CHI, October 2, 1979, pp. R5–6.

61. "Kunming PLA Unit Forbids Cadre Privileges," Kunming Provincial Service, October 27, 1979, in FBIS-CHI, November 5, 1979, pp. Q2–3.

62. Wu An-chia, "The Bourgeois Right—Its Impact on the Lifestyle," *Issues and Studies* 11:8 (August 1975), pp. 8–19.

63. "Kunming PLA Unit," FBIS-CHI, pp. Q2–3.

64. "Jiangsu CCP Committee Warns Against Misuse of Privileges," Nanjing, Jiangsu Provincial Service, December 3, 1979, in FBIS-CHI, December 7, 1979, p. O1.

65. "Gongren Daily Letters Praise Good Deeds, Criticize Bad Ones," NCNA, September 6, 1979, in FBIS-CHI, September 7, 1979, p. L4.

66. "A Tendency," FBIS-CHI, p. L7.

67. "Liaoning CCP Committee Decision on Rectifying Party Style," Shenyang, Liaoning Provincial Service, September 11, 1979, in FBIS-CHI, September 14, 1979, p. S1.

68. "Beijing PLA Studies Inner-party Discipline," Beijing Domestic Service, May 12, 1979, in FBIS-CHI, May 16, 1979, p. R2.

69. Ibid.

70. "Strengthen Unity Between Army and People, Promote the Four Modernizations," *People's Daily*, December 23, 1979, in FBIS-CHI, December 26, 1979, pp. L6–8; "Carry Out Extensive Activities to Support the Government and Cherish the People," *Jiefangjun bao* [Liberation Army daily], Janaury 15, 1980. Also see "PLA Political Department Issues Support Campaign Circular," NCNA, December 18, 1979, in FBIS-CHI, December 19, 1979, pp. L9–10; "Ministry Issues Circular on Army Support Campaign," NCNA, December 18, 1979, in FBIS-CHI, December 21, 1979, pp. L1–2.

71. "Yang Yichen Attends Heilongjiang Support-Army Meeting," Harbin, Heilongjiang Provincial Service, January 11, 1980, in FBIS-CHI, January 17, 1980, p. S1. In Liaoning's Yingkou municipality, where army-people unity was "revived and carried forward," blame was attributed to the "three supports, two militaries." This slogan referred to PLA support for the Left, industry, and agriculture. The two militaries involved training Red Guards and exercising control in some civilian institutions (see "Liaoning's Yingkou Municipality Restores Army-People Unit," NCNA, January 13, 1980, in FBIS-CHI, January 17, 1980, p. S3).

72. "Strengthen Unity," FBIS-CHI, p. L6–7.

73. "Ministry Issues Circular," FBIS-CHI, p. L1; "Yang Yichen Attends," FBIS-CHI, p. S3.

74. "Yang Yichen Attends," FBIS-CHI, p. S1.

75. "Do a Good Job of Settling Veteran Cadres Who Have Retired or Left Office for Convalescence," *People's Daily*, November 18, 1979, p. 3, in FBIS-CHI, December 11, 1979, pp. L4–6.

76. Fox Butterfield, "In China, Army Defies Government Orders," *New York Times*, October 14, 1979, p. 3. The PLA also was reported to be occupying facilities at the Beijing Institute of Hygiene, the Beijing Institute of Finance and Economics, and Sports Commission buildings.

77. "PLA Unit Agrees to Return Buildings to University," NCNA, October 13, 1979, in FBIS-CHI, October 15, 1979, p. L1.

78. "Liaoning Military District Issues Circular on Land Occupation," Shenyang, Liaoning Provincial Service, October 23, 1979, in FBIS-CHI, October 26, 1979, p. S7.

79. "PLA Cadres in Beijing Ordered to Return Occupied Houses," NCNA, May 26, 1979, in FBIS-CHI, May 29, 1979, pp. R1–2.

80. "Liberation Army Daily on Supporting Government Campaign," NCNA, December 19, 1979, in FBIS-CHI, December 27, 1979, p. L13.

81. "Guangming Daily," FBIS-CHI, p. L5.

82. Investigation Team of the Political Department of the Air Force, "Work Hard to Continue the Revolution—Investigation Report on the Leading

Group of a Certain Flight Division of the Air Force," *Red Flag* no. 12 (December 5, 1977), pp. 43–46, translated in Joint Publications Research Service, *Translations on Red Flag* no. 70536 (January 25, 1978), pp. 63–68.

83. "Study the Revolutionary Spirit of the Party Committee of a Certain Flying Division of the Air Force," *Red Flag* no. 2 (February 2, 1978), pp. 79–80.

84. Huang Shusen, "Commenting on 'Don't Forget the Workers, Peasants, and Soldiers,' " *Nanfang ribao* [Nanfang daily], August 16, 1979, p. 3, translated in FBIS-CHI, August 24, 1979, p. P6.

85. "PLA Unit Agrees," FBIS-CHI, p. L1.

86. "Air Force Employment," NCNA, October 1, 1979, in FBIS-CHI, October 26, 1979, p. L24.

87. "Navy Employment," NCNA, October 5, 1979, in FBIS-CHI, October 22, 1979, p. L22.

88. "Beijing Poster Criticizes PLA Political Affairs Office," September 25, 1979, Agence France Presse (AFP) dispatch, reported in FBIS-CHI, September 26, 1979, p. L18.

89. Ibid.

90. "Demobilized Soldiers Demand Reintegration into City Life," May 12, 1979, AFP dispatch, reported in FBIS-CHI, May 14, 1979, p. L20.

91. Ibid., p. L21.

92. Ibid.

93. "Jilin Leader Speaks at Meeting of Veteran Red Army Men," Changchun, Jilin Provincial Service, August 3, 1979, in FBIS-CHI, August 6, 1979, p. S2.

94. "Wang Feng Attends Xinjiang Congress of Retired Servicemen," Urumqi, Xinjiang Regional Service, November 15, 1979, in FBIS-CHI, November 23, 1979, p. T3.

95. Liu Zizhen, " 'The "Iron Rice Bowl" Must Not Be Broken'—Views on Comrade Xue Muqiao's 'Several Points on Employment in Cities and Towns,' " *Beijing ribao* [Beijing daily], September 18, 1979, p. 3, in FBIS-CHI, October 4, 1979, pp. L10–12; "Beijing Daily Continues Debate on Socialist Employment," NCNA, October 5, 1979, in FBIS-CHI, October 9, 1979, pp. L14–15; "Unemployed Continue Sit-in in Beijing," Kyodo (Tokyo), October 15, 1979, reported in FBIS-CHI, October 16, 1979, p. R1.

96. "Jilin City Institutes Retirement, Replacement System," Changchun, Jilin Provincial Service, in FBIS-CHI, September 6, 1979, p. S4.

97. "Chengdu PLA Discusses Lack of Confidence," Chengdu, Sichuan Provincial Service, December 2, 1979, in FBIS-CHI, December 4, 1979, p. Q1.

98. "Liaoning CCP Committee," FBIS-CHI, p. S3.

99. See "Remove Interferences, Uphold the Party's Policy Toward Cadres Who Made Mistakes," *People's Daily*, July 23, 1979, in FBIS-CHI, July 24, 1979, pp. L1–5; "When One Commits Mistakes, One Should Not Conceal Them for Fear of Criticism," *Liberation Army Daily*, August 5, 1979, reprinted in *People's Daily*, August 19, 1979, translated in FBIS-CHI, August 10, 1979, pp. L6–10.

5

Professional Military Education in the People's Republic of China

William R. Heaton

During a visit of a delegation representing the military academies of the People's Liberation Army to the United States in the fall of 1980, the head of the delegation, Xiao Ke, commander of the PLA Military Academy and vice-minister of national defense, informed his guests that the Military Academy was building new facilities. He also observed that the members of his delegation were quite old; they had not been able to retire because the devastation of military academies during the Cultural Revolution had made it impossible to properly train a generation of younger military leaders. Commander Xiao's remarks strike at the heart of the key issues for the PLA's professional military education for the 1980s: technical modernization and ideological change.

Both issues were highly controversial as the decade began. China's program for economic modernization has experienced dramatic revision, and there has been political instability at the highest levels. It is against this background that the professional military education system is expected to produce officers that are "politically conscious, professionally competent, unyielding in work style and physically strong."[1] This chapter will examine the structure and function of the Chinese professional military education system and examine the relationship of this education to the broader questions posed by modernization.

The objective of professional military education in China cited above helps to distinguish it from concepts prevalent in the West.

The views in this chapter are those of the author and are not necessarily those of the National War College or any other U.S. government agency.

Although Western scholars have dwelt on the unique aspects of military professionalism, the Chinese communist approach, owing both to Chinese tradition and to the revolutionary insurgency experience, has generally downplayed its uniqueness.[2] This important dimension will be discussed in greater detail later, but it should be noted here as we establish a background for our discussion by briefly outlining the organization of the Chinese professional military education system.

First of all, professional military education is pervasive in the PLA. At the apex are the three academies, which correspond to the organization of the high command; the Military Academy (General Staff Department), the Political Academy (General Political Department), and the Logistical Academy (General Logistics Department). All of them are located in Beijing. Below these academies are service academies for the navy and air force and specialized academies (e.g., the PLA Advanced Infantry Academy and the Air Force Maintenance Academy), which are located in various parts of China. Little is known about the organization of the remainder of the military education system, but it is quite clear from the prolific reports of various study and indoctrination efforts in PLA units that the system is extensive.[3]

Second, the curriculum of the military education system has been undergoing rapid change. The amount of time spent in studying "political" subjects has been reduced in favor of spending more time on "military" subjects. Military educators are concerned that the curriculum should reflect the objective of military modernization. Besides studying the Soviet tank offensive in Manchuria in 1945, they are desirous of giving more attention to subjects dealing with strategy and tactics in a nuclear environment, the management of combined operations, and other aspects of modern warfare.

Finally, the organization appears to be undergoing some revamping. A conference on military academies in the fall of 1980, attended by China's top military leaders, concluded that military educators must "emancipate our thinking and boldly change the content of the training and education programs" in the military education system.[4] Although the conference did not reveal precisely how the academies were to change to accomplish this objective, it did suggest that the teachers should become more innovative. Consequently, any attempt to analyze the Chinese military education system must be subject to the caveat that it is undergoing change and will probably vary in structure and purpose in the 1980s.

Rather than focusing upon the institutions that are responsible for professional military education, I have chosen to examine more closely the issues and problems military education must deal with. I believe military education is a microcosm of the many issues that are readily apparent in the other chapters of this book. Inasmuch as military education is an important vehicle for the socialization of military leaders, such issues as the relationship between ideological and technical values, the role of the military in society, and the pursuit of effective national strategy can be readily discerned in its content. The Chinese are extremely aware of the relationship between military education and socialization, and consequently, military education can reveal much about how the Chinese leaders view these questions as well as how the military responds to them. In the next few pages I will try to sketch out some of these issues.

Military Versus Civilian

The selection of military versus civilian as a principle issue area no doubt requires some justification, particularly since Chinese statements from the dawn of the revolutionary insurgency era have stressed the close relationship between the army and the masses. Moreover, because of the insurgent heritage and the overlap of Party and military responsibilities in Chinese political institutions since 1949, there has generally not been a sharp dichotomy between the military and other segments. During the Cultural Revolution, the PLA became directly involved in political administration in many areas of China, yet it would be a mistake to say that the military had staged a coup. Persons whose careers have been predominantly in the military may well have constituted a majority of the active Politburo membership in the late 1960s and early 1970s, yet this high level of military involvement in political decision making was not akin to the seizure of power by the military that occurs in many developing countries. The charge that Lin Biao was behind a "counterrevolutionary coup attempt" in 1971 (given lengthy and detailed examination during the trial of the Gang of Four and Lin's alleged coconspirators) suggests that the Chinese consider this kind of intervention to be particularly odious and repugnant.[5]

However, in recent times, a military-civilian dichotomy has become more apparent. Besides reports of anti-PLA demonstrations on university campuses where troops remained in buildings, complaints by demobilized veterans of discriminatory treatment, and other evidence, recent editorials in the *Liberation Army Daily* indicate that a military-civilian cleavage has developed over other issues as well. The military has been particularly discontented over agricultural reforms that discriminate against families with members in the armed forces by eliminating extra work points designed to compensate for the loss of able-bodied workers (and, therefore, income). A General Political

Department circular in October 1980 called for intensive efforts by the army to study the Party leadership's rural policies.[6] Furthermore, an article in the army paper on November 20 declared that cadre adherence to the Party's political and ideological line is "the most fundamental yardstick" in PLA organizational work and warned that people who had spoken out or worked against the Party line should not be retained in leadership positions.[7]

Paradoxically, much of the reason for the civilian-military cleavage appears to stem from the modernization effort. Official military spokesmen have insisted that the PLA genuinely adheres to the principle that military modernization hinges on the other modernizations, yet there is some evidence that there has been some disagreement over budgetary priorities. Thus, although military leaders have stressed the importance of developing modern and advanced weapons, civilian leaders have placed great emphasis on staying within the budget; official figures suggest that the military budget has actually been reduced.[8] But even more important than the issue of budget priorities is the question of professionalism, a key theme of military education.[9]

According to Chinese conceptualizations, there have been two broad approaches to military professionalism. The first may be referred to as the "Maoist" approach. This approach was characterized by stressing the importance of men over machines and the suppression of uniqueness among the armed forces as an institution. This approach recognized the importance of the military in providing national defense, but also gave equal emphasis to its role in society—the army's being a work force and a production force as well as a fighting force. A close relationship between the army and the people was an important value, as was the exemplary nature of military personnel.

The Maoist approach was most strongly articulated during the periods of the anti-Japanese war, the Chinese civil war, and the Cultural Revolution. It will be recalled that during much of the 1960s, the entire country was supposed to "learn from the PLA," which had correctly embodied Mao's thought. During these periods, military personnel were responsible not only for national defense but for serving as models of such values as sacrifice, selflessness, diligence, perseverance, hard work, and other "revolutionary" ideals.

The Maoist approach to professionalism may be contrasted with the "Pengist" or "Dengist" approach, which appears to be closer to Western concepts of military professionalism. This approach stresses the uniqueness of the armed forces, their specialization, and their diverseness from society. In this approach, the military stresses the importance of modernizing equipment and of developing combat expertise over ideological training. The military should concentrate more on providing national defense and less on performing other social tasks.

This approach was particularly evident during the period of the 1950s when Peng Dehuai, as defense minister, followed the Soviet model in developing professionalism among the Chinese armed forces.[10] More recently, this approach has been signaled since the death of Mao and the purge of the Gang of Four. A host of conferences, reports, and articles suggest that the drive for modernization is pushing the military toward the approach in which "expert" takes precedence over "red."[11] For example, a *Red Flag* article commemorating the thirtieth anniversary of the People's Republic of China in 1979, written by Defense Minister Xu Xiangqian, stressed the importance of expertise and demanded that training in the armed forces be "geared to the needs of actual combat."[12]

Obviously, neither approach has been followed exclusively at any given time, and both approaches to military professionalism share common aspects. Both acknowledge the importance of Party control of the armed forces; both recognize that the principal role of the military is to provide national defense. I would also argue that both accept the premise that the legitimacy of the armed forces is expressed in great measure through ideology; that is, the basis for the effectiveness of the armed forces is primarily a correct political line. Even those who stress "expertise" over "redness" do so by saying that "red" is defined by "expert." Nevertheless, the distinctions are quite apparent. The Maoist model abolishes ranks, and the Pengist-Dengist model encourages them. The Maoist approach says that military education should concentrate more on ideological study, and the Pengist-Dengist approach wants more time spent on combat training.

It has already been pointed out that in the early 1980s, the Pengist-Dengist approach was once again being favored, which poses the question of whether or not the inculcation of this concept of professionalism will create a greater civilian-military cleavage. As the military becomes increasingly unique and separate from society, will it not find that its interests diverge more from those of other institutions and sectors in Chinese society? Given the tone and content of recent statements in the official army newspaper, Chinese leaders are greatly concerned about this potential.

Consequently, China's present leaders believe that an important responsibility of military education will be to ensure the adherence of the military to Party leadership. It is implicitly assumed that as the military becomes more "expert," it will become more distinct as an interest group and that the way to deal with this factor is to ensure Party control. It is not surprising that the conference on military academies concluded that in the future, "The most important thing is: The cadres trained by military academies and institutions must have a firm and correct political orientation, firmly implement the party's line, principles and policies and resolutely obey the command of the party Central Committee and its Military Commission."[13]

Strategy and Doctrine

Strategy and doctrine are covered more completely in other chapters of this book, but it is also important that they be examined in the context of professional military education. The evolution of strategy and doctrine from "people's war" to "people's war under modern conditions" presumes that the rising generations of military leaders will be able to comprehend and apply the new concepts. Yet it is quite evident that the military education system is having some difficulty in adjusting its curriculum to explain the new concepts, perhaps because they are inherently not altogether clear.

This lack of clarity was amply demonstrated during a visit made by the author in 1979 as part of a delegation to the PLA Military Academy when we were informed that the students were expected to master Marxism-Leninism and Mao's thought in analyzing and solving problems. Military training also emphasized Mao's teachings on war. Now that the "thought of Mao" has been redefined to be a culmination of the Party's collective experience rather than merely the contributions of one individual, its all-inclusive nature may lend itself to proper study as providing some contribution on the nature of modern warfare. Nevertheless, there are probably also some pitfalls. The leaders of the Military Academy seemed to give a good deal of credence to the possibility of a massive Soviet tank offensive against China and pay special attention to the operations of the Soviet army in Manchuria in 1945. While recognizing that there are other possible Soviet military options vis-à-vis China, they strongly emphasized the view that for the Soviet Union, China was too great a problem to be handled by some kind of limited incursion or selective strike.

Without debating the merits of the Chinese view, it does appear that the PLA leaders are reluctant to modify a strategic image that they have held for some time. As other people have pointed out, the deterrent value of "people's war" is of more limited utility in projecting foreign policy, as the "defensive counterattack" against Vietnam in 1979 suggested. But in spite of the constant articles and statements calling for "people's war under modern conditions," there is apparently a bureaucratic tendency to cling to what is known.[14] During the delegation's visit to the Military Academy, we were told that the curriculum was undergoing revision so that the principles of modernization could be more fully brought into play in the program of instruction. When a reciprocal delegation from China visited the United States a year and a half later, we were told the same thing—that the curriculum was undergoing change in accordance with the demands of modernization. I do not mean to say that curriculums should not be constantly revised and updated, they quite obviously are in any good system of professional military education; but it seems that in the Chinese case, there is continuing uncertainty over just what it is one teaches in matters of strategy and doctrine in order to contribute to modernization. There were some hints that the Chinese were coming to grips with the issue in the fall of 1980 when they explained that they were trying to teach the relationship between diplomacy and military power; they were also very anxious to know how U.S. military education taught the subject of warnings of impending surprise attack. Chinese professional military education like other systems of education in China, is trying to impart greater technical and scientific knowledge. Any subjects designed to increase this knowledge, depending on how they are taught, could result in a movement away from the classical concepts of doctrine and strategy.

As Chinese military education enters the 1980s, it is still the Long March generation that has ultimate responsibility for what is taught. In spite of the great attention given to modernization in various speeches and writings, it will likely be some time before a full transition in strategic and doctrinal concepts will occur in the professional military education system. Ultimately, the current mixture of classical aphorisms on people's war, and a good deal of talk about modern conditions, will give way to a more coherent system of education in these subjects, but for the time being, there is likely to be a continuing ad hoc character to them.

Generational Change

At a speech commemorating the thirtieth anniversary of the PLA Military Academy on January 15, 1981, Xiao Ke identified the central task of the Military Academy as "to bring up a new generation of middle-ranking and senior commanding personnel."[15] Indeed, this issue is paramount throughout the professional military education system; that is, the socialization of a new generation of leaders on all levels of the military command structure. A primary function of the military education system is to transmit the values of one group of leaders to the next, and in this regard the Chinese have a unique situation.

It will be recalled that during his meetings with U.S. military educators, Xiao Ke noted the age of the Chinese delegation and suggested that they could not retire immediately because of the disruptions created in socialization during the Cultural Revolution. Yet this approach involves a paradox in that the Long March and revolutionary war generation insists on clinging to authority until they are assured that the newer generations are correctly socialized, thereby blocking a transition that is almost certainly necessary if the goal of modernization is to be achieved.

The problem is closely related to the problem of defining professionalism and strategy and doctrine discussed above. For the most part, the people who are in authority at the highest echelons of the military education system are older veterans. Very little, if any, "new blood" has been brought into the system. Consequently, although much lip service is given to modernization, both the curriculum and the teaching methodology tend toward the "tried and true" system of the past. This tendency was reflected to a great extent during our visit to various military facilities and in our discussions with Chinese leaders.

For example, during our visit to a model division near Tianjin, we were treated to tours and demonstrations illustrating the principle that the PLA is a fighting force, a working force, and a production force (indeed, one of the most impressive things about Chinese museums and exhibits in general was their ability to articulate a common theme through organization and presentation). Thus, we witnessed PLA soldiers engaged in climbing and descending walls, hand-to-hand combat, and other basic skills. We also visited the unit's fields, factories (including seeing officers' wives make vitamins), and other facilities, and were entertained by the cultural groups. Although it was obvious that this was a showpiece unit designed to impress foreign visitors, we were surprised that its presentations had changed little, if any, since the early 1970s when Westerners first visited it.

At one point, I asked the cadre in charge of political work who was conducting the tour how modernization would affect the activities we had witnessed. When he finished his answer, which stressed the importance of modernization, the necessity of improvements, and so on, it appeared that the relevance of modernization for this unit was uncertain. I was left with the distinct impression that modernization was something that might incrementally filter down to various units as time went by. I do not suggest that the same situation exists in all units. There are numerous reports in the Chinese press of unit technical innovations that supposedly contribute to modernization and of increased time spent in learning technical information. However, there is a very strong legacy of the way things are to be done that seems to have a good grip on the vast majority of units.

This fact should not be surprising. Given the public relegation of military modernization to a fairly low priority status and the fact that traditionalists head the military education system, why should units make dramatic changes in the way they go about doing things? Thus, there is a very paradoxical situation in which leaders constantly allude to the need for fresh thinking, innovation, modernization while the system itself is strongly wedded to seniority, tradition, and continuity. Although it would be unfair to say that the older generation is incapable of promoting change, it does seem true that the present socialization scheme does not augur well for the kinds of values that the Chinese leaders are saying must be inculcated.[16]

In summary, the military education system requires a new leadership that can effectively impart new values and methods if modernization is truly to become, in practice as well as in theory, a part of the system. As long as the present leaders are dissatisfied with the results of the military education system (as they have been saying they are since the criticism of the Cultural Revolution began) and are unwilling to surrender control to new and younger personnel (presuming people with the proper technical backgrounds can be found), we can anticipate that there will be only halting steps toward a revamping of the professional military education system. Consequently, the generational issue will continue to be significant in the 1980s.

The Politics of Modernization

All of the issues discussed above—military versus civilian, strategy and doctrine, and the question of leadership transition—are closely related and might conceivably be subsumed in a more general issue, that of the politics of modernization. Modernization, besides being an important slogan in the Chinese lexicon, has become an intensely political question. Debates over strategies to achieve modernization resulted in severe political cleavages and leadership change during the early 1980s, and in many respects, professional military education represented a microcosm of the larger questions under debate.

One of the major questions related to modernization was how to define China's relationship with the West. Much as the self-strengthening movement at the turn of the century sought to define the Sino-Western relationship, the current leaders of China are considering the impact of both Western technology and ideas.[17] This issue is of great importance to the Chinese military. A greater reliance on Western technology in weapons procurement, for example, would presumably necessitate greater specialization in military training. With this specialization would almost certainly come a refinement of the concept of professionalism in the armed forces; that is, a shift toward the Pengist-Dengist model discussed earlier.

Increasing specialization and changes in professionalism must necessarily have a political impact. The bifurcation of Party and military offices within the military might help to ensure the continued dominance of the military by the Party, but at the same time, increasingly specialized military technicians would demand greater influence in decisions concerning doctrine and strategy. Presumably, over an extended period of time, the PLA could evolve into something akin to the Soviet armed forces; however, given the heritage of the PLA, this evolution would require some fairly dramatic changes.

Even if it were to be assumed that the Chinese leaders had a clear idea of which way they wanted the military to evolve (which obviously cannot be assumed), the implications for military education are staggering. The military education system would somehow be expected to divorce itself from current practices and produce a group of loyal adherents to the Party who were also technically proficient managers (precisely the task that the military academies are calling for). The military education system would have to quickly resolve the question of authority between people with seniority and people with technical expertise.

Also, the whole question of political education, one of the major components of professional military education, would have to be addressed. Under the present system, the major political questions have arisen over the question of political line. Thus, the debates of the 1960s and 1970s were carried over into the content of political education. Shifts in the wind could be managed by experienced personnel responsible for political education, although during major upheavals—such as occurred during the Cultural Revolution—many of these people found themselves on the wrong side (in many instances, no matter which side they were on). A review of the General Political Department over the past few years shows many criticisms of political cadres for not being able to keep up with the correct political line; even the most adept could not escape blame altogether.

However, the issue now at stake is infinitely more complex. In addition to coping with shifts in the political line, the professional military education system faces a more profound restructuring than was envisioned during the Cultural Revolution, because the Maoist citizen-soldier model must necessarily yield to the modernization model under conditions of increased technical specialization. In the past, when the Maoist model was more closely adhered to by the PLA, the authority of the command structure was based on close identification with ideologically specified values. Repeating an observation made earlier in this chapter, Maoist ideology does not deny modernization, but it places greater emphasis on nontechnical values. In many instances, specialization violated the concept that the soldier must remain close to the masses. If we assume that technical change will result in increased specialization and that promotions, awards, recognition, and so forth, will be based increasingly on technical expertise, then what will command authority be based on? Rhetorically, we may answer that it will be based on the expertise of the commander. However, as in the case of other technologically improving military organizations in the world, this expertise will not necessarily be specific abilities in weapon systems (though of course, this skill will be important), but managerial skills.

In other words, the military education system will be called upon to provide skilled managers, not better combat technicians, political thinkers, or high-level decision makers. Unfortunately, it does not appear that this need has been fully grasped by the leaders of the military education system. Once again, however, it must be pointed out that the reason it has not been fully grasped is because the Chinese themselves are not certain that they are fully committed to a shift away from the Maoist model, in spite of the lip service that is given to modernization. The Chinese professional military education system and its curriculum are ample evidence of the tentative commitment.

By way of contrast, professional military education in the United States reflects the results of modernization. On various levels, both the organization and the curriculum have historically reflected the perceived increasing need for training in management skills, leadership, communication, and other subjects more akin to the social sciences than to scientific and technical subjects or subjects uniquely related to combat. Part of this change is due to the fact that officers with college degrees frequently have strong technical backgrounds upon which to draw, but the main reason has to do with what is perceived as necessary in order to operate a modern military force. During the visit of the Chinese military educators to Washington in the fall of 1980, the point was made that the successively higher levels of professional military education in the United States increasingly reflect emphasis on political subjects. The curriculum of the National War College, for example, stresses international relations, the development of strategy, budgetary politics, and the operation of the upper echelons of the national security system.

When the Chinese say that 80 percent of their curriculum is military and 20 percent of it is political, they mean that much of their training deals with combat operations and about 20 percent of it is indoctrination in Marxist-Leninist theory. Combat operations are stressed even at the highest level of Chinese professional military education, the PLA Military Academy. Even though the PLA has historically been heavily involved in political decision making on the highest levels, there seems to be little, if any, formal instruction in subjects such as management or public administration. An attribute of modernization it seems would imply greater attention to these kinds of subjects.

If we assume that modernization of the professional military education will contribute to specialization and a new definition of professionalism in the PLA, what will that mean about its political role, an issue mentioned briefly earlier in this chapter? Past models of the military's political role have stressed that "the party controls the gun," and present emphasis in professional military education suggests that Party leadership will continue to be important.[18] However, in the past, professional military officers were involved in the Politburo—the Party's highest decision-making organ—directly, but since the Tenth Party Congress in 1973, there has been a tendency toward a reduction of military representation on this level, a tendency that will probably continue into the 1980s. The question becomes whether the military will be willing to strive for its interests within bureaucratic and Party channels since it is losing its high-level access.

A situation could be envisioned in which the PLA—its access to top-level decision making curbed, its interests challenged, and its prestige damaged—could experience tremendous pressures to stage a coup. This would not be a Lin Biao–style coup attempt, in which a leader elicits segments of the military to challenge others for power (although another coup attempt of this type can by no means be completely ruled out), but one in which the military would seize power in order to advance its own interests—a situation that has arisen in many developing countries with problems similar to those of China. Obviously, China's leaders are desirous that such a development not occur. Therefore, we can expect to see that a problem for professional military education will be to socialize military leaders in such a manner as to minimize the possibility that they will want to circumvent normal channels in order to achieve their political objectives.

The obvious response to this problem is what the Chinese are already stressing—heavy ideological indoctrination that emphasizes loyalty, discipline, and other values. Nevertheless, for the up-and-coming generation of Chinese military leaders, who have witnessed the vicissitudes of the Cultural Revolution and the ongoing movement to "de-Maoify" Chinese ideology, finding commitment in ideologically expressed values must be somewhat difficult. There is already considerable evidence that top military leaders question the effort to denigrate Mao; moreover, there is considerable uncertainty as to where this ideological trend will lead. Just as other aspects of the political process in China have reflected turbulence over this question, so must professional military education.

Conclusions

The primary purpose of this chapter has been to look at professional military education in the PLA, especially the issues that face it in the coming decade. I have briefly considered the structure and curriculum of professional military education today but have dealt mainly with the issues that will confront it in the future. Professional military education is a microcosm of basic economic, social, and political issues in China today. The Chinese communists are committed to the modernization of China, of which military modernization has been defined as an important component. Military modernization is seen not only as the acquisition of new weaponry, but as the increasing specialization and technical expertise of armed forces personnel. At present, professional military education reflects primarily past values, which are not altogether congruent with modernization and specialization. For example, little attention is given to public administration, management, or other similar training as is typical of higher professional military education systems in most other countries, and a great deal of emphasis is placed on combat operations. Nevertheless, a good deal of lip service is given to the rubric of modernization.

Although the strategy of how to modernize has been constantly undergoing redefinition in China, and the effort to modernize the armed forces has been halting at best, it is unlikely that the commitment will diminish. The content of professional military education as expressed in the curriculum will change gradually to reflect the demands of specialization. However, the content must also cope with the changing political role of the PLA, thereby producing a generation of military leaders who are loyal and technically proficient (in managerial skills). The evidence provided in this chapter suggests that this task will be extremely tortuous. For the most part, the PLA's professional military education system seems to have done its work well in the past. At least that is the opinion of Chinese military leaders, except for their reservations about what happened during the Cultural Revolution. The next decade may well provide even greater tests.

Deng's proposed military reforms, if carried out, could have a substantial effect on professional military education. Deng has pushed for the retirement of older officers, the streamlining of the military organization, and a shift in the command structure so that the state organization will increasingly replace Party organization in the management of the armed forces. In 1981, the military academies at various levels conducted special courses of study for high-ranking officers in military theory and combat tactics. A Xinhua report in January 1982 said that these courses had helped the officers learn modern military science and how to "organize troops, reform training methods and strengthen combat readiness."[19] Throughout the PLA, movements were launched to study the resolution of Party history adopted at the sixth plenum of the Eleventh Central Committee, June 1981; there were also movements to learn from both the newly published works of Peng Dehuai and the writings of Mao. Modernization is the key word for professional military education, but the search for a happy marriage between Maoist and Dengist values in achieving modernization continues to be the key issue.

Notes

1. Xinhua (New China News Agency), November 7, 1980; Foreign Broadcast Information Service, *Daily Report* (People's Republic of China), November 10, 1980, p. L4 (hereinafter referred to as DR/PRC).

2. For a discussion of the approach to professionalism in the PLA, see Paul H.B. Godwin, "Professionalism and Politics in the Chinese Armed Forces: A Reconceptualization," in Dale R. Herspring and Ivan Volgyes, eds., *Civil-Military Relations in Communist Systems* (Boulder, Colo.: Westview Press, 1978), pp. 219–240. In this chapter, Godwin examines professionalism in the PLA in the context of various theories of professionalism advanced by Western military sociologists and also examines the issue of modernization.

3. Most of the standard Western works on the PLA have had little to say about professional military education, probably because the Chinese have revealed little. For a more extensive discussion of the present system, see William Heaton, "Professional Military Education in China: A Visit to the Military Academy of the People's Liberation Army," *China Quarterly* (March 1980), pp. 122–128. Also see my unpublished report on the meeting of a delegation of the National Defense University with representatives of the PLA Air Force Academy on May 2, 1979, in Beijing and my unpublished report on discussions with a reciprocal delegation of Chinese military educators on October 14, 1980, in Washington, D.C. For insights on training at air force academies, see Wu Jung-Ken, "Why I Fled to Freedom," *Inside China Mainland* (December 1, 1980), pp. 7–8.

4. Xinhua, November 7, 1980; DR/PRC, November 10, 1980, p. L4.

5. For example, see the editorial in *Renmin ribao* of January 26, 1981, hailing the verdict against the "Lin Biao–Jiang Qing counterrevolutionary cliques," which, among other things, argues that the crimes of the usurpers are so great that "not even all the water of the Changjiang River is enough

to wash away their crimes" (DR/PRC, January 26, 1981, pp. L24–28).

6. Xinhua, October 11, 1980; DR/PRC, October 14, 1980, p. L26. Also see the authoritative *Renmin ribao* commentator article, "Further Successfully Carry Out the Work of Giving Preferential Treatment," November 12, 1980; DR/PRC, November 20, 1980, pp. L33–34.

7. Portions of a November 20 *Jiefangjun bao* commentator article, "Attach Importance to Selecting and Promoting Cadres Who Uphold the Party Line," carried on Beijing Radio's domestic service on November 24, 1980; DR/PRC, November 25, 1980, pp. L33–36.

8. PRC Finance Minister Wang Bingqian reported to the third session of the Fifth National People's Congress in August 1980 that the 1979 defense budget totaled 22.27 billion yuan, 2.04 billion yuan above the original target, and said that the budget for 1980 would be 19.33 billion yuan, or a cut of 2.94 billion yuan (Xinhua, September 12, 1980; DR/PRC Supplement, September 23, 1980, pp. 19, 23). The Japanese news agency Kyodo cited Chinese officials as indicating that Premier Zhao Ziyang had decided to cut defense spending by 1 billion yuan in 1981 and that cuts might be even greater. Kyodo also said that China has been reducing the size of its armed forces because of budgetary reasons (DR/PRC, January 21, 1981, p. L1).

9. Compare Godwin's section on conflict over ethics in "Professionalism and Politics," pp. 229–232.

10. See Ellis Joffe, *Party and Army: Professionalism and Political Control in the Chinese Officer Corps, 1949–1964* (Cambridge, Mass.: Harvard East Asian Monographs, 1967).

11. William Heaton, "China Visit: A Military Assessment," *Army* (November 1979), pp. 22–27. Also see Chapter 4 in this book by Richard J. Latham, "The Rectification of 'Work Style.' "

12. Xu Xiangqian, "Strive to Achieve Modernization in National Defense— In Celebration of the 30th Anniversary of the Founding of the People's Republic of China," *Hongqi* no. 10 (October 2, 1979), pp. 28–33, translated in U.S. Joint Publications Research Service, *China Report* no. 74680 (November 30, 1979), pp. 49–50.

13. Xinhua, November 7, 1980; DR/PRC, November 10, 1980, p. L4.

14. For example, an article by Yi Li, "What the Afghan War Tells Us," *Hongqi* no. 1 (January 1, 1981), pp. 47–48 contains comments on the strategy of the Afghan insurgency that reflect the strong influence of Mao's military thinking. The article discusses at length why it is possible for the Afghan insurgents to fight against the Soviet Union, a formidable military foe. Among other points:

> The Afghan people are able to continue the fight against the Soviet aggressors because they have adopted correct military tactics. They have been able to overcome the enemy's superiority—concentrated forces, strong firepower and good mobility, and have given full play to the power of people's war. Their troops are scattered and hidden. They have seized opportunities to make sudden attacks upon the enemy, to intercept enemy motorcades, to skillfully seize strongholds, to burn warehouses and to attack the airport. In this way the enemy

has been put into a passive position and has been tired out by too much moving around. . . .

Fighting for the purpose of safeguarding the independence of the motherland and the survival of the nation and adopting the correct military tactics are the fundamental reasons why the Afghan people can and are still fighting in the war.

. . . The struggle of the Afghan people tells all people in the world the following truth: Despite their military strength, the Soviet social imperialists are not irresistible. When a small nation is invaded, its people can mobilize all patriotic forces and adopt military tactics which conform with the specific conditions of their own nation to deal with even such a military superpower like the Soviet Union. This is an encouragement to all countries which are being occupied, controlled, suppressed and threatened by the Soviet Union.

15. Xinhua, January 15, 1981; DR/PRC, January 16, 1981, pp. L10–11.

16. Some of China's current leaders can certainly be considered innovative, among them, Deng Xiaoping, who seems quite willing to tinker with political and social institutions. Nevertheless, for every innovator, there is an army of recalcitrant bureaucrats ready to wear down any new policy, at least if Chinese press comments can be believed. Much of the problem is related to what theorists of political socialization have termed "manifest" and "latent" socialization. The manifest aspects of socialization, consisting of numerous speeches, articles, and policy documents calling for modernization, are very prominent. The latent aspects, consisting of the organizational structure of the professional military education system, careerism, promotions, and other aspects of "how the system really works," are not as easily seen, yet have a very real impact on how military professionals conceive of the military role and their own role in the military.

17. For example, see Chalmers Johnson, "The Failure of Socialism in China," *Issues and Studies* (July 1979), pp. 22–33; see especially pp. 28–31. In the summer of 1980, a series of articles on the "westernization" movement at the end of the Qing dynasty appeared in the Chinese press. The allegorical debate had obvious significance for present issues. Some of the more notable are Qiao Huantian, "Brief Account of the Discussions on Certain Questions Regarding the Westernization Movement," *Renmin ribao* (taken from *Beifang Luncong*), July 14, 1980; DR/PRC, July 30, 1980, pp. L19–22; also Qiao's article, "A Brief Discussion on How the Westernization Group Arranged for the Building of Coastal Defenses," *Guangming ribao*, July 29, 1980; DR/PRC, August 12, 1980, pp. L13–15. Qiao generally makes a positive assessment of the "westernization" movement.

18. See the speech by PLA Chief of Staff Yang Dezhi to the graduating class of the PLA Military Academy on January 23, 1981. Among other points Yang made the following: "Every comrade must subordinate himself to the needs of the revolutionary cause, bring into full play the spirit of waging arduous struggles, practice strict economy, combat waste, build the army and run all undertakings with diligence and thrift." According to the Xinhua account of the speech, Yang "particularly stressed the importance of strength-

ening political-ideological work under the new circumstances" and asked the students to conscientiously carry out the line and policies laid down by the third plenum of the Eleventh CCP Central Committee (Xinhua, January 23, 1981; DR/PRC, January 27, 1981, p. L9).

19. Xinhua, January 15, 1982; DR/PRC, January 19, 1982, p. K6.

6
Internal Management in the Armed Forces: Confucian Anachronism or Model for the 1980s?

Harvey W. Nelsen

Chinese and Westerners alike, when speaking of the four modernizations, have referred to technology, the industrial base, raw material resources, and other tangible, quantifiable aspects of the economy. Only in the past few years has attention been focused on management practices. In industry, new plants have failed to perform anywhere near their design capacities, forcing the leadership to look at the human factors. In agriculture, material incentives have been needed along with chemical fertilizers and improved seed strains in order to prod lagging productivity. The military portion of the four modernizations quartet, when viewed by Western analysts, is still treated primarily in terms of hardware. However, the Chinese media concentrate on management problems in the PLA. The purpose of this chapter is to review the military management and personnel system in terms of its suitability for modernization. After identifying aspects that may facilitate modernization as well as those that may hinder it, my discussion concludes with a survey of the current Chinese reform efforts and their prospects for success.

We must begin by defining criteria needed for successful military modernization. Sophisticated weaponry must be backed by a strong national technological and industrial base as well as by a high level of general education. The Chinese leadership has wisely decreed that military modernization will advance only in conjunction with the general modernization of the economy. The development of professional military training and suitable doctrine and strategies are also basic to modernization. These topics are dealt with elsewhere in Chapters 2 and 5 of this volume.

In addition to hardware and the ability to use and support it, morale must be maintained, and manpower—both on active duty and in the reserves—must be adequate to meet defense needs. The armed forces must be well disciplined, both internally and in terms of executing orders from the national leadership. The society must accept the importance and legitimacy of the military and its mission. It is these aspects of modernization that we will evaluate here.

Strengths of the Present System

Recruitment

Recruiting officers all over the world have good reason to be envious of the PLA. It is blessed with a conscription system that could allow it to induct only the best young men and women, and in ample numbers. Every year at least 10 million males and an equal number of females reach the draft age of seventeen to eighteen. The minimum terms of service are three years in the army, four years in the air force, and five in the naval forces. Given an active duty force of 4 million, and assuming an overall average service tenure of five years (thus allowing for reenlistees, noncommissioned and commissioned officers), the maximum personnel requirement would be 800,000 people annually. Even if we ignore the young women of draft age, since they constitute only about 2 percent of active duty manpower, there is still a recruitment pool over ten times larger than the draft requirement. The selection process then consists of picking excellent physical specimens who have flawless political records and who wish to serve in the PLA.

Virtually all recruits are volunteers; there is no need to dragoon unwilling men into the armed forces, except perhaps for a few highly specialized personnel such as scientists and medical doctors, and even those professionals often benefit from military service. In the 1960s, the physical exam was so demanding that men were frequently refused enlistment merely because they wore glasses, had too many cavities in their teeth, or suffered from hemorrhoids. The quality of recruits could be better still but for political imperatives. First, for purposes of national integration, a certain percentage of minority peoples are enlisted even if they are not well qualified. Second, since over 75 percent of the population is rural, social justice obliges the government to induct more young men from the peasantry rather than from the better-schooled urbanites. Recent changes in the commune system that make individual households responsible for meeting production quotas rather than the collective "teams" on the village level have somewhat darkened this rosy picture. Young men of draft age are now highly valuable to the economic well being of peasant families, and parents are less eager to see them leave for military service. Overall, however, China's recruitment situation remains favorable.

Military service is popularly seen as a considerable attainment and a highly desirable honor. The family of the recruit receives special status and a few minor economic privileges. PLA duty offers many more possibilities for general and technical education than does civilian status. More important, it offers much-improved chances for obtaining the coveted prize of Communist Party membership. Military service even guarantees the love life of the enlistee. If a recruit is engaged when he enters the service, his fiancee is forbidden by law from breaking the engagement so long as the soldier is on active duty. With these attractions, the PLA is able to pay its lower-ranking enlisted men only a few dollars a month without harming morale.

Morale

It follows from the above that morale would be good, and it is— especially in the enlisted ranks. As recently as February–March 1979, the PLA proved that it could sustain heavy casualties in a concentrated time frame while engaged in a senseless conflict, battling for ground the army knew was later to be voluntarily relinquished back to the enemy. The PLA suffered about 10,000 fatalities out of 20,000 total casualties in a mere three weeks of fighting.[1] (Comparatively, in Vietnam the United States lost 50,000 from a maximum force of 550,000 personnel over a decade of war.) Despite the high rate of casualties for the PLA, there was no evidence of unit breakdown or breaches of combat discipline. During the period of 1977–1979, when wall posters were allowed that exhibited complaints about the system, some PLA men criticized poor living conditions and tyrannical officers, but their opinions seemed exceptions rather than the norm. Officer morale does have some weak spots, and although the difficulties do not now threaten combat capabilities, they may yet adversely effect modernization.

Political Control

In terms of responsiveness to national political leadership, the PLA has a good to excellent record. Civilian authority over the military was severely strained during the Great Proletarian Cultural Revolution and its aftermath, the Lin Biao affair of 1970–1971. However, the remainder of the last decade saw a gradual, but fairly steady, return to the barracks and a restoration of the pre–Cultural Revolution political status quo—especially from 1977 to 1980.

Beginning in the late 1950s, studies in comparative military systems have established that "praetorianism"—the tendency for military leaders to intervene in the political process by shunting aside duly constituted civilian leadership—is terribly damaging to military professionalism, effectiveness, and unity. The PLA, though strongly tempted toward praetorian behavior from 1967 to 1971, survived the test. Moreover, the leadership of Mao Zedong generally worked against the professionalization of the PLA, emphasizing instead a populist military line. In contrast, the present government is more amenable to professionalization and seemingly less concerned about the development of corporate behavior in the officer corps. Thus, there is less reason today for the PLA to slide toward praetorianism.

One issue threatening the corporate interests of the PLA, and thus straining civil-military relations, is resource allocations. In 1977–78, the armed forces slipped from third to fourth in the priority listing of the four modernizations. European shopping trips for Western weapons have yielded little, and the 1980 and 1981 defense budgets were cut sharply—albeit after three years of continuous and substantial increases; the 1982 budget was increased slightly. But military restiveness over resource allocations is not apt to develop into a political crisis. Even in a time of shrinking budgets, the three services can be played off against each other, and the institutions of Party control over the PLA are now as strong as ever.

Jonathan Adelman develops a well-documented argument that communist governments that come to power through long and arduous guerrilla wars develop leaderships that span the civil-military functions and reduce tensions between the two sectors.[2] This has been true for the People's Republic of China. Even though the Long March generation has only a few survivors, they cling to power, and nearly all of the remaining national leadership joined the Party prior to the accession of power in 1949. Thus, there is little reason to expect strong polarity to develop between civil and military elites as modernization proceeds in this decade.

Within the PLA itself, the political control system was severely damaged by the tumultuous history of the past fifteen years, but even in this area, there is reason for optimism.

Weaknesses and Obstacles to Modernization

Education

Not long ago, the *People's Daily* ran a small item concerning a commune work team and a newly acquired diesel irrigation pump.

Upon first using the machine to flood some rice paddies, the peasants did not know how to turn off the engine. In frustration, they first beat it with boards; when that failed, they threw the pump in the irrigation canal. Although obviously an extreme example, the case is still useful as an indicator of the low level of general mechanical and technical knowledge in the countryside. Most rural youth receive only six to nine years of education—usually of mediocre to poor quality. Thus, the average Chinese recruit requires a great deal of training in order to handle and maintain complex military equipment. His lack of mechanical and technical exposure while growing up also renders him less able to cope with those inevitable, unforeseen problems that are not specifically covered in the training manual. During the 1979 Vietnam incursion, troops were often able to do only the specific job for which they were trained and proved unable to fill in for wounded comrades. Troop training has since been modified to make it extensive as well as intensive.[3]

Another approach to the education problem is to extend the term of service and keep reenlisting specialists while promoting them to the higher ranks of the noncommissioned officers. The present leadership seems to be adopting that policy, although it has recently placed an upper limit of fifteen years of service in the enlisted ranks. Of course, as agricultural modernization proceeds and the average number of years of schooling increases, the problem of education will gradually recede in significance.

Civic Action Programs

Chinese propaganda has long portrayed the PLA as a work force as well as a fighting force. Glossy magazines frequently show military men laboring in the paddies along with the peasants, assisting in disaster relief, or being involved in some large-scale capital construction project. The inference has been that whenever military men are not training, sleeping, or eating, they are involved in some economically productive activity, either on the military base or in conjunction with civilian enterprises such as communes. The image has not survived close scrutiny. Using China's own statistics, only about one out of every ninety military workdays has been devoted to work in the civilian economic sector, and that figure probably includes the man-days of the PLA Capital Construction Engineering Corps, which are mostly devoted to major economic projects.[4]

However, the requirements for civic contributions rose sharply at the beginning of 1979. At that time, Defense Minister Xu Xiangqian announced a three-year campaign during which the PLA was called upon to assist "the policy of readjusting, restructuring, consolidating and improving the national economy."[5] Defense plants were to use "surplus productivity" to turn out light industrial commodities— especially those suited for export. According to an economic report presented to the National People's Congress in August 1980, pro- duction in the civilian sector reached 20 percent of the total output volume of defense industries in 1979.[6] Defense plants were also ordered to establish mutually beneficial relations with local communes. Finally, military manpower commitments to civilian labor seem to have risen sharply in 1979–1980, although not to the point of seriously hampering training.

Xu Xiangqian, in the above cited article, provides an argument for these extensive civic action activities. He claims that significant progress in national economic productivity has resulted in later qualitative military improvements. This result may eventually prove to be the case again in the 1980s, but the initial trend in this decade has been to reduce resource allocations to the PLA while requiring it to do more in support of the national economy. Rumors filtering out of China in the aftermath of the 1980 People's Congress indicated some disgruntlement among elements of the PLA leadership. As discussed in the section on political control, these issues are not apt to develop into a full-fledged civil-military crisis, but the current trends do not favor the PLA's modernization requirements.

Promotion System

The PLA usually promotes officers up a single vertical chain of command. For example, a company commander is ordinarily promoted to the battalion headquarters that controls his company, and so on up the line. It is possible for an officer to request a transfer, but he is actively discouraged from doing so. The selection process takes place two echelons above the post to be filled, e.g., regimental Party committees select company commanders, army corps Party committees choose regimental officers. Names of candidates are forwarded by the Party committee (or a branch of it) of the unit concerned as well as by the unit's immediate superior. Thus, a regimental committee meeting to select a company commander would have suggestions from the unit and from the unit's battalion headquarters. The most important position in the selection process is the secretary of the Party committee, although the promotion decisions are collective. The final choice, especially on administrative levels and in large units, is often based on a "sponsor-protégé" relationship. If a senior officer pushes hard for a particular subordinate to be promoted, he is understood to be responsible for that person's future behavior and performance. In turn, the subordinate owes a personal debt of loyalty to the sponsoring superior officer. If the protégé makes a serious mistake or commits an offense, it reflects badly on the sponsor. If the sponsor is demoted, suspended, or purged, it is understood that his protégés' careers will also suffer. The whole system is reminiscent of the "mutual responsibility" employed in the civil bureaucracies of the Ming and Qing dynasties.

A second element needs mention at this point to complete the picture. There was no retirement system in effect from 1958 to 1978. Senior officers did not retire at all, and even today flag-rank officers generally die with their boots on, are reassigned to thé civilian bureaucracy at an equivalent or higher grade, or are purged. Prior to 1978, field-grade officers remained at their posts for years or even decades longer than their Western army equivalents. Naturally, promotion opportunities for the great number of junior- and field-grade officers were severely limited. About the only effective way to get ahead was to hitch oneself to a star. If one's sponsor did well in terms of getting positions with extensive powers of patronage, then his protégés advanced. As officers attain high rank and extensive patronage opportunities, they are able to recruit new, talented followers into their entourage with the lures of pay raises and choice positions.[7] The end result of this promotion system is a network of competing vertical cliques built around key officers in large units, military regions, and the central military administration.

Recent PLA history has revealed serious inherent problems in this method of officer corps management. There is a general pattern of behavior, which the Chinese refer to as "mountaintopism," in which clique leaders and powerful subordinates, relying on the extralegal strength of their own networks, manipulate or even defy formal PLA organizations and bureaucratic practices. What is dubbed "back-door clique behavior" results in lowered morale, wasted talent, corruption, and weakened control over the military. Officers refuse to accept transfers or remain in luxurious housing accommodations even after being ordered to leave by a military district headquarters.[8]

Worse still, the cliques engender outright corruption. The elder statesman of the PLA, Marshal Ye Jianying, is infamous within China for his personal extravagances; e.g., a birthday party for himself in 1981 that cost thousands of dollars. His son is widely rumored to be guilty of rape or murder in Beijing, but he is protected by his father and lives free in Guangzhou. During travels in China in 1981, this writer was surprised at the general public's knowledge of Ye's alleged malfeasance, the willingness to discuss it (privately) with a foreigner, and the combined sense of concern and frustration in coping with such problems. On lower levels, the national media have publicized

PLA unit leaders who have requisitioned civilian goods and then shared the spoils among themselves or have used income from unit sideline production for lavish parties and banquets for the officers rather than for the intended purpose of improving unit housing and recreational facilities.[9] However, the public still perceives the top-level leaders as being above the law. This situation may change for the better after the promulgation of the new national constitution in 1982, which emphasizes that all persons are equal before the law and that the Party apparatus is subject to the provisions of the constitution.

Where there is a breakdown of consensus, or when bureaucratic routine is disrupted, cliques tend to be pitted against one another in a no-holds-barred political war.[10] If one clique gains ascendency in a military region or in the Central Military Commission, wholesale dismissals, suspensions, and demotions of rivals disrupt assignments all the way down to the tactical-level units. Three thousand military cadres who had incurred the wrath of Lin Biao were transferred for "reeducation" to Yunnan, where they were severely mistreated resulting in the death of 7 and serious injury to 300.[11] Also, during the Cultural Revolution, 42 percent of General Political Department (GPD) cadres were imprisoned, and an undisclosed number died.[12] As late as 1974, the GPD was still described by its new director, Zhang Chunchiao, as "paralyzed." Unfortunately, Zhang went on to say that the paralysis was a good thing: "We must not be afraid of factionalism . . . some problems can only be solved if we fight a civil war."[13] The disruption of GPD operations did not end with the purge of the Gang of Four. In 1978, Hua Guofeng revealed the existence of a three-year rebuilding program for the army political organization, and the *Liberation Army Daily* expressed concern about the factionalism that still weakened the GPD.[14]

Another nettlesome case was in the Guangzhou Military Region, which, like the GPD, had been torn with factionalism from early in the Cultural Revolution until at least as late as 1978. In addition to the headquarters, infantry divisions and military schools were affected; some 800 cadres were "persecuted." Following the death of Lin Biao, efforts were made to rehabilitate the victims of the struggle, but the clique in power feared that rehabilitation would lead to acts of vengeance and a jeopardizing of their positions. With the reshuffle of military region commanders at the end of 1973, the power struggle was resumed, but it was only in November 1977—with the personal intervention of Deng Xiaoping, Ye Jianying and other unnamed leaders of the Central Military Commission—that the Guangzhou Military

Region finally agreed to rehabilitate 70 percent of the dismissed cadres.[15]

A final disadvantage of the promotion system lies in the narrow career patterns of the officer corps. When officers are promoted up a single chain of command, they have very little exposure to operations of other PLA branches and services. Military schools in the regions and on the national level ameliorate, but cannot fully solve, this problem. Likewise, combined-arms training exercises help broaden military expertise, and the PLA in the 1970s did increase the frequency and scale of such training, although the level remained well below that of most advanced armed forces in other nations.

It can be argued that the PLA adopted and perpetuated its promotion and assignment system because of the force of cultural tradition. Also, the decentralized command and control over the dispersed field armies from 1928 to 1949 prevented the formation of a national bureaucratic system of personnel management. It could be further argued that the high level of political consensus in the early years of the PRC and the absence of any extensive bureaucratic breakdown allowed the perpetuation of the system since there was no imperative to change. William Whitson and Chinese Nationalist observers have also noted that any efforts to radically change the system would probably either have failed or would have caused a severe political-military crisis since the most powerful PLA leaders would have had the most to lose in any reform of the promotion and assignment system.[16]

I do not wish to challenge the above-mentioned analyses, but I do want to add that the system does have some advantages, which also help explain its perpetuation. The most important pluses are in military capabilities. First by retaining officers and enlisted men in a single chain of command, training effectiveness is greatly improved. Last year's training is still valuable for all but the new recruits. With regular and frequent rotation of men and officers, last year's training in individual skills may endure, but unit training does not. Second, officers and enlisted men know each other and their specific jobs better than in Western armies. Social psychologists since World War II have agreed that in the stress of battle, it is primary group solidarity that sustains morale and the will to fight when rational behavior would lead men to freeze in place or flee. The PLA personnel system should ensure tightly knit primary groups and small-unit effectiveness, especially since the divisive aspects of clique behavior are manifested primarily at much higher echelons. On a related point, the units have a high esprit de corps, and the men and officers can develop a real

identification with a unit's history and accomplishments. Such pride
of unit is also very helpful in enduring wartime stresses.

Chronological Survey of Efforts to Reform PLA Management

China's leadership has been deeply concerned about problems of
factionalism within the PLA, and several efforts have been made to
change the system. This dissatisfaction began with political problems
during the Cultural Revolution, and the first man to attempt systemic
change was Mao Zedong. In 1968, he is said to have decreed that a
policy of regular geographic rotation of both officers and units would
be undertaken, presumably as soon as the Cultural Revolution had
ended. If thoroughly implemented, that policy would have quickly
destroyed regionally based military factions and would have eroded
away vertical cliques in the central PLA organizations. No program
of personnel rotation was implemented. Flight units of the air force
did completely relocate at the end of the Cultural Revolution, and a
few of the army corps that were the most deeply embroiled in factional
strife were separated from one another.[17] If one compares the current
unclassified order-of-battle maps with those of the Cultural Revolution
period, it is remarkable how few units have moved and the relocations
have been for strategic military purposes rather than as part of a
systematic program of periodic relocation. There were only two
redeployments in the 1970s. First, three army corps from southern
military regions moved to the north—a result of the China-U.S.
détente, the end of the Vietnam War, and the heightened Soviet
menace.[18] Second, approximately three army corps relocated to the
Sino-Vietnamese border in late 1978 and early 1979, preliminary to
the invasion of Vietnam.[19]

After the Lin Biao affair, little was done to reform the PLA
management. Instead, the emphasis was on regaining civilian control
over the armed forces and returning the military to the barracks.
However, the December 1973 reshuffle of military region commanders
was a major achievement and it beheaded the regional cliques as well
as removing an overly influential military presence from the provincial
leadership. Military region commanders were forbidden to hold provincial Party or government posts in their newly assigned territories,
but at least some were allowed to become the Party secretaries of
their military regions. If they had not been allowed to assume that
post, their power to break up existing cliques would have been
weakened. Yet, as Party secretaries, they could presumably begin to
build new patronage systems, which eventually might become as

powerful as those they had been transferred from. Neither option would seem very attractive from Beijing's viewpoint.

From 1974 to 1976, the PLA was buffeted by policies pushed by the Gang of Four. These policies were not intended to reform PLA management and personnel practices as such; rather, they seemed geared to weaken the power of the established leadership and of the military in general. So-called helicopters and childrens' corps disrupted the seniority system in promotions, and "earthquakers" ruined discipline by openly challenging command authority on political grounds. Many, if not most, of the higher-level military organizations were disrupted, and an unknown number of military units—down to at least division level—were also affected.

Current Reform Efforts

In the three years following the purge of the Gang of Four, a clear national policy gradually emerged that is intended to reform internal PLA management practices. First, a strongly professional orientation was ordered for the PLA for the first time since the mid-1950s. A three-year program was undertaken to reconstruct the GPD and the political system on all echelons and to return the GPD to its original functions, i.e., the maintenance of discipline and morale and improving the education, indoctrination, culture, and welfare of the troops. Since 1977, *Liberation Army Daily* editorials have repeated ad nauseam the need for unity, discipline, training, and military expertise. Second, in 1978, the retirement system was reinstituted—presumably based on the 1955 military service law. Retirement should do much to open the channels of promotion, although at present it seems the law is not being enforced at the higher echelons. If another directive, first mentioned in 1978, is implemented, it would also serve to facilitate upward mobility. The *Liberation Army Daily* called for demotions to take place when promotions occurred, which was probably seen as necessary for the elimination of "helicopters" and "earthquakers" from responsible positions. With that campaign now concluded and with the reinstatement of the retirement system, the call for simultaneous promotions and demotions may no longer be seen as valid. However, in the summer of 1979, Hua Guofeng publicly criticized the iron-rice-bowl psychology of cadres in general and restated the concept of a linkage between promotions and demotions.[20] Thus, the issue is not dead. The practice would be useful as a means of carrying out another officer corps rectification, avoiding the Janowitz "diamond-shaped" rank structure (too many field-grade officers), or even as an experimental means of defeating the Peter Principle. A disadvantage is the sense of insecurity that such a policy would engender in the officer corps. This sense of insecurity could easily further the sponsor-protégé relationships and clique behavior.

Also in 1978, a central directive ordered that the Party secretaries of regional, provincial, and prefectural Party committees should automatically assume the political commissar post at the equivalent military administrative echelon; e.g., the Party secretary of a province would automatically become the political commissar of the military district. This is not a new policy, but a reimplementation of the pre–Cultural Revolution system. In the military regions, districts, and subdistricts, the civilian political commissars do not normally serve as Party secretaries to these important PLA echelons—the commander usually assumes that role. This situation is unfortunate since an "objective" civilian referee might mediate promotions and assignments, thereby weakening the personal loyalty systems within the PLA. Merely serving as "nominal political commissars," as Mao called them, is not enough to undercut the cliques—at least the presence of such men from the mid-1950s through 1966 had no appreciable effect.

Finally, a new promotion system has been put forward as a model, although it has not yet been adopted on a national basis. Appropriately enough, the Guangzhou Military Region Headquarters which suffered so under the old system, created the new one. The initial step remains the same: Candidates for promotion are recommended by the Party branches or committees of the echelons concerned. Following this procedure, there is open discussion of the nominees by the "masses," and all nominees are publicly scrutinized on the basis of Mao's five criteria for revolutionary successors. Individuals who are reluctant to publicly criticize nominees are encouraged to write the Party committee considering the promotions. The slate of candidates is then revised on the basis of the semipublic assessment and submitted to a higher level. Thus, according to the Guangzhou Military Region Headquarters, "the promoted cadres come to know that their powers are given to them by the Party and the people, not by a certain leader."[21] On the same issue, the GPD editorialized against the method of "change of ministers when a new emperor ascends the throne." Leaders should not appoint only those they know as subordinates, and they should not take former subordinates with them when they are transferred or promoted.[22]

Possible Further Reform Measures in the 1980s

All of the above mentioned measures, while helpful, are probably insufficient to break down the cliques. Systematic personnel rotation seems the obvious solution. However, if implemented, two radical changes would be entailed. First, a centralized system of personnel management would have to be established. At present, national-level PLA organizations directly administer the careers only of division commanders and above. Second, and more important, the unit- and administrative-level Party committees would lose much of their power over the officers in their units.[23] This latter result may prove to be the sticking point in the 1980s. Party control over the military is as primary a principle to Deng Xiaoping as it was to Mao. If the unit Party committees lose control over the promotion and assignment of officers and men in subordinate echelons, the Party function may become formalistic. Perhaps the best compromise would be to have the committees render officer efficiency evaluations and to leave assignment, promotion, and demotion to some central authority, such as the GPD.

One alternative to periodic officer rotation might be the election of cadres by their subordinates and/or peers. The new Guangzhou promotion method is a step in that direction, and the policy has been implemented on a limited basis in the civilian sector. Hua Guofeng recommended its extension. However, senior officers would probably resist the application of elections to the PLA on the grounds that elections might undermine discipline and officers might be selected more on the basis of popularity than competence. The election technique, like cadre rotation, would also serve to weaken the power of the unit Party committees.

It remains to be seen if the national leadership will settle for the present palliatives or dig in and overhaul the system. Deng Xiaoping is committed to a deep-rooted reform of the civilian Party management practices, which suffer from many of the same problems as the PLA officer corps. If he succeeds in that sector, the PLA will not be far behind.

Notes

1. Daniel Tretiak, "China's Vietnam War and Its Consequences," *China Quarterly* no. 80 (December 1979), pp. 740–767.

2. Jonathan Adelman, "Origins of the Difference in Political Influence of the Soviet and Chinese Armies: The Officer Corps in the Civil Wars," *Studies in Comparative Communism* 10:4 (Winter 1977), pp. 347–349.

3. Radio Guangzhou, October 21, 1979, in Foreign Broadcast Information Service (henceforth FBIS), October 24, 1979, p. P6.

4. Xinhua, September 28, 1979, in FBIS, October 3, 1979, p. L26.

5. *Hongqi* no. 10 (October 1979) in FBIS, October 18, 1979, p. L13.

6. *Beijing Review* no. 38 (September 22, 1980), p. 31.

7. *Liberation Army Daily*, October 13, 1978, in FBIS, October 19, 1978, p. E8.

8. Ibid.

9. See for examples, FBIS, April 22, 1978, p. L4 and December 8, 1978, p. E22.

10. William Parish, "Factions in Chinese Military Politics," *China Quarterly* no. 56 (October–December 1973), pp. 667–699.

11. *Asiaweek* (Hong Kong), November 2, 1979, pp. 28–29 (citing Beijing wall posters).

12. *Liberation Army Daily*, August 25, 1978, in FBIS, August 25, 1978, p. E2.

13. *Ming bao* (Hong Kong), August 19, 1978, p. 11.

14. *Liberation Army Daily*, August 25, 1978, in FBIS, August 25, 1978, p. E2.

15. Guangzhou Radio, September 30, 1978, in FBIS, October 3, 1978, pp. H5–7.

16. William Whitson, *The Chinese High Command* (New York: Praeger Press, 1972).

17. H. Nelsen, "Military Forces in the Cultural Revolution," *China Quarterly* no. 51 (July–September 1972), pp. 444–474.

18. The Forty-seventh Army moved from the Guangzhou Military Region to the Lanzhou Military Region, the Fifty-fourth Army moved from the Kunming Military Region to the Wuhan Military Region, and an unidentified army went to Xinjiang.

19. None of the corps moved to the Vietnam border were publicly identified, but two were probably from the Fujian Front and one from elsewhere in the Guangzhou Military Region.

20. Hua Guofeng's report to the Fifth National People's Congress, Xinhua, June 20, 1979, in FBIS, June 21, 1979, p. L8.

21. Guangdong Provincial Radio, December 12, 1978, in FBIS, December 27, 1978, p. H2.

22. *People's Daily* (Beijing), March 8, 1978, in FBIS, March 8, 1978, p. E14.

23. Harlan Jencks, *From Muskets to Missiles: Politics and Professionalism in the Chinese Army, 1945–1981* (Boulder, Colo.: Westview Press, 1982), p. 245.

Part 4

The Militia

7
The Chinese People's Militia: Transformation and Strategic Role

June Teufel Dreyer

Introduction

The media of the People's Republic of China regularly criticize discredited Chinese leaders for having disparaged the value of the militia. Former Defense Minister Peng Dehuai, for example, is said to have characterized the militia as outmoded and to have advocated that it be reduced in size. Lin Biao, Peng's successor as defense minister and heir apparent to the aging Mao Zedong, allegedly described the militia as a "heap of loose flesh." Following Lin's demise, the so-called Gang of Four reportedly belittled the role of the militia in war, charging that its leadership was incapable and its training inadequate.

In contrast to the unanimously negative views of the militia attributed to out-of-power leaders, the same leaders, while in power, have uniformly praised the militia for its loyalty and value to the PRC. Underlying these apparent inconsistencies are a variety of unresolved questions regarding the optimum size of the militia, its proper role in society, its relationship to the regular military forces on the one hand and to the Party on the other, and the priority that the militia should claim in resource allocation. This chapter will analyze the nature of these controversies, describe the institutional arrangements associated with the proponents of different views of the militia, and attempt to predict the role of the militia in China's future defense policy.

Role of the Militia

In War

The Chinese militia is a paramilitary organization with both wartime and peacetime functions. Its role in war is, at least in theory, extremely important. Chinese defense strategy is based on Mao Zedong's theory of people's war, which calls for the coordinated use of three organizations—the main forces, regional forces, and militia—against an enemy. Militia units are, in general, expected to operate in their native areas; hence, their members' familiarity with the local terrain enhances the militia's value as a guerrilla force.

Militia will be used to harass and weaken the enemy through such activities as ambush, sabotage, minelaying, and the disruption of supply lines. Militia members are to immobilize enemy tanks, serve as snipers, and engage in tunnel and barricade warfare and in street fighting. These techniques, aiming at the gradual attrition of a more powerful enemy, are an important component of the protracted war concept of Maoist military doctrine.

The militia is expected to provide reinforcements for the regular forces and to supply them with medical and logistic support. Individual militia members are to be available as replacements for main force and regional force units, and selected militia units may be upgraded to regional force status, allowing some regional force units to be upgraded to main force status. Militia personnel will also aid in combating the effects of air raids, in maintaining public order in combat areas, and if necessary, in the evacuation of civilians from the combat areas.

In its capacity of a bridge between the civilian populace and the regular military organizations, and as an aid to both, the militia thus plays an important part in people's war doctrine.

In Peace

In peacetime, the militia's roles center around providing a leading force for the increase of production and as an aid to public security work. In the former capacity, militia may be used as a shock force to lead a production campaign, to conduct emergency repairs to a damaged facility, and to help cope with the ravages of natural disasters. The militia's public security role involves coordinating with People's Liberation Army and public security departments in such roles as preventing sabotage, suppressing rebellion, reporting suspicious persons, conducting surveillance of those people in a community who have been deemed undesirable elements, carrying out patrol and sentry duties, and apprehending illegal emigrants. At the same time, militia members are expected to carry on their normal work activities.[1]

As will be obvious on a moment's reflection, the different roles assigned to the militia are not always compatible with one another. Time spent in military training is time lost from economic production. And the surveillance, informer, and apprehension functions inherent in the militia's public security duties often contribute to the masses' suspicion of militia members rather than building a bridge between the civilian and military populations. Thus, the question of the amount of time to be allotted to these various functions touches on the fundamental priorities of Chinese society.

Size and Organization

The militia consists of politically reliable, able-bodied men between the ages of sixteen and forty-five, and women between sixteen and thirty-five. Since meritorious service in the militia is viewed as bettering one's chances of acceptance into the PLA, and since membership in the PLA has been an important channel of social mobility in China, there generally has been no shortage of recruits for the militia. Recently, however, policy changes that downgraded the attraction of a military career have also adversely affected militia recruitment.

Although the Chinese media have not disclosed the total size of the militia, information obtained from refugees indicates that approximately a quarter of the Chinese population is enrolled. Since the Chinese population is now estimated at over a billion, a militia of upwards of 250,000,000 persons is implied. This staggering figure does not, however, accurately represent the actual power of the militia in Chinese society. The militia is divided into three main categories: ordinary, backbone or basic, and armed. Slightly over half of all militia members receive no, or virtually no, training. Participation in the ordinary militia involves little time. Members may be asked to serve in holiday rallies, such as those on National Day or at the New Year, and they may be pressed into service in time of drought or flood. The ordinary militia has little significant military value.

The basic, or backbone, militia, composes slightly less than half of total militia membership. Its members are slightly younger than are those of the ordinary militia (sixteen to thirty for males and sixteen to twenty-five for females). More of them, perhaps three-fourths of the total, are male, and many are demobilized soldiers. Unlike the ordinary militia, the basic militia does receive regular training, although the types of training and amount of time devoted to it vary considerably according to area and current Party line. Some units receive a half-day's instruction per month; others, several days once or twice a year. The instructors may be cadres of a commune's People's Armed Forces Department or PLA officers assigned from local military garrisons. Typically, basic militia members do not possess weapons except while on patrol or during training exercises.

The armed militia is a select group, composing perhaps 1½–2 percent of the militia as a whole. Western estimates of the total size of the armed militia range between 12 million and 15 million. Its members are about 90 percent male, between the ages of eighteen and twenty-five, and have been chosen from the basic militia on the basis of military ability and political reliability. Not surprisingly, a large number of the armed militia members belong to the Communist Youth League and/or are former members of the PLA.

A higher proportion of the militia, pehaps as much as 3 percent of the total, will be in the armed category in border and coastal areas. Typically, the weapons they possess and the training they receive will be superior to those prevalent in less strategically important interior areas.[2] Armed militia personnel may train for as much as a month to six weeks each year and are usually instructed by PLA members. Many are on full-time duty for their commune or county and carry weapons during duty hours.

Militia weapons are generally of inferior quality, even by the relatively unsophisticated standards of the PLA. Often they are of World War II vintage or are PLA castoffs. There have been persistent complaints that militia weapons are inadequately maintained. Commitments made in the late 1970s to modernize the militia arsenal[3] had to be abandoned due to the budget cuts of 1980.

Although the militia is a paramilitary organization, the units into which it is divided bear little resemblance in size or organization to the corresponding PLA units. Rather, militia units such as platoons, companies, and battalions correspond with civilian production units. No militia order of battle is known to exist. Typically, a commune's production team or factory shop will raise a militia platoon or company; a brigade or factory will form a battalion or company; a commune will sponsor a division, regiment, or battalion; and a county will sponsor a division. There are no known militia units above division level, and in fact, during peacetime, units above the battalion level probably exist only on organizational charts. Unit sizes vary widely in accordance with the population and strategic significance of an area. A battalion, for example, may comprise anywhere between 100 and 1,000 persons; a regiment, between 1,000 and 15,000.

At present, command over the militia is believed to be exercised by the PLA's General Staff through its Mobilization Department. On lower levels—including military district, subdistrict, and county—organizations known either as People's Armed Forces Departments (PAFDs) or People's Armed Departments supervise militia work. The CCP committee on any given level theoretically exercises dual leadership with the PAFD. As will be discussed later, the matter of how much control shall be exercised over the militia by the Party and how much by the army, and under what circumstances, has caused considerable controversy among the Chinese elite. Both Party and army have been accused of apathy toward militia work on the one hand and of attempts to usurp all power over the militia on the other.

Militia leaders appear to be selected by the PAFDs, presumably after consultation with Party authorities. Command positions are predominantly held by demobilized PLA personnel. An ambitious young militia member's best road to upward mobility is entrance into the PLA rather than rising within the militia command.[4] The advanced age of militia officers has been a common complaint of late, and allegations have been made that many are so elderly and infirm that they cannot perform their duties properly.

Transformation of the Militia

The previous section describes the militia in general terms. In fact, the militia has served different functions at different times. These changes have shaped the militia into the entity it is today, molding behavior patterns and imposing constraints on its capacities. Thus, an understanding of the historical development of the militia is important to an understanding of its present and future capabilities and limitations.

The controversies over the proper size, organization, and role of the militia have led to frequent shifts in policy that have had an enormous impact on the militia. Often these shifts have been manifestations of basic ideological differences that have had a wider import than the surface changes in the militia would seem to indicate. Therefore, the changing profile of the militia is closely connected with the confrontation of fundamental beliefs underlying their holders' visions of Chinese society as a whole. This section will attempt to analyze these twists and turns in ideology as they have affected the militia.

Early communist theorists favored the creation of a strong militia. Desiring to avoid reliance on a professional military whose interests might be divorced from, or even antithetical to, those of the masses, they saw the concept of "every citizen a soldier" as a solution to the defense of the socialist state. Friedrich Engels believed that under socialist society,

> every member of society who is fit for war can be taught, along with his other activities, to master the use of weapons, as much as is needed, not for taking part in parades, but for defending the country. . . . In the event of war, a member of such a society . . . must defend his *real* motherland, his *real* home, and will consequently fight with a spirit, resolution and bravery that will put to rout like chaff a modern, mechanically trained army.[5]

Subsequently, Lenin also espoused the idea of arming the entire population, adding that this act would be necessary even where a professional army existed. In his 1917 essay "On the Proletarian Militia," Lenin opined that "it would be a deceitful and lying evasion to say that it is superfluous to arm the proletariat when there is a revolutionary army, or that there are 'not enough' arms. What is needed is to begin immediately to organize a general militia on a really universal basis, which will master the use of arms even though there are 'not enough' arms for all."[6]

The concept of relying on an armed citizenry was enthusiastically espoused by members of the infant Chinese Communist Party. Firsthand experience with warlords, many of whose mercenary armies killed and looted with scant concern for the well-being of the civilian population, reinforced the appeal of a people's army to CCP members. In his 1927 "Report On an Investigation into the Peasant Movement in Hunan," Mao advocated building up a peasants' armed force, pointing out these "irregular household militias" could overthrow landlord tyranny.[7]

Despite Mao's words of praise, the militia did not play a major role in CCP strategy until the late 1930s. In the course of the Chinese communist struggle against the Japanese invaders, and in the Party's drive to seize power from Chiang Kai-shek's Kuomintang (KMT) government, the CCP greatly expanded the size and activities of the militia groups. Once having secured a base area, CCP leaders began to propagandize the local population. Noting those elements of the populace that were receptive to the Party's message, communist leaders selected the most capable and organized them into self-defense teams. The militia was formed from among the most outstanding of these teams. Militia personnel carried messages and supplies through blockades, performed patrol duty, and assisted the regular army on an ad hoc basis.[8]

By 1945, the militia had moved beyond its original, basically civil defense kinds of activities to become a large, diversified guerrilla-type force involving an estimated 10 percent of the people under CCP control. In that year, which also saw the defeat of Japan, the Party expanded its activities against Chiang Kai-shek's troops, and the militia was called upon to do its part. The militia was placed under the same military authorities as the CCP's main and local forces in order to facilitate the lateral movement of people from one group to another. When large numbers of peasants were needed to support a military campaign, the militia was assigned to lead them. However, during the civil war with the KMT, the militia was still a relatively ad hoc organization.

Not until two years after the CCP assumed control of the Chinese mainland did it move to regularize militia groups. In 1951, the Party set up a militia organization under the PLA's Mobilization Department. That department was in turn subordinate to the Revolutionary Military Council, which was the predecessor of the present-day PLA General Staff. On the lower levels—including the military district (generally composed of one province), subdistrict, and county—PAFDs were to supervise militia work.

The militia's chief functions during the early 1950s included providing "volunteers" for the Korean War, helping the PLA to guard China's frontiers, and serving as a leading force for the sweeping reforms the CCP was instituting. However, with the end of the civil war, militia activity was hardly needed on the scale of the late 1940s. In consequence, militia membership was greatly reduced, to approximately 5 percent of the total population. This smaller size and the expanded domestic role of the militia appear to have caused no particular controversy among the members of the elite group.

China's experiences during the Korean War convinced some, though not all, members of the CCP elite that the defense of the PRC could not be ensured without a substantial upgrading of the country's military capabilities. Measures taken in support of this conviction included increased professionalism and specialization within the PLA and a downplaying of the role of guerrilla warfare by civilian soldiers. The size and prestige of the militia declined proportionally.

In the late 1950s, several policy decisions were made that sharply reversed the militia's fortunes. First, in 1957, the government issued new regulations on conscription and demobilization that substantially enhanced the prestige of militia membership. According to these new rules, people eligible for conscription but not selected for the PLA automatically went into the militia, and people who were selected for the PLA were to be assigned to the militia after completion of their tour of duty. In effect, these regulations made the militia into the reserves of the PLA. Since membership in the PLA was highly esteemed, membership in the militia was perceived as desirable. Thus, the 1957 regulations increased both the size and the prestige of the militia.

During the following year, other changes were made that, while reversing many of the 1957 regulations, further augmented the size and role of the militia. Over strong minority dissent, Mao Zedong and a group of his radical followers instituted a massive socioeconomic program that was intended to fundamentally transform Chinese society. Known as the Great Leap Forward, its aims included reducing the specialization and professionalization that had grown so rapidly since 1949 and substituting ideological for material incentives to production.

In consequence, control over the militia was transferred from the PLA to the Party. Marshal Peng Dehuai, then minister of defense, was subsequently criticized for having alleged that the militia system was outmoded. Thus, this shift from army to Party control may have been part of the radicals' efforts to undercut the power of conservative, professionally oriented elements within the army's high command. The PAFDs, their functions gone, were no longer mentioned by the media and apparently ceased to exist. Formally, at least, the militia no longer functioned as a reserve for the PLA.

In 1958 also, Mao Zedong issued the first of what were to become known as his "two great directives on militia work," an order to "organize the militia on a large scale." The media enthusiastically touted his directive as "a creative application of the Marxist-Leninist thesis on arming the people."[9] However, more than a desire to creatively develop Marxist-Leninist thought appears to have been involved in Mao's decision to expand the militia. One reason was economic. Mao envisioned the revitalized militia as a device to mobilize the masses to expand production and to help establish the institutional innovations that were part of the Great Leap Forward.

The second cause for the expansion of the militia was a military one. In addition to being the year in which the Great Leap Forward was instituted, 1958 saw the beginning of a new, more aggressive period in Chinese foreign policy. Consonant with Mao's assessment that the east wind was prevailing over the west wind, and that China would have to seize this opportunity or risk losing it, the PRC adopted a more militant stance toward, among others, Taiwan and India. Denouncing the machinations of imperialist cliques who created tensions everywhere in order to advance their schemes, Mao urged the need to turn everyone into a soldier.

At the time, most observers assumed that the imperialist cliques mentioned by Mao referred to leaders of capitalist states; subsequent events revealed that the Soviet Union was included as well. An interesting sidelight to the belief that Mao's perception of a Soviet threat prompted him to expand the PRC's militia is provided by a Japanese journalist who toured China in 1975. He was told that Mao had decided on this expansion after receiving, and rejecting, a Soviet proposal that the USSR share in the command of the Chinese military forces.[10]

The response to Mao's call was immediate. Within a few months, the militia system was reportedly established in virtually every commune, factory, mine, school, and government office. By late 1958, it allegedly had 177 million members; by mid-1959, 220 million, or an incredible 35 percent of the Chinese population at that time. The media described the role of the militia in glowing terms. "With a hoe in one hand and a rifle in the other," militia members were portrayed as leading an enormous drive to increase production while simultaneously guarding China against external attack.

Despite these heroic efforts, the Great Leap Forward was an abject failure. Severe shortages of food and other basic commodities brought the PRC's economy to the brink of collapse. In this desperate situation, the government ordered a nationwide concentration on agricultural production. In the case of the militia, this emphasis entailed a virtual halt to military training. In some areas, militia organizations effectively ceased to exist as their erstwhile members bent all their efforts to raising vegetables. In other areas, militia members found other ways to satisfy their hunger. Using weapons they had been legally issued, or those they had managed to steal from militia stocks, armed bands terrorized and robbed the citizenry and looted government warehouses.

The government took a series of steps to bring the militia under control. In December 1959, a Three Year Program for Military Organization was announced; one of its aims was the consolidation of militia work. In April 1960, a national conference on militia work was convened to discuss strengthening the organization and ideological construction of the militia.[11] Obviously dissatisfied with the results of these efforts, Defense Minister Lin Biao undertook a rectification movement for militia work. In January 1961, the Party's Military Commission issued a directive reiterating that militia training should not interfere with production and calling for:

1. the purification of "bad elements" within the militia,
2. a thorough accounting for militia supplies and weapons,

3. strict control over utilization of the militia, and
4. the consolidation of militia organization.[12]

These tasks were to be accomplished within three years. However, new regulations for militia work that were issued in July 1961 indicated that difficulties were being encountered. At the end of 1961, what was originally envisaged as a three-year task came to be referred to as "long-term, arduous, and difficult." By mid-1962, the condition of the militia prompted Mao to issue the second of his major directives on militia work, that the work be implemented in three ways: organizationally, politically, and militarily.[13] At this time also, in what was a clear setback for radical views and a victory for conservative elements within the elite, control of the militia was removed from the Party and returned to the army.

A noticeable increase in militia training and military activities took place in 1962 and 1963, though this increase probably occurred for reasons other than the renewal of the PLA's supervisory role. First, the recuperation of the economy in 1962 allowed more time for military activities. Second, deteriorating relations with both India and the Soviet Union had increased the possibility that the PRC might be attacked.

In 1963, in what appeared to be a move to undercut military control over the militia, public security forces began to assist in militia training. The following years saw an increasing emphasis on the political role of the militia and efforts to bring it more closely under Party control. Both moves are associated with a rise in the fortunes of radical ideologues. An August 1964 article in *Beijing Review* noted that Mao Zedong had both founded and fostered the army and the militia and that "both forces are under the firm leadership of the CCP."[14] In October, the PLA's General Political Department convened a national conference which concluded that "to put the work of the militia on an unshakable organizational, political and military footing, the political factor should come first, since this decides whether the gun is entirely in the hands of those who are politically reliable."[15] This apparent platitude on the need to put politics first was later to become the focus of much controversy.

The conference also emphasized the importance of strengthening militia building through the socialist education movement, pointing out that although the militia was an instrument for China's protection against attack from the outside, "internally, it enables China to exercise the proletarian dictatorship. Thus, consolidating militia building in the course of the socialist education movement will remain the key task in militia work for a long time."[16] This statement is not to imply that military training ceased entirely in favor of political education as 1964 and 1965 saw a number of marksmanship contests among militia units and foreign visitors to China were often taken to demonstrations of militia skills. But training was definitely subordinate to political study and production work.

Press commentary in early 1965 indicated relative satisfaction with the results of ideological work within the militia. According to one report, "the political consciousness of the people's militia has been greatly enhanced, its ranks made purer and sounder, and its organization and discipline strengthened. The fighting power of the militia has been greatly improved."[17]

The months preceding the Cultural Revolution saw a quickening and intensification of trends noted in earlier years. Contests between militia units and demonstrations of skill ceased as of November 1965, being criticized as representative of the "bourgeois military line." Actual training exercises, however, continued into early 1966, possibly as a response to U.S. activities in Vietnam. The idea of a well-trained militia is not, of course, antithetical to radical views, since these envision an army of citizen-soldiers. In fact, opposition to training the militia has typically come from conservative elements within the army as they favor a specialized, professional military and resent the time spent to train amateurs of doubtful ability. However, in general, and particularly in view of the serious deficiencies in militia behavior noted after the Great Leap Forward, radicals felt that raising the political and ideological level of the militia should be given first priority. Arguing that the skills of the militia could actually be harmful unless directed to the proper goals, the radicals pressed for more thorough political education.

The onset of the Cultural Revolution was accompanied by reports of militia groups, like most other groups in China, denouncing favorite targets such as Teng To and Wu Han. Militia units also dutifully made pledges to support the Left and carry through the Cultural Revolution to the end. The militia was described as sponsoring revolutionary rallies, disseminating Mao Zedong's thought, and organizing study teams.

Unfortunately, however sincere militia units were in their vows to support the Left, it was often difficult to know who represented the true Left, and in many cases, the militia's behavior was not exemplary. Militia weapons were an important source of arms for warring factions during the Cultural Revolution, and militia groups, often of substantial size, used these weapons in factional struggles. Sometimes the militia acted under orders of local Party committees; at other times, at the behest of military authorities.

On some occasions, militia behavior was judged to be misguided. Shanghai Radio, for example, described the story of a 200-strong militia detachment that had been "hoodwinked" into taking its grievances to Beijing.[18] At other times, militia elements were judged guilty of purposeful crime. For example, the New China News Agency charged on January 25, 1967, that Shanghai militia personnel willfully

> planned and carried out the "three stoppage conspiracy" to block water supplies, power, and communications and, whistling up an evil wind of economism, they incited the uninformed masses to lay siege to banks, make withdrawals by force, steal, rob, and occupy building [*sic*] by force. Group after group of workers were incited to march on Beijing to make accusations and stage strikes.[19]

During the period that radicals refer to as the "February adverse current" and the "evil wind of March," the army was ordered to assert control over militia groups. Shanghai Radio announced that "the militia must actively take part in the struggle to seize power under the command of the local PLA units or local militia department."[20] Given this control, the army tried to utilize the militia to bolster an economy that was somewhat shaken by the disruptions of the Cultural Revolution. A directive of the Central Committee's Military Commission directed PAFDs to use the militia "as the backbone of spring cultivation, to play the vital role of a production shock team."[21]

However, this "adverse current" was soon reversed, and the militia was again exhorted to support leftist causes. The results of these exhortations were not necessarily beneficial to leftists. Militia members reportedly seized a railway train in Guangxi in mid-1968, detaining and killing several of its passengers. Other militia members, described as fully armed, allegedly attacked revolutionary rebel organizations and seized arms from a local garrison force, injuring members of the garrison in the process.[22]

Some militia units were considered so unreliable that they were officially disbanded. Several attempts to confiscate militia weapons were made during the course of the Cultural Revolution, apparently without significant effect. This failure to confiscate militia arms may be partially explained by inefficiency engendered by the administrative chaos attendant upon the Cultural Revolution. However, in some areas, it was deemed necessary for the militia to possess arms: When the Cultural Revolution led to the collapse of the public security system, militia units were mobilized to assume peacekeeping and guard duties.

Allegations that several ranking members of China's elite sabotaged militia building were among the many charges made by proponents of the Cultural Revolution. They believed the chief proponents of these erroneous views to be head of state Liu Shaoqi, former Minister of Defense Peng Dehuai, and former chief of the PLA's general staff, Lo Ruiqing. The radicals' accusations not only contradicted one another, they were often internally inconsistent as well. However, because many of the practices the Liu-Peng-Lo group allegedly advocated were later declared correct, and because some of the "crimes" they committed were later held to be committed by their accusers as well, the charges are worth examining.

An article in *Liberation Army Daily* in August 1967 charged that the Liu-Peng-Lo group distrusted the militia and regarded it as a "great hindrance for them in usurping the party, military and political power, and in bringing about capitalist restoration." Further, the group "either directly opposed the arming of the masses and the organizing of contingents of the people's militia on a big scale, or advocated the purely military viewpoint in the course of militia building, and opposed giving prominence to politics in a vain attempt to transform the people's militia to fit the bourgeois outlook."[23]

It is immediately apparent that a group that viewed the militia as an obstacle on its road to power and was philosophically opposed to arming the masses would be unlikely to advocate "the purely military point of view," involving intense training for the militia. Apparently untroubled by the inconsistency of its argument, the article further accused the "capitalist roader" group of

> using such vicious means as hoodwinking, deception, threats and incitement in vainly attempting to pull certain militia cadres and militia members to the side of the bourgeois reactionary line. . . . They attempted to make use of militia to arrest, beat up and detain people, and they incited militia members to take part in struggle by force. They attempted to incite militia members in rural areas to suppress the proletarian revolutionaries there. They even attempted to direct militiamen to undermine production, communications, and social order.[24]

The implications of that assertion are that the Liu-Peng-Lo group, while regarding the militia as opposed to its plans to seize power, nonetheless attempted to make the militia a tool for its power seizure and that it succeeded in that the militia were following its orders to arrest and assault people and to undermine social order.

An equally puzzling article on the militia appeared in the same newspaper a little more than two years later. After routine criticisms of Liu Shaoqi and Peng Dehuai for having opposed arming the masses, denying the strategic role of the militia, and criticizing Mao's 1958 directive to organize the militia on a large scale, the article launched into a detailed criticism of Lo Ruiqing's response to Mao's 1962 directive that "militia work should be carried out organizationally, politically, and militarily." Mao, according to the article, had pointed out that "the first thing was organizational, the second, political, and the third, military." Lo, however, had reversed these priorities.

> He alleged that in doing militia work, the first thing was to do it politically, and that this should serve as the basis for doing it organizationally and militarily. This is just waving the red flag in order to oppose the red flag! Militia members are armed masses who are not divorced from production, so it is impossible to carry out militia work politically before carrying it out organizationally. In fact, Lo Ruiqing was consistently opposed to giving prominence to proletarian politics, and to militia members' lively study and application of Chairman Mao's works.[25]

The article concludes by exhorting the militia to intensively study Mao's teachings, citing the chairman's statement that "politics is the commander, the soul in everything"—a sentiment that appears to agree with Lo's giving priority to political work and says nothing about the primacy of organizational work.

It would seem, therefore, that Lo did not, in fact, distort Mao's priorities on the rectification of the militia, but that these priorities themselves changed in response to changing circumstances, and that in order to mask these changes, official propaganda attributed them to a discredited leader. In 1962, when Mao first issued his directive to carry out militia work organizationally, politically, and militarily, the militia organization had suffered severely from the impact of "three lean years" of economic hardship. In many areas, militia organization had completely disappeared. It was necessary to bring the militia back into existence before political indoctrination could be given; hence the sequence of organizational, political, and military work. Since Maoist ideology clearly and repeatedly declares the primacy of politics, the Chinese press said little about Mao's order of priorities. Later, as conditions in China recovered and the militia was reconstituted, more attention could be devoted to political indoctrination. With the approach of the Cultural Revolution, pressures for ideological purity grew, and the political activities of the militia tended to crowd out organizational and military activities.

The PLA emerged from the Cultural Revolution in a relatively strong position. The militia, by contrast seemed to have ceased to exist as an organizational unit. For several years, no training activities or militia conferences were reported, although in 1968, scattered reports from several different provinces indicated that rectification movements were being carried out within individual militia groups.[26] The powerful influence of the PLA and the border clashes with the USSR, which began in March 1969, seem to have provided the impetus for resuscitating the militia ranks that had been decimated by the Cultural Revolution; the organization had to be re-rebuilt—hence the *Liberation Army Daily*'s renewed emphasis on the primacy of the organizational factor.

The rebuilding of the militia as an aid against attack from the Soviet Union was closely supervised by the PLA. The close relationship between army and militia was described by a militia member in an article in *Beijing Review* in August 1969. Entitled "We Poor and Lower-Middle Peasants Have the Greatest Love for the PLA," it states:

> Guided by this great thinking of Chairman Mao's, we . . . have sent our best sons and brothers to join the PLA. In our brigade, practically everyone is now a member of the militia, hoe in one hand and rifle in the other. Day and night, winter or summer, at the river bank or in the hills, our militia always stand guard shoulder to shoulder with the PLA, keeping a vigilant watch on the enemy and defending the borders of the motherland. . . . We are determined to study and apply well Chairman Mao's great thinking on people's war, diligently take part in combat training and form a gigantic net of people's war . . . we . . . vow to unite closely with the great Chinese PLA.[27]

The author, while praising Mao's teachings on people's war, scarcely mentions the Party and never mentions its role with regard to the militia. Several radio broadcasts during 1969 voiced the need to build the militia into a more powerful reserve force to assist the PLA,[28] and army units were reportedly helping militia groups to study the concepts of people's war and to repudiate the Liu-Peng-Lo plot to sabotage army-people unity.[29]

This renewed emphasis on the militia, on its close connection with the PLA, and on its need for combat training as well as political education continued through mid-1973. Toward the end of that year, however, another major shift in militia form and function occurred. On September 29, joint editorials in *People's Daily* and *Liberation Army Daily* praised Shanghai's militia building program. Said to be based on the experiences of that city's Number 21 Cotton Mill and to have been successfully adopted in Liaoning Province, the model was clearly intended for large-scale imitation throughout China.

The new model had a number of interesting characteristics. First, it involved a much greater political role for the militia. Specifically, the militia was to serve as a leading force for revolution and against revisionism. Second, the Party's role in supervising the militia was stressed. Since the military had exercised de facto control over the militia for many years, the Shanghai model in fact entailed a major shift in militia command and control.

Third, the Shanghai model entailed the abolition of PAFDs and put militia work under the control of a new organization, the militia headquarters. Critics of the model later alleged that its proponents, the Gang of Four, had attempted to establish militia headquarters even on the central-government level. Presumably, this action would have removed the PLA, and specifically its PAFDs and Mobilization Department, from any control over the militia.

Fourth, the public security role of the militia was greatly enlarged. In keeping with its expanded political role, the militia was to exercise control over ideological deviance, thus involving it in public security patrols. A fire-fighting role was added as well. In what was called the three-in-one concept, militia began to incorporate public security and fire departments.

Fifth, the new model was urban based. Previous militia building campaigns had focused on the peasants—for example, Mao's 1958 drive to raise large militia contingents to help organize the communes. The post–Cultural Revolution campaign to rebuild the militia had also focused on the peasant, as is evident in the August 1969 *Beijing Review* article cited earlier.

Sixth, the Shanghai model stressed that militia units were to be armed. Although militia serving in sensitive border areas or guarding strategically significant installations were frequently armed, the large-scale use of armed militia in an urban, nonstrategic context was unusual. Moreover, the militia's role in national defense was scarcely mentioned.[30]

Meetings were held in several provinces to discuss the new militia model, and the media reported uniformly positive responses. If the military resented a reassertion of Party control over the militia, there were no overt manifestations of such resentment. In Liaoning, for example, a radio broadcast described PAFD members—their positions apparently not yet abolished by the militia headquarters—as saying, "Following Chairman Mao's teaching, our principle is that the party commands the gun and the gun must never be allowed to command the party. . . . [We] consciously accept the party committee's centralized leadership."[31]

The Gang of Four was later accused of subverting Mao's teachings on the militia by destroying the good relations between army and militia in order to serve the gang's own purposes. However, just a few weeks after the Chinese media began to devote attention to the Shanghai model of militia building, a major transfer of PLA commanders was announced. Designed not so much to purge as to remove from their bases of political power military leaders who were simultaneously first Party secretaries, the transfer was widely interpreted as a Maoist effort to return political power to the Party. It seems likely that the reorganization of the militia in accordance with the Shanghai model was intended to achieve the same goal and that Mao, far from being "hoodwinked" by the Gang of Four, was consciously supportive of the reorganization.

The first major political campaign to absorb militia attention was that to criticize Lin Biao and Confucius; militia study groups were also organized to discuss Mao's latest instructions when they appeared. Meanwhile, rural areas were reportedly applying Shanghai's experience in building an urban militia to the countryside. However, apart from militia members in the countryside "earnestly studying the experience of participating in class struggle in society accumulated by urban militia of Shanghai and scathingly criticizing Lin Biao's counterrevolutionary crime of undermining militia-building,"[32] it is not clear how this urban model was transposed. What percentage of the country's militia organizations adopted the Shanghai model, including its incorporation of public security and fire-fighting roles, is not known, but it is unlikely to have been universal. The larger cities were most apt to conform while rural areas postponed or ignored directives on reorganization of their militia units.

Both the principle of subordinating the military to Party control and that of relying more heavily on a nonprofessional military for national defense were enshrined in the new state constitution adopted by the Fourth National People's Congress in January 1975. In fact, Article 15 of the document raised the militia to a position of parity with the PLA, stating that "The Chinese People's Liberation Army and the people's militia are the workers' and peasants' own armed forces led by the Communist Party of China; they are the armed forces of the people of all nationalities."[33] In line with this desire to lean more heavily on the militia for national defense, the Chinese press in 1975 published frequent reports of militia training exercises. Whatever the attitude of the professional military toward this activity, numerous sources confirmed the active involvement of the PLA in training the militia.

Political activities continued, and the militia was heavily involved in the "learn from Dazhai" campaign. The greater attention given to militia training activities in 1975–1976 vis-à-vis 1973–1974 is, however, unmistakable. It almost certainly results from the PRC's increasing perception of threat from the Soviet Union. Press reports from the later two years express markedly greater concern about an attack from the USSR. The Soviet media responded by denouncing the education of the militia "in an atmosphere of hatred toward the Soviet Union" but, curiously, reserved their main criticisms for the alleged domestic excesses of the militia.[34]

The descriptions of militia activity found in Soviet sources during 1975 and 1976 closely parallel those found in Taiwan publications for the same years. It is, of course, wise to be skeptical of analyses emanating from both Moscow and Taibei, but given the essential compatibility of their accounts with allegations made after Mao's death by his successors, it is worthwhile to examine these descriptions.

The USSR's media depicted the militia as being overzealous in its role of guardian of ideological orthodoxy, to the point of ransacking the courtyards of homes and ensuring that barbershops cut hair in the officially approved manner. Soviet analysts advanced two reasons for these uses of the militia: first, that Mao was attempting to neutralize anti-Maoist tendencies in certain circles of the PLA and, second, that widespread popular dissatisfaction with Maoist policies had increased the necessity of dealing harshly with dissent.[35]

Taiwan sources advanced the same reasons for utilizing the militia in this manner, but added that the reorganization of the militia under Party control was one technique Mao Zedong had devised to ensure the succession of his wife, Jiang Qing, to the chairship of the CCP.[36] Jiang and Wang Hongwen, another member of the Gang of Four, were variously named as leaders of the militia. Taiwan analysts also portrayed the militia as an unreliable tool in the hands of its directors, with one commentator describing Wang Hongwen as "riding the tiger's back."[37]

One instance supporting Taiwan's view of militia unreliability has been well documented by Western sources. During the summer of 1975, there were serious clashes between rival militia units in which both sides used mortars and automatic rifles. A joint Central Committee–State Council "Resolution on Problems of Zhejiang Province" was issued on July 24 of that year, ordering the suppression of counterrevolutionary elements who disrupt production, disrupt communications, incite armed struggles, harrass [*sic*] movements, dispense counterrevolutionary propaganda, and commit counterrevolutionary crimes, as well as all those active counterrevolutionaries proven to have committed murder, arson, or poisoning, and all landlords, rich peasants, counterrevolutionaries, bad elements, and rightist elements plotting to usurp authority.[38]

The PLA, acting on the orders of Vice-Premier and Chief of the PLA General Staff Deng Xiaoping, was sent in and eventually, with difficulty, put down the violence. The militia, its arms confiscated, was disbanded, and PLA units took over militia patrols in the streets of Hangzhou and the safeguarding of the railroads in that area.[39] The issues that prompted the Hangzhou militia disturbances remain unclear, but the outcome is not: It was a victory for conservative elements within the PLA, and specifically for Deng Xiaoping.

The next well-documented major incident involving the militia was the infamous Tiananmen Square demonstration of April 1976. Here the outcome was exactly the opposite of the Hangzhou disturbances: The militia's behavior was quite reliable, and Deng Xiaoping was clearly defeated. On April 5, during the Qing Ming holiday, demonstrators commemorating the recently deceased premier Zhou Enlai, "openly hoisting the ensign of supporting Deng Xiaoping, frenziedly directed their spearhead at our great leader Chairman Mao, attempted to split the party Central Committee headed by Chairman Mao [and] tried to change the general orientation of the current struggle to criticize Deng Xiaoping."[40]

According to the official NCNA account, tens of thousands of worker-militia men and women from among Beijing's million-strong members had surrounded the square two hours after they had received orders from the municipal militia command. Charging "into the square from both sides like two irresistible torrents . . . they surrounded the handful of counterrevolutionaries [who], their arrogance now deflated, were shivering all over and received due punishment at the hands of the worker-militia."[41] It should be noted that the prefix "worker" is not normally used before "militia," and its inclusion indicates Xinhua's conscious decision to draw attention to the urban composition of the militia.

After describing various acts of heroism on the part of members of the worker-militia, the news agency declared that the worker-militia's suppression of the Tiananmen incident demonstrated the value of that group's participation in the class struggle in society at large and added that the worker-militia was now taking part in running, reforming and building up the city and in consolidating the dictatorship of the proletariat. . . . To deal heavy blows at conspiracies and sabotage by imperialism, revisionism, and reaction, tens of thousands of worker-militia men and women are patrolling and guarding the capital, day and night in all weather. They are to be seen in the streets, alleys and parks, and at railway stations and bus stops. Defending the people against the class enemies, they are praised by the masses of the people as pathbreakers in production and defenders of the capital.[42]

While the militia emerged as the heroes of Tiananmen, Deng Xiaoping was the villain. Two days after the incident, the CCP's Central Committee named Hua Guofeng as first vice-chairman of the Party Central Committee and premier of the State Council and dismissed Deng from all his posts both inside and outside the Party.[43] During the ensuing weeks, anti-Deng rallies were held in major Chinese cities, in what was called a "high tide of criticism" against him. Among his many alleged crimes, Deng was said to have opposed militia participation in the class struggle and to have declared that the Shanghai model of militia building was applicable only in that city.[44] In addition, whereas the militia's experience at Tiananmen had "confirmed the need for a militia headquarters," Deng had consistently opposed the creation of such a headquarters.[45]

During the summer of 1976, as Mao Zedong's death approached, the militia was mobilized in Beijing, Shanghai, and Tianjin. The Beijing correspondent of the Toronto *Globe and Mail* reported that the number of militia patrols in the capital was increasing weekly. Feeling that the immediate cause for this increasing militia presence was mounting concern about lawbreakers, he nonetheless added that "the calls for additional, larger, and better-trained militia units mean that radical circles will turn to the militia for support in any succession crisis."[46]

If this was the radicals' strategy, it was ill conceived. An article published in the Taiwan journal *Studies on Chinese Communism* at approximately this time stated that the militia had been called upon to quell general strikes in a number of cities and had been found lacking. The article also denigrated the role of the Beijing worker-militia in suppressing the Tiananmen incident, attributing the real credit to the army and the police.[47]

For whatever reasons, the militia proved unable to save either the radical ideologues or their own organization when the succession crisis arrived. Shortly after Mao's death in September 1976, Hua Guofeng announced that the Party had "smashed the scheme of the 'Gang of

Four' to usurp party and state power, thus removing from the party a bunch of hidden traitors, ridding the country of a big scourge, and redressing the grievances of the people."[48] Although the worker-militia was listed among those groups present at the celebration/denunciation rally, it disappeared from mention immediately thereafter.

Several months later, in early 1977, the militia began to slowly reappear, albeit in greatly changed form. Many of its leading cadres and a smaller percentage of its rank-and-file members were purged and imprisoned for their role in supporting the Gang of Four. The PAFDs were re-created, with new directives stressing that Party and PAFDs should exercise dual authority over militia work. Militia headquarters were abolished, it being explained that they had been a tool of the Gang of Four to usurp power for their own ends. The new militia was also rural based, and the presence of its urban-industrial component was no longer stressed. Moreover, the revived militia no longer assumed the work of the public security and fire departments. Interestingly, Liaoning, which had been the earliest province to publicly emulate the Shanghai model, was also the first to hold criticism meetings on the Gang of Four's theories of militia organization. The *Liberation Army Daily*, commending the reorganization work done thus far, likened the reactivation of the militia to a "kite that has had its string cut flying again" and stressed the importance of the militia.[49]

The new state constitution adopted in March 1978 reaffirmed the primacy of the PLA, referring to the PLA (and, in contrast to the 1975 constitution quoted earlier, the PLA alone) as the workers' and peasants' own armed forces. In a manner nonetheless meaningful for its subtlety, the militia was removed from the position of parity with the PLA it had been given by the 1975 document. However, the new constitution promised that the militia would be strengthened and also supported the three-in-one (field armies, regional forces, and militia) concept of defense, which was not present in the 1975 document.[50] In fact, the Gang of Four's attempt to elevate the militia to a position of parity with the PLA was subsequently denigrated as an attempt to destroy the three-in-one concept devised by Mao. This three-in-one defense concept should not be confused with the identically named militia organization scheme advocated by rebels, in which the militia incorporated public security and fire-fighting departments.

In support of the new constitution's pledge that the militia would be strengthened, in April, just a month after the constitution had been passed, the PLA's General Staff held a symposium on militia political work. The deliberations stressed the need for better organization and discipline in the militia, and participants agreed that the focus of rebuilding should be on the grass-roots level. Only "when conditions warranted"—meaning, presumably, imminent attack by a foreign power—should militia work be extended beyond the company level. Leaders of both Party and military organizations were told to devote major efforts to militia work, since success therein would be regarded as an important yardstick for measuring their performance.[51]

In July and August, the PLA held a second high-level conference on militia work in Beijing. Lasting for three weeks, it was attended by virtually every important member of the elite group, including Hua Guofeng and Deng Xiaoping. Hua and several other ranking figures wrote hortatory inscriptions on militia work, and major speeches were delivered by Vice-Chairman of the Military Commission Nie Rongzhen, Deputy Chief of the PLA General Staff Yang Yong, and several other military leaders. All speeches stressed the value of the militia, arguing in an almost suspiciously strident manner that the more modernized a war, the greater the role of the militia. Nie Rongzhen's speech was particularly insistent on this point, referring to the militia as a "revolutionary heirloom" to be passed down from generation to generation.[52]

In essence, the conference called for a better-organized militia with younger officers. Better training, particularly for the armed militia, was stressed, the goal being the armed militia's ability to assemble instantly in combat readiness.[53] For the militia as a whole, military training was to be combined with production work and public security functions.[54] Those people who concentrated on appearances rather than on results were criticized,[55] as were those who "feel that to do militia work means they are inferior to others, and that it means a lack of faith in them by their organizations."[56] This statement, plus several others urging the military to take its training role more seriously,[57] indicates that the PLA was still reluctant to allocate time and officers to militia training.

As a corrective measure, provincial military districts and subdistricts were put on notice that their work would

> be checked and rated on the basis of whether their number one and number two leading members [are] concentrating their main efforts on militia work and whether the vast majority of their cadres are doing militia work. At the same time, their performances will also be judged by the results of putting militia work on a solid basis organizationally, politically, and militarily, to see if the militia under their command is able to assemble quickly at the first call, and is capable of fighting and winning.[58]

Other issues addressed included discipline problems, which were to be remedied by better education and training plus a strict system of evaluation. Weapons maintenance and weapons control problems were also to be remedied by better systems of accounting and responsibility.[59] A persistent area of contention, that of the proper remuneration for militia work, was briefly addressed: armed militia personnel and militia cadres participating in military training were to be regarded as on duty; they were to be given wages or work points "and be evaluated and commended as usual."[60] Presumably, other militia personnel would not be compensated for their work.

During the ensuing months, militia work conferences were held at military region and district levels to publicize the decisions of the national-level conference and to discuss the experimental implementation of these decisions. In general, the conference members reported enlarging the armed components of their militia units and giving them more specialized training. Zhang Caijian, a deputy chief of the PLA General Staff, revealed that "in certain key areas," the armed militia had "not only infantry companies but also antiaircraft artillery [AAA], machinegun and mortar, antiaircraft machinegun, heavy machinegun, communications, antichemical, reconnaissance, and antitank units."[61] Antichemical and AAA training for militia units were reported in a number of areas throughout China. Zhang also stated that great improvements had been made in the militia's equipment, not only quantitatively but qualitatively as well. However, his next statement averred that the militia's equipment was now "better than our army's weapons and equipment during the war of liberation."[62] Foreign military experts, remembering the motley assortment of World War II and prewar U.S., Japanese, and Soviet equipment—augmented by an occasional flintlock or vintage cannon—the 1945–1949 war of liberation had been won with, may well have contemplated what the attainment of this new technological level would mean to the militia's combat effectiveness. However, other high-ranking army officials mentioned plans to equip the militia with arms equivalent to those possessed by the present PLA within a few years.

It was presumably members of the newly retrained armed militia who were active in China's February 1979 attack on Vietnam, some of them in combat roles.[63] Although the militia's performance received much praise in the Chinese media,[64] there are also indications that militia confusion in a number of battle scenarios posed problems for the PLA.

The Militia in the 1980s

As the 1980s began, the militia's position in the PRC's foreign and domestic policies seemed well defined. The constitution itself sanctioned the militia's place in the nation's defense—alongside field armies and regional forces—and pledged that it would be strengthened. The importance of the militia's role in people's war and the continuation of people's war as the basis of the PRC's defense strategy were also reaffirmed. Domestically, purged of members deemed guilty of using it to influence internal power struggles, the militia would serve as a leading force in social causes, such as the achievement of the ambitious goals of the four modernizations drive. And, in its newly purified form, the militia would aid public security forces to maintain order. Control over the militia was to be exercised by Party and army jointly.

In fact, the militia in the 1980s will not be able to play the role envisioned for it. The plans outlined above have already been, and will continue to be, significantly modified in practice—first, by constraints imposed on the militia by its previous development and, second, by the changes in the political-economic environment in which the militia must function.

The most salient recent example of constraints imposed on the militia by its past history relates to the militia's role in public security work. Militia members, for eminently understandable reasons, were most reluctant to perform public security duties. Party propaganda since the fall of the Gang of Four had emphasized the evil conspiracy behind the gang's desire to combine militia, public security, and firefighting capacities, and large numbers of militia members had suffered for their involvement in this alleged plot. Also vivid in the public memory was the Tiananmen incident of April 1976. The militia, initially lauded as the heroes of Tiananmen, had been quickly transformed into its villains. At the same time, the demonstrators and Deng Xiaoping, previously branded as counterrevolutionaries, had not only been rehabilitated but praised. It is therefore hardly surprising that militia members have been attempting to avoid public security duties. Government propaganda has stressed that these reluctant comrades have "misunderstood" the role of the militia in public security work, but the explanation that one must distinguish between the militia's proper involvement in public security duties and the misuse of the militia's public security role by the Gang of Four has not proved convincing to many.[65] It is simply too difficult for militia members to distinguish between use and misuse of this role at any given moment.

Given the level of social unrest in China as the 1980s began, the militia's reluctance to perform public security duties posed problems for the government: When not even the combination of militia and public security forces could quell the unrest, the regular army was assigned to patrol duty in the PRC's major cities.[66] Even more worrisome than the militia's reluctance to put down public unrest was its penchant to participate in it. At best, this behavior is merely mischievous and wasteful—for example, in Shandong, militia weapons and ammunition were improperly requisitioned to provide background noisemaking for the birthday celebration of an elderly lady.[67] At worst, major problems of law and order have been involved. On Hainan Island, a dispute between the children of two villages escalated to involve the villages' adults, who were armed with militia weapons. Nearly 700 people took part in the dispute; 6 were killed, and there was a substantial amount of property damage.[68] Militia weapons are also frequently involved in instances of armed robbery, petty theft, and the settlement of personal grievances.

Another important constraint on the militia's ability to play the role envisioned for it in the 1980s is an economic one. The overly ambitious and often poorly managed economic development schemes initiated by the post-Mao government led to budget deficits, inflation, and unemployment. These problems in turn had adverse effects on both the militia's domestic work and its combat readiness. As part of a budget-balancing effort, military funds were cut drastically, thus ending previous hopes of equipping the militia with weapons comparable to those of the PLA. In addition, newly established economic incentive schemes increased the potential remuneration from productive labor, while proving a disincentive to participating in militia training exercises. The official media reported militia members avoiding training duties because they received so little pay for them. Although some such dispatches chided the militiamen for ignoring the glorious revolutionary traditions of their organization in pursuit of crass material gain,[69] other press releases seemed almost sympathetic, noting that militia members could not be expected to concentrate on militia work when they could not afford to purchase basic food supplies.[70]

The government, aware that time spent in militia training was time lost from productive labor attempted to formulate a compromise plan. Ordinary and basic militia were to concentrate on production, to further the goals of the four modernizations, and, not incidentally, to help alleviate growing shortages of food and other basic commodities. Meanwhile, training activities would focus on the armed militia, which would concentrate on specialized activities, such as AAA and anti-chemical work, deemed appropriate to fighting people's war as modified by modern technological innovations.

All militia activities considered not strictly necessary, such as participation in parades, were to be curtailed, and the yearly training period was set at fifteen to twenty days. Moreover, training activities were to be tailored to fit the needs of the specific areas in which the units resided. One unit, for example, was told to eliminate flat-trajectory firing and anti-tank maneuvers from its training exercises since its members lived in a semimountainous area where such firing was of limited value and tanks were unlikely to penetrate.[71] Elimination of such maneuvers will, however, limit the degree to which militia units can be deployed outside their own areas. Also, allowing local militia units to design their own training activities is likely to reinforce the localist tendencies that are always present in Chinese society.

Although the government's new measures have surely 'helped to alleviate some of the burdens militia work has imposed on China's citizenry, problems continue to exist. In the fall of 1980, one county in Shandong reported that only 60 percent of its militia companies were able to fulfill their stipulated training missions.[72] Two months later, the provincial government announced a provincewide cut in the number of militia trainees and a further simplification of training exercises. No one over the age of twenty-five was to receive training, and even members of the armed militia were excluded from their yearly training period if they had received training in the past.[73] As for those people who did participate in the training exercises, their pay had to be cut.[74] Another province, Anhui, postponed all live ammunition practice to save money and fuel.[75]

In the spring of 1981, a militia conference held in Henan announced that the province's militia organization "is not yet very well suited to the modernization drive and future opposition to a war of aggression."[76] In light of all the evidence, it is plausible that Henan's admission that its militia organization is not equal to either the civil or the military tasks it has been assigned may be taken as a fair description of the general state of the militia in the PRC at the beginning of the 1980s.

Conclusions

That the size, functions, and institutional control mechanisms of the Chinese people's militia have changed drastically and repeatedly over the years is fact. However, one need not accept the contentions of leaders in power that their predecessors, in ordering these changes, were motivated by sinister desires to sabotage the militia or to use it to bring themselves to power.

The militia prior to 1949 had a clear-cut function: to help the CCP attain power. Therefore, from the point of view of the Party, the militia's size was noncontroversial: the bigger, the better. Since Party and army goals were closely intertwined, there were few areas of conflict between them with regard to the militia. After 1949, the functions of the militia were less clear. With peace achieved, the militia's military function bcame a matter of potential rather than of present use. Still, given the Korean War and the tensions with Taiwan, a military role for the militia could not be ignored.

Since militia members were among the more able-bodied citizens of China and since the economy was in a shambles, a role for the militia as a spearhead of production was indicated. Since its members were among the more enthusiastic proponents of the new government, propaganda and public security roles were also indicated.

All of these roles were enshrined in ideology, with no indication of how much time and effort should be allocated to each. Therefore, although intra-elite arguments about the militia have been characterized by charges that one side or the other has abandoned ideological principles, legitimate differences of opinion may exist on the mixture of the militia's roles.

For example, the small, reasonably well-trained militia of the mid-1950s reflected a conscious decision among the elite that the best use of the militia was as a reserve force for the PLA. In the late 1950s, this perception changed in favor of a large, production- and ideology-oriented militia to expedite the Great Leap Forward. In each case, the decision was opposed by some members of the elite who sought to reverse the changes and discredit the people who had made them. Similarly, the army's supervision of the militia in the late 1960s and early 1970s was a natural outgrowth of the breakdown of public security during the Cultural Revolution and of an increased perception of threat from the Soviet Union.

The Gang of Four's elevation of the militia to a position of parity with the PLA was an attempt to undermine what they may have sincerely believed to be inflated military power that ran counter to the principle that the Party must control the gun. Their creation of militia headquarters may have been due less to a selfish desire to usurp power for personal reasons than a wish to wrest power away from what they saw as PLA-dominated PAFDs. Although it is plausible that militia members did overstep the authority given to them in their public security capacity, and did themselves become disorderly occasionally, they did not necessarily do so at the direction of ideological zealots any more than the militia units that stole and terrorized during the three lean years of economic hardship did so on the orders of the predominantly conservative government of that time.

The present mixture of militia roles emphasizes careful military training for the armed militia and a predominantly production-centered role for the other components of the militia. Dual control is to be exercised by the Party and the army, the latter acting through PAFDs. In the short run, this arrangement may be an acceptable mixture of the roles, provided, of course, that economic conditions improve enough for militia work to be properly carried out. However, the solution is unlikely to be completely satisfactory for the long run. The fact that the militia's propaganda role is almost completely lacking must displease a number of people, and tensions will inevitably arise over the prerogatives of Party versus military in their joint control of the militia.

Because the size and organization of the militia are strongly influenced by local population and area factors, problems of central control have always existed. The present emphasis on adapting militia functions to local needs is likely to exacerbate localist tendencies. The abolition of militia headquarters now criticized as an evil innovation of the Gang of Four, may be expected to further reinforce local variations and cause command and control problems for the central government.

These and other problems concerning the militia are likely to prove enduring. In a society with many more pressing concerns, militia work does, and will, receive a relatively low priority, and the morale of militia members will probably not be high, particularly since militia work detracts from productive activities with potentially more lucrative material benefits. In the case of the armed militia, a feeling of inferiority to the PLA may also influence morale. One province, Hebei, has called for linking the militia system with the reserve system of the PLA[77] and if generally applied, this plan might help improve morale. However, it will also involve improving the present sagging spirits of the PLA itself.

The concept of dual leadership by Party and military over a relatively low-prestige organization leads to an evasion of responsibility by both except when one group feels that its prerogatives are being usurped by the other. At present, repeated exhortations in province after province that Party and military "must realistically place militia work on their daily agenda[s] and devote sufficient attention to it"[78] indicate the central elite's concern about indifference to militia work.

Although lack of enthusiasm for militia work and interest in labor that produces more immediate material benefits limit the militia's domestic role, its present military role is also problematic. In the event of war, even the armed militia could probably not be made combat ready in less than a month; the basic and ordinary categories, not for several months. Given an improvement in the PRC's present economic difficulties, it may be possible to implement previously formulated plans to improve militia weapons and training. This improvement in turn may enhance the militia's combat capabilities, but the process is apt to take many years. The modernization of the PLA occupies a higher priority, and it too is proceeding far more slowly than many leaders feel is desirable. Moreover, the PRC government's stated priority is that of increasing agricultural production, and most militia training activities come at the expense of this production. In short, the PRC faces substantial difficulties in elevating the militia to a reliable, combat-effective element of the three-in-one concept of forces on which current Chinese defense strategy is based.

The militia's traditional role has been in people's war, but there are strong indications that the Chinese elite is now rethinking the concept of people's war. However, for the foreseeable future, China will remain militarily inferior, and public espousal of the doctrine of people's war, despite its deficiencies, can be construed as making a virtue of necessity. People's war is, in addition, a relatively inexpensive form of defense. Given the continuation of this concept, even a marginally trained militia will, of course, be of some value in time of hostilities. For the present, however, the militia, for all that it has been the source of much contention among the Chinese elite, is, in Nie Rongzhen's words, a revolutionary heirloom. However precious its memory, it is an organization whose value to the society is marginal.

Notes

1. A complete discussion of militia functions may be found in Nie Rongzhen, "The Militia's Role in a Future War," *Beijing Review* (henceforth *BR*) 21:35 (September 1, 1978), pp. 16–19.

2. See Harvey W. Nelsen, *The Chinese Military System* (Boulder, Colo.: Westview Press, 1977), pp. 177–189.

3. See, for example, Wuhan Radio, November 7, 1979, in Foreign Broadcast Information Service, China (henceforth FBIS-CHI), no. 219, 1979, p. P3.

4. The organization of the militia is outlined in *Handbook on the Chinese Armed Forces*, DDI-2680-32-76 (Washington, D.C.: Defense Intelligence Agency, July 1976), pp. 2–15, A–22.

5. Karl Marx and Friedrich Engels, "Elberfeld Speeches," February 8, 1845, in *Works* (Moscow: State Publishing House of Political Literature, 1955), 2:539.

6. V. I. Lenin, "On the Proletarian Militia," in *Works* (Moscow: State Publishing House of Political Literature, 1949), 24:51.

7. *Selected Works of Mao Zedong* (Beijing: Foreign Languages Press, 1965), 1:41–42.

8. For an account of the process of militia formation in Inner Mongolia, see *Nei Monggol ribao*, October 4, 1979, in FBIS-CHI-79-216, p. R1.

9. See, for example, Liu Yuncheng, "The Militia in Chinese People's Revolutionary Wars," *BR* 7:34 (August 21, 1964), pp. 20–25.

10. Inagaki Osamu, "Militia Organization in China," *Translations on the PRC*, no. 335, Joint Publications Research Service (henceforth JPRS) 66532, January 7, 1976, pp. 31–34.

11. Nanning Radio, February 14, 1978, in FBIS-CHI-78-34, p. G4.

12. Yang Lu-hsia, "The Chinese Communist Militia," Part 1, *Issues and Studies* (Taibei) (June 1973), p. 56.

13. Nanning Radio, February 14, 1978, in FBIS-CHI-78-34, p. G4.

14. Liu, "The Militia," p. 20.

15. Conference report, "Strengthening Militia Work," *BR* 7:48 (November 27, 1964), p. 27.

16. Ibid.

17. Liu Yuncheng, "The Role of People's Militia," *BR* 8:6 (February 5, 1965), p. 18.

18. Shanghai Radio, January 13, 1967, New China News Agency (henceforth NCNA).

19. Shanghai Radio, January 25, 1967, NCNA.

20. Shanghai Radio, March 5, 1967, NCNA.

21. Beijing Radio, February 24, 1967, NCNA.

22. "The Chinese Militia, 1965–1969," *China Topics* (Hong Kong) YB 537 (November 1969), p. 10.

23. *Liberation Army Daily* (henceforth *LAD*), August 7, 1967, p. 3, NCNA.

24. Ibid.

25. *LAD*, November 27, 1969, quoted by NCNA.

26. See, for example, Changsha Radio, September 25, 1968, and Lanzhou Radio, December 5, 1968.

27. Jiang Daiyuan, "We Poor and Lower-Middle Peasants Have the Greatest Love for the PLA," *BR* 12:35 (August 29, 1969), pp. 9–10.

28. See, for example, Xian Radio, January 17, 1969, NCNA.

29. Hohhot Radio, June 17, 1969, NCNA.

30. A complete translation of the joint editorial may be found in *Chinese Law and Government* (White Plains, N.Y.: International Arts and Sciences Press, 1974), pp. 58–61.

31. Shenyang Radio, November 23, 1974, in FBIS-CHI-74-230, p. L5.

32. Changchun Radio, November 21, 1974, in FBIS-CHI-74-228, p. L1.

33. *BR* 18:4 (January 24, 1975), p. 15.

34. See, for example, Radio Peace and Progress (Moscow), November 5, 1975, in FBIS-SOV (Soviet Union)-75-215, p. C3; Radio Moscow, June 24, 1976, in FBIS-SOV-76-123, p. C1.

35. *Pravda*, July 31, 1976, p. 5, in FBIS-SOV-76-151, p. C2; Radio Peace and Progress, November 5, 1975, in FBIS-SOV-75-215, p. C3.

36. "Maoist Struggle Against the Military in 1974," *Peking Informers* (Hong Kong), January 1, 1975, pp. 1–3.

37. L. Chen, "Wang Hongwen on Tiger's Back," *Asian Outlook* (Taibei) (October 1975), pp. 40–41.

38. "Joint Central Committee–State Council Resolution on the Zhejiang Problem," *Translations on the PRC*, no. 335, JPRS 67524, June 30, 1976, pp. 1–3.

39. C. L. Sulzberger, "The Bear in the China Shop," *New York Times*, August 10, 1975, p. 1V–15.

40. *BR* 19:15 (April 9, 1976), p. 4.

41. NCNA, April 11, 1976 in FBIS-CHI-76-77, p. K5.

42. Ibid., p. K6.

43. *BR* 19:15 (April 9, 1976), p. 3.

44. Shanghai Radio, June 29, 1976, in FBIS-CHI-76-120, p. G9.

45. Mao Gengdi, "Build Militia Headquarters in the Cause of Struggle," translated in U.S. Consulate General, *Survey of People's Republic of China Press*, CMP-SPRC-76-27 (Hong Kong, July 1976), pp. 148–150.

46. Ross Munro, "Hints of Unease and Indiscipline Appear in China," *New York Times*, July 26, 1976, pp. 1, 11.

47. *Iyue zabing*, "Gongren minbing" [Monthly review: "Worker-militia"], *Zhonggong yanjiu* [Studies on Chinese Communism] (Taibei) (May 1976), pp. 4–7.

48. *BR* 19:44 (October 29, 1976), p. 7.

49. *LAD*, September 29, 1977, p. 3, NCNA.

50. *BR* 21:11 (March 17, 1978), pp. 8–9.

51. *LAD*, April 13, 1978, p. 1, NCNA.

52. NCNA, August 7, 1978, in FBIS-CHI-78-154, p. E2.

53. NCNA, August 8, 1978, in FBIS-CHI-78-156, p. E8.

54. Ibid., p. E5.

55. Ibid., p. E8.

56. FBIS-CHI-78-154, p. E9.

57. FBIS-CHI-78-156, pp. E6, E7.

58. Ibid., p. E9.

59. Ibid., p. E8.

60. Ibid.

61. Beijing Radio, October 3, 1978, in FBIS-CHI-78-192, p. E1.

62. Ibid.

63. Nanning Radio, April 23, 1979, in FBIS-CHI-79-81, p. P1.

64. Beijing Radio, June 2, 1979, in FBIS-CHI-79-108, pp. L15–16.

65. See, for example, *Yunnan ribao*, March 27, 1978; Guangzhou Radio, January 9, 1978, in FBIS-CHI-78-6, p. H7.

66. See, for example, Agence France Presse (AFP), Hong Kong, December 23, 1979, in FBIS-CHI-79-250, p. L7.

67. Jinan Radio, June 13, 1980, in FBIS-CHI-80-116, p. O4.

68. Haikou Radio, March 21, 1980, in FBIS-CHI-80-59, p. P7.

69. *Xinhua ribao* (Nanjing), February 26, 1981, in *Translations on the PRC*, no. 194, JPRS 78177, May 28, 1981, pp. 37–38.

70. *Dazhong ribao* (Jinan), October 14, 1980, in *Translations on the PRC*, no. 155, JPRS 77155, January 12, 1981, pp. 21–22.

71. *Zhejiang ribao* (Hangzhou), June 14, 1980, in *Translations on the PRC*, no. 106, JPRS 76253, August 19, 1981, p. 30.

72. *Dazhong ribao*, October 14, 1980, in *Translations on the PRC*, no. 155, JPRS 77155, January 12, 1981, pp. 21–22.

73. *Dazhong ribao,* December 9, 1980, in *Translations on the PRC,* no. 164, JPRS 77401, February 17, 1981, pp. 42–43.

74. *Dazhong ribao,* December 17, 1980, in *Translations on the PRC,* no. 166, JPRS 77474, February 27, 1981, p. 18.

75. Hefei Radio, March 18, 1981, in FBIS-CHI-81-52, p. O1.

76. Zhengzhou Radio, May 8, 1981, in FBIS-CHI-81-90, p. P3.

77. Shijiazhuang Radio, May 26, 1981, in FBIS-CHI-81-109, p. R3.

78. See, for example, Nanjing Radio, March 2, 1979, in FBIS-CHI-79-44, pp. G1–2.

About the Contributors

June Teufel Dreyer is professor of politics and director of East Asian programs at the Center for Advanced International Studies at the University of Miami, Coral Gables, Florida. Previously she served as a Far East specialist at the Library of Congress. She is the author of *China's Forty Millions* and a frequent contributor to scholarly journals.

Paul H.B. Godwin is associate professor of Asian studies at the Air University, Maxwell Air Force Base, Alabama, where he teaches Chinese military and political affairs at the Air War College and the Air Command and Staff College. He is a coauthor of *The Making of a Model Citizen in Communist China* and a contributor to *Studies in Comparative Communism, Comparative Politics, Problems of Communism,* and other journals.

William R. Heaton is professor of national security affairs at the National War College. He has taught at the U.S. Air Force Academy and has held the position of research fellow at the National Defense University. He is a coauthor of *The Politics of East Asia* and a contributor to *The Defense Policies of Nations: A Comparative Study* as well as to a number of scholarly journals.

Richard J. Latham is a major in the U.S. Air Force and a member of the political science faculty of the U.S. Air Force Academy. He has held a number of assignments in Asia including assistant air attaché in Hong Kong. He is completing a Ph.D. dissertation at the University of Washington in the field of modern Chinese politics.

Harvey W. Nelsen is professor of international studies at the University of South Florida, Tampa. He is the author of *The Chinese Military System* and a frequent contributor of articles on Chinese military affairs to a number of scholarly journals.

Jonathan D. Pollack is an analyst at the RAND Corporation, specializing in Chinese political and strategic problems. He is coeditor of *Military Power and Policy in Asian States: China, India, and Japan,* and his numerous articles on Chinese national security and military policy have appeared in the *China Quarterly,* the *Bulletin of the Atomic Scientists, Problems of Communism,* and other scholarly journals and books.

David L. Shambaugh is a doctoral candidate in political science at the University of Michigan and has analyzed Chinese military and international policy for the U.S. Senate, the Department of State, and the National Security Council. His articles on China's military industries have appeared in *Contemporary China* and other journals.

Index

Westview Special Studies on East Asia

The Chinese Defense Establishment:
Continuity and Change in the 1980s
edited by Paul H.B. Godwin

Complex issues of national security and defense modernization continue to be a major preoccupation of the PRC leadership. In the 1970s, especially during the second half of that crucial decade, critical decisions were made that led to Beijing's alignment with the West against the USSR and a revitalization of its armed forces. This book looks at China's defense establishment in light of those decisions and evaluates the problems the Chinese must overcome to achieve their objectives. The authors go beyond narrow issues of weapons and military equipment to explore the interrelationships of defense, national security, professional military education, command and management, army and society, the militia, and revised conceptualizations of people's war, thus bringing the future of China's defense establishment into broader perspective. In all of these areas, the past weighs heavily on China's future and places severe restrictions on what Beijing can hope to achieve within this decade. This book, therefore, addresses both current patterns of change and the continuing legacy of the past.

Paul H.B. Godwin is associate professor of Asian studies at the Air University, Maxwell Air Force Base. Dr. Godwin is author of *The Making of a Model Citizen in Communist China* (1971).